MODERN INDIAN EDUCATION
Policies, Progress and Problems

MODERN INDIAN EDUCATION

Policies, Progress and Problems

Dr. C. P. S. Chauhan
Professor of Education
Aligarh Muslim University
ALIGARH

KANISHKA PUBLISHERS, DISTRIBUTORS
NEW DELHI-110 002

KANISHKA PUBLISHERS, DISTRIBUTORS
4697/5-21A, Ansari Road, Daryaganj
New Delhi -110 002
Phones : 2327 0497, 232 8 8285
Fax : 011-2328 8285
E-mail : kanishka_publishing@yahoo.co.in
kanishkabooks@gmail.com

Modern Indian Education:
Policies, Progress and Problems

First Published-2004

Edition-2023

ISBN : 978-81-7391-616-0

PRINTED IN INDIA

Published by Madan Sachdeva for Kanishka Publishers, Distributors, 4697/5-21A, Ansari Road, Daryaganj, New Delhi-110002, Typeset by Sunshine Graphics, Delhi, and Printed at G.S. Printers, Delhi.

Preface

The present book is a by-product of my long experience of delivering lectures to under-graduate and post-graduate students, for the period of more than two decades since 1980, as a part of my teaching duties in two Central Universities of India—Benaras Hindu University and Aligarh Muslim University. When I joined the latter institution in 1985 as a Reader in Education, I was assigned the teaching work of a subject, which was in a way, new to me. But, I took it, not only as a challenge, but also as a great opportunity to study the issues and problems facing the system of education in India. During the process of discharging my duties as a teacher, I had to make an intensive study of various problems and issues associated with different aspects of education. While discussing with my students, I sometimes felt that there was acute dearth of latest data based literature on development of Indian education. The existing books available in the market on the subject were either outdated or deficient in presentation and/or coverage. This situation prompted me to make a humble beginning in this direction.

My first book on the subject entitled "Higher Education in India: Achievements, Failures and Future Strategies" was published in 1990, and was warmly received by the academic fraternity and served the interests of students and researchers. Professor Malcolm S. Adiseshiah, an eminent Indian educationist, in his review of this book, remarked, "This publication is an important addition to the growing documentation on Higher Education in India." The academic community and the research scholars owe a debt to the author for this synthesis of what is available so far in this area. This kind of feedback encouraged me to make further attempts in this direction.

The present publication is the second in the same series. The approach of presentation of the subject-matter is historical, and hence, indicates a major diversion from the conventional mode of writing books. Organized into twelve chapters, the book covers all aspects of Indian education from Pre-primary Education to Higher Education. The discussion starts with major highlights of the historical development of Indian education since the Ancient Period, which has been presented in the First Chapter. In addition, separate chapters have been devoted to subject-matter areas like Early Childhood Care and Education, Compulsory Elementary Education, Eradication of Illiteracy, Secondary Education and 10+2+3, Higher Education, Teacher Education, Education of the Weaker Sections, Distance Education and Educational Finance. The policies adopted by the Government of India in respect of these areas, during the last more than five decades since independence, have been discussed in the respective chapters along with programmes of action launched, the progress achieved, and the problems faced while implementing the policies and programmes.

The entire discussion is data based and analytical. In order to collect necessary data, all the national level organizations including the University Grants Commission (UGC), Ministry of Human Resource Development, and National Council of Educational Research and Training (NCERT), were approached. Various other reports of the commissions and committees appointed by the Government of India from time to time were also consulted. The trends that emerge from the data have also been thoroughly discussed. A salient feature of the book is that it contains 35 tables, which present quantitative information about various developmental aspects of education at all levels. Each table is followed by references of the sources from where the data have been taken/compiled. The quantitative data have been presented within the text in tabular form through these tables, so as to make the discussion more meaningful and intelligible to the prospective readers. This book will be very useful to the students of education at all levels, teachers, researchers, administrators and policy planners.

I consider it my sacred duty to express my heart-felt and sincere gratitude to all those academicians, colleagues and friends who have directly or indirectly encouraged me to undertake and successfully complete such an important project. During the last three years since the present work was started, I have been continuously benefited from the writings and personal discussions of some scholarly persons. I express my sincere gratitude to all of them. I also feel highly indebted to my teachers, Professor R. G. Mishra and Professor R. N. Mehrotra, both educationists of international repute, whose blessings have always been a source of inspiration for me. Special thanks are also due to Professor R. P. Singh, former Dean (Research), NCERT, New Delhi, and presently, President, All India Association of Teacher Educators (AIATE), for his continuous encouragement and guidance during the preparation of the manuscript.

I hope that the book will be of immense utility for the students, teachers, researchers, educational administrators and policy planners. Although, authentic references have been quoted wherever necessary, yet, I assume full responsibility for the views and ideas expressed in the book. However, any suggestions, comments, and constructive criticisms from the readers for the improvement of the book, will be gratefully acknowledged.

Finally, I express my sincere thanks to Kanishka Publishers, Distributors for bringing out the book in such a short period and in such a beautiful shape.

Aligarh

C.P. S. Chauhan

Contents

1

From The Pages of History

As far as population is concerned, India is the largest democracy in the world. Geographically, we are a vast country spread over 329 million hectares of land supporting 1045 million people (2002 estimate), about 1.25 times the total population of Europe. During the last five decades, our number has tripled. With the birth of 48,000 children per day, 18 million are added every year to our population. This addition is more than the total population of Australia. With only 2.4 per cent of the total global land and 2 per cent of the total world's income, we bear the burden of 16.7 per cent of the total population of the world. We are essentially the land of youth and children as about 50 per cent of Indians are below the age of 20 years. Population explosion is one of the most serious problems facing our nation, which tends to nullify our progress on several socio-economic fronts. Even after 50 years of sustained efforts to develop and expand education, about 35 per cent of the people are illiterate. The corresponding figure for women is 46 per cent. According to NSSO Report (1999-2000), 26 per cent of our people live under the poverty line.

This is, however, only one side of the coin. If we look at the other side, we find that India has made remarkable progress in certain fields. We have achieved self-sufficiency in food. At present, we are tenth most industrialized country of the world and rank third as producer of scientifically and technologically trained manpower. Having acquired nuclear capability, we are fully capable of protecting our territorial integrity, without being unnecessarily offensive and aggressive towards others. This has been possible because of our education system, which despite many serious flaws, has functioned as a powerful tool of socio-economic transformation and development. Let us have a glance over the historical development of our education system before studying its other features. The developmental history of Indian education may be studied in three main phases: ancient period, medieval period and the modern period. We will discuss them in that order.

THE ANCIENT PERIOD

Learning has been deeply rooted in the Indian traditions. The term education was used both in wider and narrower sense as is also done these days. In its wider sense education meant self-culture and self-improvement, which processes would go on to the end of one's life. A true teacher was supposed to be a student to the end of his life. In its narrower sense education denoted the instruction and training, which a youth received during his student life before he settled down to his career or profession. Education was recognized as a source of illumination, which provided correct lead in the various spheres of life. According to the contemporary thinking, education was the 'third eye' of man, which gave him insight into all affairs and taught him how to act. As mentioned in 'Mahabharata', there was no "eye" that matched education (Altekar, 1951, p 4). It valued democratic ways of life by removing prejudices, and made a man more reasonable and considerate by enabling him to understand and accept the viewpoints of others. It strengthened man's moral nature and enabled him to stand the severest temptations of life. Due emphasis was laid on physical education, and exercises like "Pranayama" and "Surya Namaskara" formed an integrated part of curricula at all stages of education.

While the major goal of education was to achieve illumination through knowledge, the "bread giving" role of education was not ignored. It also prepared the learners for living as respectable and self-supporting citizens. Infusion of a spirit of piety and religiousness, formation of character, development of personality, inculcation of civic and social duties, promotion of social efficiency, and preservation and spread of national culture may be described as the chief aims and ideals of ancient Indian education. Our society not only had always enlightened itself but also had profound influence on other parts of the world.

Education and Caste System

Even in the ancient times, the organization of the society was divided into four castes—Brahmins, Kshatriyas, Vaishyas and Shudras, did not undermine the significance of learning. This classification of people indicated the ways in which they would serve the society or community. The Brahmins, who were at the top of the caste hierarchy, were supposed to devote themselves to the cause of education. They were assigned the pious duty of acquisition, conservation and transmission of knowledge for the benefit of coming generations. The human life was divided into four stages or ashramas—Brahmacharya (student life), Grahastha (married life), Vanaprastha (retired life) and Sannyasa (life of renunciation). Brahmacharya ashrama or student life, comprising childhood (aged 5-13 years) and adolescence (aged 14-18 years), was a period to be devoted to education in its entirety. During this period, every individual was expected to observe celibacy, which was a characteristic feature of this period. A student was referred to as brahmachari as he ought not to marry during his course of study and lead a celibate life in order to realize his educational ideals and ambitions. Roughly, this period constituted one-fourth of a man's lifetime. Education was free of cost but accessible to only upper three castes—Brahmins, Kshatriyas and Vaishyas. It was largely denied to Shudras, the lowest in the caste hierarchy. Being regarded as the best agency of social change, education was made available to all that were qualified to receive it. To ensure literary education to the largest possible number of people, the Upanayana ceremony, which marked the initiation of a child into the literary and religious education, was made obligatory for all the Aryans, both males and females. Every Aryan, i. e.

every Brahmin, Kshatriya and Vaishya, thus received elementary literary and religious education. The institution of caste was the main vehicle of professional/vocational education because every family used to train its children in the traditional vocation of their family.

Girls were also allowed to receive education. It is on record that Atreyi studied the Vedanta with Lord Rama's sons Lava and Kusha in Valmiki's ashrama. Sometimes, women advanced so much in education that they challenged men in public debates on philosophy and metaphysics. Gargi challenged Yajnavalka in the court of Janaka to answer two questions, which he could not, and later admitted defeat (Vakil and Natarajan, 1966). Kaushalya—the mother of Rama, Tara—the wife of Bali, Draupadi—the wife of Pandavas, are some of the examples of educated women in ancient India.

Educational Management and Finance

Education was free from the interference of the state because rulers were not directly involved in the educational matters, but they financed education with land or money grants. The management of education was completely a private matter under the control of a Brahmin (teacher) who maintained himself on presents, called guru-dakshina received from his students. Each learned Brahmin was an educational institution by himself. Famous capitals like Taxila and Benares were centres of a number of famous scholars, but they also imparted instruction in their individual capacity and did not combine to form an institution or a college. Corporate educational institutions were first evolved in ancient India in connection with Buddhist monasteries, which developed into big establishments from the time of Ashoka onwards. They naturally developed into centres of education as counterparts of Hindu Gurukulas. One of the most significant features of ancient Indian education was the "Gurukula System" under which it was necessary for the student to stay away from his home. A student had to live with his teacher, as a member of his family or in the boarding house under teacher's supervision, till the end of his education. He was supposed to observe celibacy and live in poverty by begging alms. The practice of begging alms taught him humility and made him feel indebted to the society for his education. Another important effect of begging alms was that consciousness of caste hierarchy was minimized because all, rich and poor, had to live together and beg alms. Both, the teachers and students were held in high esteem by the society including the kings. Teachers were revered even more than parents in ancient Indian society as it was believed that parents gave a child physical birth, but teacher gave him intellectual birth in terms of knowledge and wisdom.

Funds for education were received from the public in the form of Vidyadana, which meant "donation for the cause of education". Vidyadana was pronounced to be the best of all gifts having a higher religious efficacy than even the gift of land. This had a profound religious appeal on the public as well as the rulers who donated money for the cause of education, which was sufficient to support free education at least to all poor students who wished to benefit from it.

Stages of Education

Education was divided into two main stages—lower and higher. Lower education imparted knowledge of Vedas necessary for everyday social interaction, while higher education included subjects like history, mythology, mathematics, grammar, logic, polity, astronomy, science (of war and worship), and fine arts. There were two-stage objectives of education: immediate and ultimate. The immediate objectives included preparation of individuals for their caste-based vocations, which was supposed to be their immediate need. The ultimate objectives of education, however, were "self-realization" and " liberation of the soul".

Ancient Indian universities were mostly residential in character, but not as structured and managed as modern universities. These existed in the form of small clusters of teachers and students living and working together, in pursuit of knowledge and its creation, conservation, and dissemination. Students were admitted to the higher level courses on the basis of admission tests, which were stiff ones in view of the education being imparted free of cost. Even the very idea of charging fees was vehemently condemned by one and all. The best-known places of higher education in ancient India were: Takshashila,

Nalanda, Vikramashila, Vallabhi, Nadia, Kanchi, and Benaras—all associated with religious places. Nalanda, Vikramashila, and Vallabhi were associated with Buddhist viharas, while Nadia and Kanchi were connected with temples. Takshashila was situated near Peshawar (now in Pakistan) and was named after the ruler of Kandahar (then Gandhar). This was a great seat of learning associated with Hindu and Buddhist cultures, but attracted students from far off places in India and abroad. The curriculum at Takshashila included the study of Vedas, sciences, medicine and surgery, archery and agriculture. This institution flourished till it was destroyed by Huns, who invaded India in 455 AD. Nalanda—another famous seat of learning, was founded by a disciple of Nagarjuna during the Gupta period. It was situated near the old capital of Magadha about 40 miles away from Patliputra (present Patna) in Bihar. It was an excellent centre of Buddhist studies and attracted students from different parts of the world. Students from India, China, Burma, Tibet, Java, Sumatra, Japan and Turkistan received higher education at Nalanda. It is on record that during the later half of the seventh century AD, Nalanda had about 1500 teachers and 8500 students. This shows that it was a large institution with different faculties. The students were admitted on the basis of an admission test, which was passed by only 20 or 30 per cent of the candidates. Besides religious studies, the curriculum included many subjects such as philosophy, logic, linguistics, yoga, grammar and medicine. The building of Nalanda had 8 big halls and 300 small blocks where 100 lectures could be delivered everyday on various subjects, and free debates and discussions were held on them (Vakil and Natarajan, 1966). Gupta kings had donated 100 villages whose revenues were used to maintain this great seat of learning. Bakhtyar Khilji destroyed Nalanda University at the end of twelfth century AD, during the period of Mohammed Ghauri.

Teaching and Examination

In the absence of paper and printing technology, books were not available to the teachers and students; the prominent method of teaching and learning was oral interaction, mostly individual, between the teacher and the taught. Recitation and recapitulation formed an important part of daily routine of the student life. This method resulted in tremendous development in the memory of the students. Debates and discussions were held for clarifying doubts and understanding the complex aspects of the subject matter. Lecture method had a very significant role in the teaching-learning process. Debates, known as Shastrartha, were organized, which proved to be very effective in developing abilities of reasoning, analysis and power of speech among the learners.

A characteristic feature of ancient Indian education was the "Monitorial System" in which teachers took the help of advanced and brilliant students in effective management of teaching-learning process. An advanced student, designated as Monitor, guided the studies of their juniors or less advanced students under the general supervision of the teacher. This system placed a high incentive before the students. It provided the brilliant students with ample opportunity to learn the art of teaching, and thus indirectly performed the same function as the Teachers' Training Colleges of modern times are discharging. Later on this system was experimented upon and followed in England.

Assessment of achievement was done continuously. There was a daily examination of every student and no new lesson was given until the old one was thoroughly mastered. There was no annual examination and mass promotion at fixed intervals. At the end of his education the student was presented to the local learned assembly where occasionally questions were asked. The evaluation was internal and mostly done by the teacher who taught the students. No degrees or diplomas were awarded in higher education and competition was limited.

Criticism of Ancient Indian Education

The ancient education system was criticized on several grounds. The present life of a human being was considered as Maya (unreal) and the ultimate aim of education was "liberation of the soul" from this maya. This belief led the educated people to think of some future life and ignore the present one. The rigid and caste-based vocational training precluded social and occupational mobility. Therefore, all members of a particular caste had to be educated to follow their own vocation irrespective of their interest or aptitude. The exclusive dominance of Brahmins on education created a wide gap between them and the other castes. Brahmins enjoyed the position of superiority and prestige, and the rest of the population was in the darkness of ignorance and illiteracy. Consequently, both the development of the society and advancement of knowledge were arrested. Vedas were considered as the final authority, which provided answers to all the questions of social and religious life. Every bit of social change was checked by Vedic sanctions imposed by Brahmins. This resulted in the retardation of all kinds of social change and progress. Some of the British scholars have been very critical of the system of education in the ancient India. Sir Philip Hartog (1938) presents his impression of indigenous education in India in the following words:

> Picture to yourself a group of some twenty or thirty men and boys in Indian dress, in a large room in the University of Calcutta; all are seated on the ground except two small boys who stand, and with rhythmical movement up and down of their outstretched palms, chant by heart verses from the Veda, with intonations that, I imagine, go back for 3000 years or more. That is one of my earliest impressions of Indian education.

THE MEDIEVAL PERIOD

During the ancient period, as mentioned earlier, Brahmins organized education. A Brahmin, imparting instruction to his pupils, was called a "pundit"—meaning the one who has knowledge. Likewise, during the medieval period characterized by Muslim domination, education was imparted by "maulvis". An educational institution was normally associated with a mosque and was named "Maktab" or a "Madarsah". As in ancient Hindu period, education was completely a private matter, and rulers supported it by donating land, money, and other material. The agency that managed the mosque also managed the maktab associated with it. These maktabs and madarsahs imparted religious instruction to the children of the Muslim residents of the locality surrounding the mosque. The maktabs provided for a lower level of education comparable to school education, and madarsahs were meant for higher education. The curriculum and teaching in maktabs was based on reading and recitation of those portions of Quran, the holy book of Muslim faith that were necessary for daily prayers. Every pupil was expected to learn these portions of the Quran by heart. Madarsahs, in addition to reading and recitation of the Quran, carried out teaching in Arabic and Persian, which was essential for meeting social demands.

The education of a child began with a ceremony comparable to "upanayana" practised by Hindus in ancient India. This ceremony was called "bismillah". The maulvis, who imparted instruction in maktabs, had certain minimum knowledge of Quran, which they had memorized. About maulvis, Adam (1836) has written:

They do not pretend to be able even to sign their names; and they disclaim altogether the ability to understand that which they read and teach, and what they teach is all they know of written language, without presuming or pretending or aiming to elicit the feeblest glimmering of meaning from these empty vocables.

The madarsahs, on the other hand, imparted much higher level of instruction including the study of grammar, courses of reading on rhetoric, logic, law, geometry, astronomy, philosophy, metaphysics, and fundamentals of Islam. Mohammed Ghauri, the first Muslim conqueror of India, established his kingdom at the end of twelfth century. He is reported to have established mosques and madarsahs at Ajmer for providing education in the fundamentals of Islam and principles of Islamic law. His successors, Kutubuddin, Altamash, Raziya Begum, Nasiruddin, and Balban—all encouraged the establishment of maktabs and madarsahs, and provided liberal grants to maintain them. The famous madarsahs founded during Muslim rule were at Ajmer, Allahabad, Bidar, Bijapur, Burdwan, Calcutta, Delhi, Lahore, Lucknow, Multan and Murshidabad. These madarsahs attracted students from all parts of the country.

The Mughal emperors also took keen interest in education and established educational institutions. For instance, Akbar used to invite learned scholars to his court and hold discussions with them on matters of public interest. He honoured educated men of all religions and communities. He also had many Sanskrit books, such as Ramayana, Mahabharata, Atharvaveda and

Leelavati, translated into Persian. In his regime many Hindus learned Persian to find jobs in government offices because all official accounts were kept in Persian. Jahangir and Shahjahan also took keen interest in education and established maktabs and madarsahs. It is on record that the approach of Aurangzeb, the son of Shahjahan, was different. He destroyed schools attached to Hindu temples in which, Sanskrit and Vedic education was imparted. He also prohibited Hindu teaching and worship at Banaras and some other holy places of Hindus. On the contrary, he encouraged the establishment of maktabs and madarsahs attached to mosques.

There were no maktabs or madarsahs exclusively meant for girls. The Muslim girls received education in the recitation of the holy Quran in their homes. However, girls from royal families received education of a good quality. After the death of Aurangzeb, the Mughal Empire also approached its end. Consequently, many maktabs and madarsahs attached to mosques and pathshalas attached to temples were closed down. However, some maktabs and pathshalas had their impact on education for some time to come.

THE MODERN PERIOD

The modern system of education in India germinated in the attempts of Christian missionaries to spread their religion. The first among them were the Roman Catholic Missionaries, who organized educational activities in the territory under the possession of Portuguese. Most of the missionary schools were attached to churches or to the missionary offices. Francis Xavier, a famous missionary, arrived in India (1542) and started to organize street classes for instruction in Christian religion. The main aim of his efforts was to convert the native Indians to Christianity. But, Xavier faced some severe difficulties in his mission. He wrote to one of his associates:

> The natives are so terribly wicked that they can never be expected to embrace Christianity. It is so repellent to them in every way that they have not even patience to listen when we address them on the subject; in fact, one might as well invite them to allow themselves to be put to death as to become Christians.

It was during this period that the first books were printed in Tamil, an Indian vernacular, in 1577. Portuguese established a college at Bandra near Bombay, and later converted it into a university. But, later on, they destroyed it (1739) to prevent it from being used as a fort by Marathas. This was, in fact, the first modern university established in India. Robert de Nobili (1605-1656), an another missionary who worked at Madurai, pretended to be a Western Brahmin and claimed to have brought with him a lost Veda. Obviously, he did so in order to misguide the native people including Brahmins. But, his attempts did not meet with expected success.

In 1760, a great German missionary C. F. Schwartz visited India and established a number of schools in Madras, the present Chennai. Similar efforts by missionaries continued for some more time, and by 1800, about 1000 Indian children were receiving instruction in missionary schools.

The East India Company

The East India Company, which was established on 31st December 1600, started a factory at Surat (1662), and began to propagate Christianity after a decision of its Court of Directors (1659) to that effect. The Court of Directors of the Company explicitly stated that it was their earnest desire to spread Christianity among the people of India and allowed missionaries to embark upon their ships. It undertook no educational activities for nearly one hundred years of its existence. The Company even looked at the efforts of the missionaries with suspicion and remained non-committal. But, in the early years of the eighteenth century, the company made a definite beginning of the educational activities in India. The Charter Act of 1698 gave two important directions to the Company:

> It directed the Company to maintain ministers of religion at their factories in India and to take a chaplain in every ship of 500 tons or more. The ministers were required to learn the Portuguese language, which was then commonly understood by the inferior servants of the factories who were to be instructed.

It also directed the Company to maintain schools, wherever necessary, in all their garrisons and the bigger factories.

However, these provisions were mainly meant for the children of the European servants of the Company. Indians had limited or no access to them. The unwillingness of the Company to accept the responsibility of educating the Indian people was justified on the ground that it was mainly a trading concern and, thus had nothing to do with education. A body of merchants could not be expected to educate the people it traded with (Nurullah and Naik, 1943).

The renewed Charter of the Company had a new clause requiring the officers of the company to learn the native language to enable them to instruct better the Indian workers. This led to the need for establishment of the charity schools at the Presidencies of Calcutta, Bombay and Madras. The first such school was founded at Madras (1715) and was named St. Mary's Charity School. Similar schools were set up at Bombay (1718) and Calcutta (1731) for the education of the children of the British soldiers and those of the Europeans. After this, some more charity schools were opened for the same purpose. Later on, the children of some Indian officers of the company were also allowed to receive English education in these schools. One such institution, Male Military Orphans Asylum, was started near Madras (1787) in which the old Indian Monitorial System of education was experimented upon by Dr. Bell who later on published a book (1797) on this new experiment. This system was tried and adopted in selected schools in Britain. The curriculum of these schools was mostly limited to the acquisition of the 3Rs and the principles of Christian religion, and the funds for these schools was made available from the subscriptions and donations from philanthropic and religious persons and by the grants paid by the Company. These schools may be regarded as the beginning of the Company's educational activities in India.

By the middle of eighteenth century, the situation had considerably changed. The Company had emerged as a ruling power after the grant of Diwani in 1765 after successfully pushing back its European competitors—the Portuguese, the Dutch and the French. It was only after this that the Company began to encourage education among the Indian natives amidst some debates and controversies. On the one hand, the Directors of the Company were unwilling to accept the responsibility for educating the Indians, and on the other hand, the officers of the Company were agitated to persuade them to accept it, because of possible political advantage. Another conflict was that the missionaries wanted to come to India to spread Christianity, but the Directors of the Company were not willing to permit them to do so due to the fear that their proselytizing activities might arouse opposition among the people. However, the situation changed after the battle of Plassey (1757) when the British took over the administration of Bengal, Bihar and Orissa from Emperor Shah Alam. With this, the Company became a ruling power.

The Company was reluctant to take up the responsibility of educating Indian due to political fear lest it should lead to some trouble arising out of the religious feelings of the natives. But, the Company felt continuous pressure not only from outside but also from inside. Charles Grant, himself a Director of the Company, wrote a book in 1792 urging the Government to introduce Western education in India. Consequently, in 1793, the House of Commons accepted a Resolution, which stated that measures aught to be taken for securing advancement of India in "useful knowledge" and "religious and moral improvement". But, the proposal providing for sending sufficient number of schoolmasters and missionaries to India, to be maintained by the Company, was rejected.

As in Bombay and Madras Presidencies, educational development also took place in Bengal. In 1781, Warren Hastings, the first Governor General of India, founded Calcutta Madarsah aimed at cultivating the Arabic and Persian studies, in order to conciliate the Muslims of Calcutta. It was the first important Government educational institution in India of which the main and special object was "to qualify the sons of Mohammedan gentlemen for responsible and lucrative offices of the State", which were that time largely monopolized by Hindus. For two years, Hastings paid the cost of the institution from his own pocket, which was afterwards repaid by the Government.

Similarly, in order to conciliate Hindus and to cultivate the Sanskrit learning, the Banaras Sanskrit College was established in 1791, by Jonathan Duncan, the Resident at Benaras. The government officers were divided into two camps, one favouring English education in India and the other opposing it. Wilberforce carried a resolution in British Parliament (1793) asking the government to provide useful knowledge to Indians for their religious and moral development by sending out missionaries and schoolmasters from England. But, the other party opposed it saying that Hindus had a good system of faith and morals, and it would be dangerous to attempt their conversion or to give them education in Christianity. One of the Directors of the Company observed that they (the British) had lost America due to this folly in having allowed the establishment of schools and colleges, and suggested that natives should be required to go to England for education. Later on in 1797, Charles Grant pleaded for imparting education through English language. He argued:

> The Mohammedan, from the beginning of their power, employed the Persian language in the affairs of the government and in public departments. This practice aided them in maintaining their superiority.... The natives readily learnt the language of the government, finding that it was necessary....they next became teachers of it; and in all the provinces it is still understood and taught by numbers of Hindus.

But, the Company did not agree to Grant's ideas of propagating Christianity through the teaching of English because it would arouse suspicion about its motives among the people and provoke opposition to the Company's rule. The Court of Directors of the Company proposed to follow the principle of religious neutrality and refused to encourage any attempt to propagate Christianity through education. In the meantime people had come to realize the importance of English education in the contemporary sociopolitical situations. Particularly, the well to do sections of the society started believing that it is necessary for them to learn English and western science in order to overcome their backwardness in the contemporary phase of Industrial Revolution in Europe.

The Indigenous System

During the first quarter of nineteenth century, the then government conducted educational surveys in all the Presidencies in order to assess to contemporary status of indigenous education in India. Sir Thomas Munro, the Governor of Madras, asked all the Collectors in the Madras Presidency (1822) to collect information about the working of the schools in their districts. The reports of the Collectors showed that in 1826 there were 12,498 schools, for a population of 12.85 million, providing instruction to 188,650 pupils. There was 1 school for every 1000 of the population, and 1 pupil for every 67 (Vakil and Natarajan, 1966, p 23). Based on these reports, Munro suggested certain educational reforms such as, appointment of a Committee of Public Instruction, and improvement in curriculum and textbooks.

In Bombay, a similar inquiry was ordered by Mount-Stuart Elphinstone (1823), then Governor of Bombay, who was an advocate of promoting useful knowledge among the natives through the vernacular languages with provision for learning of English. The earliest official statistics for the whole Province for the year 1829 state that the total number of schools in the province was 1705 with 35143 scholars while the population was stated to be 46,81,735. These figures indicated that there was 1 school for every 2700 of the population, and that the progress of education in Bombay was only one-third as compared to Madras. There was no trace of female education as was the case in Madras. The government maintained only 25 schools enrolling 1315 students, and there were 1680 village schools with 33838 students.

William Adam (1835-38) conducted a similar survey of native education in Bengal and Bihar. Lord William Bentinck gave him this assignment at his own suggestion. Adam found that in 1835 there were 100000 village schools in Bengal and Bihar for a population of 40 million people, that is, 1 village school for every 400 of the population and for every 63 children of school going age. If girls were excluded, there would be 1 village school for every 31 or 32 boys. In his reports, Adam also revealed that in areas of Bengal, which he surveyed, the adult male literacy percentage was 9.8, and in Bihar it was 4.9. These reports were later on rejected as a "myth" by Philip Hartog (1939) on the ground that Adam's estimates of population and number of schools might not be based on reliable statistics. Adam also agreed that his calculations were based on uncertain premises and were only distant approximations to the truth.

The findings of these surveys indicate that indigenous education had strong roots till the end of the eighteenth century. Both, Hindus and Muslims had their own systems of religious education as well as they studied languages of each other. However, the indigenous system of education started decaying rapidly after it. The major reason for this decay was non-availability of adequate financial support from the traditional landlords and other rich people. The private agencies, along with some small amounts paid by students, constituted the most important source of educational finance those days. In this regard, Adam's Report said:

> The means of the manufacturing classes have been of late years greatly diminished by the introduction of our own European manufacturers in lieu of the Indian cotton fabrics.... The greater part of the middling and lower classes of the people are now unable to defray the expenses incident upon the education of their offspring, while their necessities require the assistance of their children as soon as their tender limbs are capable of the smallest labour.

Anglicists-Orientalists Controversy

In 1816, Raja Ram Mohan Roy formed an association for setting up an institution, which would provide education in European languages and western science. Although, he was a scholar of two oriental languages, Sanskrit and Persian, yet strongly opposed the establishment of a Sanskrit college at Calcutta. Gradually the government also realized the positive change in the minds of natives regarding English education. The young men and women developed a taste for English and demanded English education.

In the meantime, the Charter Act of the Company was renewed (1813) and the question of education in India figured in the discussions held in this regard in the British Parliament. The most important subject of discussion was the agency for the spread of education in India, and subsequently, a new provision was made in Article 43 of the Act. According to this provision, the Company was directed 'to accept the responsibility of the education of Indians and to spend not less than Rs. 100,000 a year for this purpose'. This event was an important milestone for future development of western education in India. In fact, this was the beginning of the State system of education in India under the British rule (Nurullah and Naik, 1943). The Charter Act of 1813, therefore forms a turning point in the history of Indian education because it ended the agitation carried out by Grant and Wilberforce, the education of Indians accepted as a duty by the Company, and missionaries were allowed to come to India for opening English schools, thereby laying the foundation of modern system of education.

In the meantime, inside the Bengal Committee of Public Instruction, a bitter struggle arose between the "Orientalists" who desired to give all higher teaching through the medium of the classical languages of India (Sanskrit for Hindus, and Arabic and Persian for Muslims), and the "Anglicists" who wished to give higher teaching through the medium of English. Mountstuart Elphinstone, then Governor of Bombay, who was an advocate of promoting useful knowledge among the natives through the vernacular languages with provision for learning of English, issued his famous minute in 1823 in which he made very useful recommendations for the improvement of education. He expressed his ideas about the strategy for education in India before the Lord's Committee in 1830. In a letter to the Secretary to the Commissioner for India Affairs (1832), he wrote:

> I conceive that it is more important to impart a high degree of education to the upper classes than to diffuse a much lower sort of it among the common people...it will be much easier to make the lower orders desirous of learning to read, after a spirit of inquiry and improvement shall have been introduced among their superiors. The most important branch of education, in my opinion, is that designed to prepare natives for public employment.

Elphinstone had realized that Indians, both Hindus and Muslims were very sensitive to their religion, and any attempt to tamper with their religious beliefs through education might be counterproductive. He was of the view that conversion of the natives into Christianity could not be expected through English education, and no direct attempt should be made to achieve this end. Regarding missionary activities, he wrote:

> To the mixture of religion, even in the slightest degree, with our plans of education, I must strongly object.... I am convinced that the conversion of natives must infallibly result from the diffusion of knowledge among them. Fortunately, they are not aware of the connections, or all attacks on their ignorance would be as vigorously resisted as if they were on their religion. The only effect of introducing Christianity into our schools would be to sound the alarm, and warn the Brahmins of the approaching danger.... The result of educating natives, both in English and in their own language, must be favourable to the progress of Christianity.

Elphinstone favoured the education of Indian natives through both English and vernacular languages. He also favoured the involvement of natives in administration and governing bodies. He started engineering and medical classes at Bombay for both Indians and Europeans. Regarding employment of natives in offices of the Company, he wrote to Sir Thomas Munro (1822):

> Besides the necessity for having good native advisors in governing natives, it is necessary that we should have the way for the introduction of the natives to some share in the government of their own country.... It will not be possible to confine them to subordinate employment; and if we have not previously opened vents for their ambitions and ability, we may expect an explosion which will overturn our government.

The people of Bombay raised a fund of over two lakhs of rupees (1827), and asked the government (1831) not to appoint any native, after a time, into a government office, unless he could read, write and speak English. The said fund raised by the public was used to establish the Elphinstone College at Bombay (1834) in the memory of the services of Mount Stuart Elphinstone to the Bombay Presidency. In the meantime the Charter Act of the Company was renewed again in 1833.

The above discussion brings out the fact that the period between 1813 and 1833 has been a period of discussions, controversies and experiments in the field of education in India. The main objectives of education, as defined in the Act of 1813 included the revival and improvement of literature, the encouragement of the learned natives of India, and the introduction and promotion of knowledge of sciences among the inhabitants of the British territories of India. But, no indication was given in the Act regarding the methods to be followed for achieving these objectives. This resulted in controversies among the Europeans who were concerned with the affairs of India. These controversies gave rise to three different schools of thought (Nurullah and Naik, 1943 p 68):

(i) The first school endorsed the ideas of Warren Hastings and Minto, and advocated the encouragement of Sanskrit and Arabic studies and suggested that Western science and knowledge should be spread in India through the medium of these languages.

(ii) The second group consisted of men like Elphinstone and Munro who believed in encouraging education through the medium of the modern Indian languages, and argued that this was the only way to take the Western knowledge to the mass of Indian people.

(iii) The third school of thought included those who endorsed Grant's ideas of spreading the western knowledge through the medium of English. This group consisted of the missionaries and the younger civilians in the employment of the Company.

The enlightened Indians joined these groups also according to the bent of their thinking, though their opinion in these issues mattered little. For example, Raja Ram Mohan Roy in Bengal favoured the ideas of the third group. In fact, the Court of Directors of the Company was the final authority as far as long-term policy on education was concerned. But, it remained indifferent to these matters and allowed the provincial governments to follow their own programmes. It is for this reason that this period is known as the period of experiments. However, the experiments carried out in different provinces led to certain significant developments in education.

Influenced by different viewpoints, the General Committee of Public Instruction was divided into two groups on the question of its education policy particularly regarding the medium of instruction. Out of the ten members of the Committee five favoured the policy of encouraging the study of Oriental literature and were termed as 'Orientalists'. This group was headed by H. T. Princep who was then the Secretary of Government of Bengal in the Education Department, and consisted mainly of older members of the Company's service. The other group of five members who supported the adoption of English as a medium of instruction was termed as 'Anglicists'. This group consisted mainly of younger servants of the Company and had no definite leader, but looked forward to the support of Macaulay who was the President of the General Committee of Public Instruction. The first group was of the view that the British policy of education in India should encourage the oriental/classical literature along with study of western science through vernacular languages. They argued that Indians has a prejudice against the European knowledge and science and would not accept it unless presented through their own classical language. The second group, on the other hand, pleaded for providing western knowledge by teaching science through the medium of English. The Orientalists were extremely keen on preserving the existing institutions of Oriental Learning, while the Anglicists proposed to abolish them. Being aware of the weakness of their case the Orientalists were ready to accept a compromise formula under which the students might be given option to choose between English and the Oriental education.

The period between 1813 and 1835 was, therefore, a period of controversy between the two groups over the issues related to educational policy including the medium of instruction.

Macaulay and his Minute (1835)

Thomas Babington Macaulay, a member of the British Parliament, who had studied the problems of British education in India in sufficient details, made an important statement before the House of Commons. He said:

> Are we to keep the people of India ignorant in order that we may keep them submissive? Or do we think that we can give knowledge without awakening ambition? Or do we mean to awaken ambition and to provide no legitimate vent? Who will answer any of these questions in affirmative?.... The destinies

of our Indian Empire are covered with thick darkness.... It may be that public mind of India may expand under our system until it has outgrown that system, that by good government we may educate our subjects into a capacity for better government, that having become instructed in European knowledge, they may, in some future age, demand European institutions. Whether such a day will ever come I know not. But...whenever it comes, it will be the proudest day in English History.

Macaulay was a profound scholar. He came to India in 1834 as Legal Member of the Governor's Executive Council. The saying that he was the father of modern Indian education, is not an exaggeration. His study of the psychology of Indian society and problems of British education in India was remarkable. He also supported the theory of 'downward filtration' advocated for by Elphinstone and stated:

> In one point, I fully agree with the gentlemen whose general views I am opposed to. I feel with them that it is impossible for us, with our limited means, to attempt to educate the body of the people. We must at present do our best to form a class who may be interpreters between us and the millions whom we govern, a class of persons Indian in blood and colour, but English in tastes, in opinions, in morals, and in intellect.

This statement of Macaulay was pregnant with meaning, and reflected the purpose of British education in India. The purpose was not to promote socio-economic or cultural development of the people of India, rather, to produce low cost man-power to run the British factories in India and Britain, and to help the rulers govern the natives of this land. He was a vigorous advocate of providing instruction through the medium of English, and of superiority of western science and literature. He had stated once:

> We have to educate a people who cannot at present be educated by means of their own mother tongue. We must teach them some foreign language.... In India, English is the language spoken by the ruling class. It is spoken by the higher classes of natives at the seats of government. It is likely to become the

> language of commerce throughout the seas of the East the natives are desirous to be taught English and are not desirous to be taught Sanskrit or Arabic...that it is possible to make natives of this country thoroughly good English scholars, and that to this end our efforts ought to be directed.

In 1835, Macaulay suggested the government a detailed plan, popularly known as Macaulay's Minute, of British education in India. Through his famous Minute, he urged the government to undertake a formal western type of education imparting knowledge of western literature and science through English as a medium of instruction. He also proposed to utilize total educational grant to achieve that goal, and to use the existing educational institutions of oriental learning for the promotion of western education. He addressed the issues involved in the controversy between the Orientalists and the Anglicists and Section 43 of the Charter Act 1913 in his own way. The following statement of Nurullah and Naik (1951) is worth mentioning:

> Macaulay argued that the word 'Literature' occurring in this section could be interpreted to mean English literature, and the epithet of a 'learned native India' could also be applied to a person versed in the philosophy of Locke or the poetry of Milton, and the object of promoting a knowledge of sciences could only be accomplished by the adoption of English as the medium of instruction. If this interpretation was not accepted, Macaulay was willing to propose an Act rescinding Section 43 of the Charter.... Referring to the question of the alleged prejudices of the Indian people against English education, Macaulay argued that it was the duty of England to teach Indians what was good for their health, and not what was palatable to their taste. Even assuming that the taste of the people should be consulted, Macaulay argued that Indians had given sufficient evidence of their love for English.

In this way, the Anglicists emerged triumphant in their fight for supremacy over the Orientalists. Macaulay's Minute became a major guideline for future education in India under the British rule. The plan proposed by him was not only endorsed by the government, but also widely accepted by enlightened Indians. Therefore, it is considered as an important landmark in the history of Indian education. English language and western science started receiving increased importance in every sphere of life. It made the affluent classes realize that material progress was more important than preservation of traditional cultural values. Macaulay was very confident of obtaining the desired results. He wrote to his father (1836):

> Our English schools are flourishing wonderfully. We find it difficult to...provide instruction to all that want it...the effect of this education on the Hindus is prodigious. No Hindu, who has received English education, ever remains sincerely attached to his religion...and some embrace Christianity. It is my firm belief, if our plans of education are followed up, there will not be a single idolater among the respected classes in Bengal thirty years hence. And this will be effected without any efforts to proselytize.... I heartily rejoice in the prospect.

The controversy between the two groups was decisively settled by Macaulay's Minute. In perfect agreement with the views expressed by Macaulay, Lord William Bentinck, then Governor General of India, issued a resolution (1835) saying that the great object of the British government ought to be the promotion of European literature and science among the natives of India, and that all the funds appropriated for the purpose of education should be best employed on English education.

The decision of Lord William Bentinck was reaffirmed by Lord Auckland (1839), the next Governor General, and subsequently, by the Despatch of the Court of Directors (1841) on the subject. Lord Auckland's main emphasis was on communicating through English language a complete education in European Language and Literature, Philosophy and Science to the greatest number of students who may be found ready to accept it. His document was perhaps the clearest in its emphasis on what is popularly known as "downward filtration theory", because he believed that the way to reach the masses was through the educated classes.

These developments led to the pacification of the Anglicists-Orientalists controversy with the position of the Orientalists considerably weakened. The schools for Oriental learning were maintained, but translations into Sanskrit and Arabic were discontinued. The system of "English Education" was adopted and encouraged by the Government, and developed alongside the vernacular schools.

However, in some quarters, the British policy of giving education in English and western science was looked at with suspicion. It was taken as a conspiracy of the then government to undermine the religious and cultural traditions of India and directed to convert the natives to Christianity. Those few who rushed for English education were isolated from the common people. This resulted in an unfortunate division of Indian people into two classes—English knowing and non-English knowing. The English knowing educated class developed a superiority complex, and did not mix up with the rest of the people. This phenomenon proved to be the just opposite of the one contemplated in the "downward filtration theory". This disappointed the then government a little.

Hardinge's Resolution (1844)

After the adoption of Macaulay's Minute as a Policy of British education in India, the Government announced its policy of giving every encouragement to educated Indians by employing them in the government service. In order to reinforce the favourable results of the implementation of the provisions of Macaulay's Minute, Lord Hardinge issued a proclamation in 1844, which stated that in every possible case, a preference would be given, in the selection of candidates for public employment, to those who had been educated in the institutions established for English education, and especially to those who had distinguished themselves therein by a more than ordinary degree of merit and attainment. The proclamation stated:

> The Governor General having taken into his consideration the existing state of education in Bengal, and being of the opinion that it is highly desirable to afford it every reasonable encouragement by holding out to those who have taken advantage of the opportunity of instruction afforded to them, a fair prospect of employment in the public services, and

thereby not only to reward individual merit, but also to enable the state to profit as largely and as early as possible, by the result of the measures adopted of late years for the instruction of the people as well by the government as by private individuals and societies, has resolved that in every possible case a preference shall be given in the selection of candidates for public employment to those who have been educated in the institutions thus established, and especially to those who have distinguished themselves therein by a more than ordinary degree of merit and attainment.

Hardinge's resolution gave a big boost to the English education in India. Thereafter, the study of English became a kind of "vocational education" because it guaranteed jobs in the government offices. There was a great rush of Indian youth from upper and upper-middle classes to English schools, which also mushroomed as a result of the government proclamation. Hardinge's proclamation was another important landmark in the history of Indian education.

The foregoing discussion indicates that the period of 1833-53 was a period of controversies rather than of achievements. The Company was busy in trade and commerce, conquest and consolidation, and did not devote much attention or money to the cause of education. The discussion regarding the aims of education, the agencies to be employed and the medium of instruction consumed most their time.

Wood's Education Dispatch

Company's Charter came up for revision in 1853. Upto this time; the Company's policies regarding education had neither a definite direction nor a clear-cut planning. There was hardly any system of government funding or administration of education. The revised Charter led to definite acceptance of the education of Indians as the responsibility of the government, and consequently, to the issuance of an education dispatch by Sir Charles Wood, then President of the Board of Control of the Company. Wood's Dispatch (1854) covered the entire field of education—primary, secondary, and university, and gave a definite direction for its development. It was issued by the Court of Directors of the Company on 19th

July 1854 and is considered to be a document of great historical significance. It provided, in fact, a very comprehensive scheme of British education in India. At that time, there were no universities or institutions of higher learning. There were about 25 colleges in the whole country and total enrollment in schools and colleges was about 40,000. Through this Dispatch, the Court of Directors reiterated the main objective of education, as diffusion of European knowledge of less high order, but of such a character as might be practically useful to the people in different spheres of life. The Dispatch proposed:

(i) That English language would be taught wherever it was demanded, and vernacular languages would be used as media of instruction for the great mass of the people. It was, in fact a compromise formula to settle the controversy of the Orientalists and Anglicists groups on the issue of language and the medium of instruction.

(ii) That the Departments of Public Instruction would be created in each province to streamline educational administration and management, which would function under the administrative control of a Director of Public Instruction (DPI) appointed by the government. The DPI would be required to submit to the government an annual report on the progress of education in his province.

(iii) That universities would be established at Bombay, Calcutta and Madras (or at any other place) on the model of London University to conduct examination and award degrees in literature, arts, and science for the students receiving education in the colleges affiliated to them. The senates of these universities were to consist of a Chancellor, a Vice Chancellor, and Fellows—all nominated by the government.

(iv) That the government would take active measures to provide the great mass of the people useful and practical knowledge suited to every station of life, by establishing a network of graded schools in every district and by encouraging indigenous schools. This meant that the government would set up a large number of high schools which gave instruction through English or through a

modern Indian language, and indigenous primary schools to provide instruction through vernacular languages. The government, by this time, had realized that the downward filtration theory, which was adopted earlier had not paid dividends and a more egalitarian approach to education policy was needed.

(v) That the local bodies under effective control of the government, would be encouraged to establish and manage educational institutions, and a system of grant-in-aid would be introduced. This was done under government's plan to encourage indigenous system of education at lower level. This policy presupposed that the schools opened by the local bodies would impart secular education, possess a good management, abide by the rules and regulations of the government and levy a fee, however small, from the pupils.

(vi) That a system of training of school teachers would be introduced through specially set up normal schools on the pattern of similar schools being run in Britain.

(vii) That educated persons would be preferred to uneducated ones for government jobs and candidates for employment on such jobs would be selected through selection tests wherever feasible.

(viii) That the government would encourage establishment of institutions of professional education (engineering, medicine, etc.) in areas where they did not exist, and support them where they existed.

(ix) That public education would be entirely secular without any provision of religious instruction in the institutions aided by the government, but the education of Muslim minority and girls, however, would be supported.

The Dispatch of 1854 laid the foundation on which the future Indian education was to be built. Some people have described it as the 'Magna Carta' of Indian education. Mr. H.R. James described the Despatch as 'the climax in the history of India education: what goes before leads to it: what follows flows from it'. With this Dispatch, all the controversies regarding aims of British education, medium of instruction, oriental learning, and religious education came to an end. The proposals of the Dispatch had three important features—the rejection of the downward filtration theory, the adoption of the modern Indian languages as media of instruction at the secondary stage, and the inclusion of indigenous schools as the very foundation of a national system of education. Sir Philip Hartog (1939) summarized the provisions of the Dispatch in the following words:

> It imposed on the Government of India the duty of creating a properly articulated system of education, from the primary school to the university; and perhaps its most notable feature was the emphasis, which it laid on primary education, and therefore its implicit repudiation of the more extreme forms of the "Filtration Theory". In order to carry out its policy, the Dispatch prescribed the following measures: the constitution in each presidency and lieutenant governorship of a separate department for the administration of education, with an adequate system of inspection; the institution of universities in the presidency towns; the establishment of institutions for training teachers for all classes of schools; the maintenance of the existing government colleges and high schools, and the increase of their number when necessary; increased attention to vernacular schools, both for secondary and for primary education; and the introduction of a system of grant-in-aid. The Dispatch laid great stress on the importance of encouraging the study of vernaculars as the only possible media for mass education, and recommended the institution of a comprehensive system of scholarships to connect all grades of the educational system. It further expressed sympathy for the causes of the female education and Muhammadan education; it advocated the opening of schools and colleges for technical instruction; and it insisted on a policy of perfect religious neutrality. It should be added that the Dispatch looked forward to a time when any general system of education provided by Government might be gradually discontinued, with the advance of the system of grant-in-aid, and when the management, especially of higher institutions, might be handed over to local bodies under the control of, or aided by, the state.

As a follow-up of the Dispatch, during the period of Lord Dalhousie, the Departments of Public Instruction under the Directors were created (1855); universities were established at Bombay, Calcutta and Madras (1857) as examining bodies with powers to affiliate colleges, on the model first adopted by the University of London; and the system of grant-in-aid was introduced. Later on, it was felt by the government that the system of grant-in-aid had failed to achieve its objective of producing a system of primary schools. In this connection a Bengal officer, Henry Woodrow, made the following observation:

> ...the poorest classes do not want schools at all, because they are too poor to pay schooling-fees and subscriptions, and the labour of the children is required to enable them to live. The middle and upper classes will make no sort of sacrifice for the establishment of any but English schools.

However, there were certain other issues to which no attention was paid while drafting the Dispatch. For instance, the Despatch did not even refer to the ideal of universal literacy, though it proposed to spread education among the masses through the system of grant-in aid. It did not talk of compulsory education for all children up to a certain age. It also did not talk of development of talent through education, provision of education for leadership, and preparation of natives for self-governance. Therefore, the net achievements were insignificant (Nurullah and Naik, 1943, page 178) as compared with the vastness of the population and the backwardness of its education. Even as late as 1855, the total number of educational institutions managed, aided, or inspected by the Company was as small as 1474 with only 67,569 pupils, and the total expenditure on education was not even one per cent of the total revenue.

Indian Education Commission (1882)

After the First War of Independence (1857), the Government of India was transferred from the Company to the Crown, and the Department of Education was transferred to the Provincial Governments (1871). By a government resolution, education of the masses was claimed to be the greatest duty of the state. After the Dispatch of 1854 there were hectic activities in the field of education. In order to review the progress of education during the period since 1854, Lord Ripon appointed the Indian Education Commission in 1882, with Sir William Hunter as its Chairman. The Commission was required to 'inquire particularly into the manner in which effect had been given to the principles of the Dispatch of 1854 and to suggest such measures as it might think desirable, with a view to the further carrying out of the policy therein laid down' with special reference to primary education and grant-in-aid system, which had produced results far more rapidly in secondary than in primary education. By 1882, there were in Bengal alone 156 high schools under Indian management of which 96 received grant-in-aid. The Commission undertook a comprehensive review of the progress of education since the advent of the British rule and submitted its report in 1884. The major recommendations of the Commission included:

(i) Encouragement and support to indigenous schools for extending elementary education by declaring elementary education of the masses as the most important priority—area in education to which strenuous government efforts should be directed;

(ii) Allocation of a large part of government funds, meant for education sector, to elementary education for its rapid and healthy growth;

(iii) Revision of standards of primary education in order to introduce practical subjects such as arithmetic, accounts, mensuration, natural and physical sciences, and their applications to agriculture, health and industry;

(iv) Freedom to the management committees for choosing vernacular language as a medium of instruction depending on the local needs;

(v) Establishment of secondary schools by the state, for instruction in English based on the system of grant-in aid, and setting up of primary schools with the support of local people;

(vi) Gradual transfer of all government secondary schools to local native management committees with due consideration of maintenance of standards and quality of education;

(*vii*) Bifurcation of secondary education into two streams—one leading to the entrance examination of the universities and the other of a more practical character preparing the students for commercial jobs;

(*viii*) Institution of an examination in the principles and practice of teaching, success in which to be made a condition for a permanent employment as a teacher in any secondary school;

(*ix*) More preferential employment of the Indian graduates, especially those who graduated in European universities, than they had hitherto been, in the government colleges.

This Commission had some distinguished Indian representatives who said that while every branch of education could justly claim the fostering care of the government it was desirable in the contemporary circumstances of the country to declare the elementary education of the masses, its provision, extension, and improvement, to be that part of the educational system to which strenuous efforts of the state should have been directed in a still larger measure than theretofore. They also suggested that primary education should be regarded as having an almost exclusive claim on local funds set apart for education, and a large claim on provincial revenues and proposed that aid to primary schools should be regulated to a large extent according to the results of examination, except in the backward areas (Hartog, 1939).

Regarding the secondary school curriculum, the Commission remarked, 'It has been felt that the attention of the students is too exclusively directed to university studies and that no opportunity is offered for the development of what corresponds to the "modern side" of the schools in Europe. It is believed that there is a real need in India of some corresponding course which shall fit boys for industrial or commercial pursuits, at the age when they commonly matriculate, more directly than is effected by the present system'.

Indian Universities Commission (1902)

In pursuance of the recommendation of Indian Education Commission (1882-84), the government considered seriously the ways and means to develop primary education, and technical education at high school stage. The progress of education during the period from 1882-84 to 1901-02 was reviewed during the period of Lord Curzon (1902), then Viceroy of India. Specifically, in order to review the contemporary conditions of the universities, Lord Curzon appointed the Indian Universities Commission in 1902. On the basis of the recommendations of this commission and the Conference of Provincial Directors of Public Instruction (1901), Indian Universities Bill was introduced in the Viceregal Council (1903), and consequently, the Government of India Resolution on Indian Educational Policy was issued in March 1904. This resolution expressed a grave concern at the defects of education, as it existed, such as pursuing higher education for entering government jobs exclusively, dominance of examination on teaching, too much emphasis on memory training, neglect of the vernaculars and too much emphasis on literary aspects of the curriculum. Special attention was paid to primary education in the Resolution. In view of the importance of primary education as mass education, it was proposed that it should be expanded and should attract more funds from government revenue. The progress on this front was unsatisfactory since only 22.2 per cent of boys and 2.5 per cent of girls of school-going age attended school, and 10 per cent of male population and only 0.7 per cent of female population were literate. The resolution proposed to strengthen secondary education by laying down certain conditions for recognition, funding, and affiliation to the examining universities. The introduction of diversified courses to meet the demands of industrial development was also proposed. Regarding learning of languages and medium of instruction at school level, the resolution said:

> As a general rule, a child should not be allowed to learn English language until he has made some progress in the primary stage of education and has received a thorough grounding in his mother tongue. It is equally important that when the teaching of English has begun, it should not be prematurely employed as the medium of instruction in other subjects....The line of division between the use of vernaculars and of English as the medium of instruction should, broadly speaking, be drawn at a minimum age of 13.

The Resolution indicated far-reaching decisions of the government regarding university education. It proposed to reconstitute Senates and Syndicates of universities by limiting the number of ex-officio fellows and by reducing the maximum number of senators. In addition to examination function, the universities would arrange for teaching work. The colleges seeking affiliation to the universities would be required to fulfil certain minimum requirements as prescribed by the concerned university. Affiliation would be granted only when the colleges had a regular governing body, qualified teachers, adequate building and equipment, staff quarters, sufficient financial resources and a rational fee policy. Affiliation once granted might not be permanent and might be reviewed through a proper inspection.

Important proposals were also made to improve technical, vocational, and commercial education so as to make it more practical and relevant to the local needs of the people of India. Agricultural education was also proposed to be expanded. The need for the training of secondary school teachers was emphasized in order to make school teaching more efficient and non-mechanical.

Gokhale's Bill (1910-12)

Gopal Krishan Gokhale, the champion of compulsory primary education in India, moved a resolution for compulsory education (1910), which was withdrawn on the assurance of the government that it would be examined carefully. The next year (1911) again, Gokhale introduced a private bill in the Imperial Legislative Council which, was debated for two days and turned down by clear official majority mainly because of opposition from the Indian States. The bill came up again in 1912, and was again turned down, though it enjoyed the support of many prominent Indians in the Central Legislation. However, the repeated failure of Gokhale focussed the public attention on the problem of compulsory primary education, and paved the path of complete success (Chauhan, 1990) achieved at a later date. Gokhale had stated:

> My Lord, I know that my Bill will be thrown out before the day closes, I make no complaints. I shall not even feel depressed. I know too well the story of the preliminary efforts

> that were required even in England, before the Act of 1870 was passed. Moreover, I have always felt and often said that we, of the present generation in India, can only hope to serve our country by our failures. The men and women who will be privileged to serve her by their successes will come later. We must be content to accept cheerfully the place that has been allotted to us in our onward march. The Bill thrown out today will come again and again, tell on the stepping-stones of its dead selves, a measure ultimately rises which will spread the light throughout the land.

The efforts made by Gokhale gave positive results shortly. The government Resolution on Educational Policy (1913) provided for sufficient expansion of lower primary schools with a simultaneous opening of upper primary schools. It proposed to streamline inspection and supervision, appoint trained teachers, subsidize Maktabs and Pathshalas, improve school facilities, and encourage girl's education. The Resolution also provided for expansion of university education considering the existing 5 universities and 185 colleges as insufficient. The universities were to be relieved of responsibility of granting recognition to high schools, and new teaching universities were to be opened in addition to the affiliating ones.

Calcutta University Commission (1917-19)

Calcutta University Commission was appointed by the Government of India in 1917 to inquire into the condition and prospects of Calcutta University with Dr. Michael Sadler as Chairman. Those days, the Matriculation Examination, which marked the end of school stage and constituted an entrance examination to the universities, was conducted by the universities. After two years, another public examination was held (also by the universities) which was called Intermediate Examination. This was followed by the First Degree examination. The problem was studied by the commission in depth and the following conclusions were drawn (Hasan, 1975):

(i) That the Intermediate stage was really a part of the school course and that the students at this stage could be more

effectively taught by school methods than by college methods; and

(ii) That the standard of under-graduate education in the university was so poor that the first degree in India was not really comparable to the first degree in the advanced countries.

The Commission, therefore, recommended that:

(i) the dividing line between the university and the secondary courses is more appropriately drawn at the Intermediate Examination than at the matriculation;

(ii) the duration of under-graduate courses for the first degree should be increased to three years with a provision of Honours courses;

(iii) a Board of Secondary and Intermediate Education should be established for the purpose of reorganizing High School and Intermediate education on the lines recommended by it and for holding the Matriculation and Intermediate examinations;

(iv) the universities should, thus, be left to their proper sphere, namely, the provision of under-graduate and post-graduate education and holding of examination for the first, second and research degrees;

(v) a teaching and residential university be established at Dacca to reduce the examination burden of Calcutta University;

(vi) the internal administration of the university should be improved by setting up a representative Court and Executive Council to replace Senate and Syndicate respectively. An Academic Council and Board of Studies be set up to make academic decisions in different faculties to be created;

(vii) a full time salaried vice-chancellor be appointed. A special selection committee, including external experts, be constituted to appoint Professors and Readers;

(viii) the universities should have Departments of Education with provision of teaching "Education" as a subject at B.A. level. Calcutta University was empowered to have a special Board of Women Education; and

(ix) an Inter-University Board (IUB) be established to coordinate the work of different Indian universities.

EDUCATION AND THE FREEDOM MOVEMENT

The rise of National Freedom Movement gave birth to the concept of the National System of Education, which implied (i) Indian control of education, (ii) inculcation of patriotism, and (iii) disregard of western education. Coupled with non-cooperation movement, the concept of "national system of education" led to the establishment of several institutions on national lines. The notable among them were: Banaras Hindu University (1916), Aligarh Muslim University (1920), Gujarat Vidyapeeth, Kashi Vidyapeeth, Jamia Millia Islamia and Tilak Maharashtra Vidyapeeth.

In 1919, the Government of India Act was introduced which, in effect, devolved considerable responsibility to the provinces. The Act created "Diarchy" or "Rule of Two" leading to greater representation of elected members. In 1921, the Department of Education was transferred to an Indian Minister responsible to Legislature. Being unable to receive sufficient funds from the government, these ministers could not provide the expected results. The continuous pressure for educational improvement resulted in the appointment of Hartog Committee (1928), which made wide-ranging proposals for development of both, general and professional education.

Wardha Conference (1937)

Mahatma Gandhi published his radical proposals about education in "Harijan" as a series of articles in 1937. These, in turn, led to the First Congress of National Education at Wardha in October 1937 (Steele and Taylor, 1995). Gandhi's basic idea was for education to become self-supporting through craft, agriculture, and other productive work, thereby by-passing potentially the need for government funding support. The scheme called "Basic Education" was outlined at Wardha Conference (1937) as follows:

(i) There should be free and compulsory education for seven years for all children on a national scale.

(ii) The medium of instruction should be the mother tongue.

(iii) The education should centre on manual and productive work and all other abilities to be taught should be related to the central handicraft.

(iv) The education should be self-financing through the production of some necessary material item like khadi, which could pay the cost of the teacher and the material.

This conference appointed a committee of educationists headed by Dr. Zakir Hussain to work out the details of the curriculum. The report of this committee received in 1938 was placed before Indian National Congress the same year and was readily accepted. The first "Basic School" was established at Sevagram near Wardha in 1938 under Gandhji's personal supervision. As stated by Steele and Taylor (1995), Basic Education was opposed by Congress leaders (under Nehru) and the industrialists (whom Congress Party represented), who showed a great reluctance in moving from the existing colonially derived system to Basic Education. They objected to the emphasis on vocation condemning it as "child labour" and offered instead a broad-based curriculum for elementary education and expansion of facilities for technical education.

Post-War Plan of Educational Development (1944)

After the end of Second World War, the Central Advisory Board of Education (CABE) in India published a comprehensive report on the "post-war educational development" in the country. This was the first systematic and national level attempt (Aggarwal, 1984) at taking the problems of education as a whole. It is also known as Sargent Plan after John Sargent, the then Educational Advisor to the Government of India. It is worth mentioning here that this plan was proposed by the British Government in order to counter the attempts made by leaders of the freedom movement to evolve a National System of Education (such as Wardha Scheme). The Sargent Plan proposed to provide for:

(i) free and compulsory universal primary education for all children of the age group 6-14 years, divided into two stages—Junior Basic and Senior Basic, and preceded by pre-primary education for 3-6 age group;

(ii) selective admission to secondary education both in academic and technical streams based on merit and ability;

(iii) selective admission to three-year degree courses on the basis of merit in general and professional education;

(iv) full-time and part-time courses in technical, professional, and commercial education available on merit;

(v) facilities for liquidation of illiteracy through adult education with special provision for the education of the handicapped;

(vi) adequate provision for training of teachers and improvement of their socio-economic and service conditions; and

(vii) adequate support services such as employment bureaus, health services, recreational facilities, mid-day meals, and milk supply and guidance the requirements of the colonial rule. Hardly any attempt was made toward mass services.

Sargent Plan was one of the most comprehensive schemes of education ever proposed by the British Government after the Despatch of 1854. Through this, the government had proposed a detailed outline of the educational programmes to be undertaken by the government during the following 40 years from 1944 to 1984. As the freedom movement was at its full swing those days, this plan could not be implemented because of political turmoil in the country. With India achieving freedom in 1947, this Plan became only a matter of historical significance.

THE SCENARIO IN 1947

The quantitative development of education in India is summarized in Table 1.1 (compiled from Misra, 1962). As mentioned earlier, the official funding of educational institutions began after the creation of the system of grant-in aid in 1954 on the recommendation of the Wood's Education Despatch. It was after this event only that the government made some serious attempts to develop the system of education, which had been established by that time. In 1855-56, the total number of primary schools in India was 3400, which enrolled 97000 children. The number of secondary schools (including middle schools) was about 280 with a total enrollment of 33800 children. The number of colleges was 26 enrolling 2250 students. There were no universities those days. By 1870-71, the number of primary schools increased to 18600, which enrolled 16.74 lakh children. Secondary schools had also increased to 3020 with a total enrollment of 1.25 lakh. The number of colleges also increased to 42 having a total enrollment of 3570 students. By that time 3 universities had also been established (1857). By the turn of the Nineteenth Century (1901-02), the number of primary schools had increased to 97850 having a total enrollment of over 32 lakh. The secondary schools had also increased to 5500 having enrolled 6.23 lakhs of students. There were 191 colleges and 5 universities with a total enrollment of about 23000 students.

The development of education was faster during the first quarter of the Nineteenth Century and by 1931-32, the number of primary and secondary schools had increased to 201570 and 13740 respectively with a total enrollment of 96.84 lakh. There were 317 colleges and 16 universities, which had enrolled about 99500 students. After this, the progress of education slowed down because of certain socio-political problems in the country. The national freedom movement had acquired an aggressive dimension, which diverted the attention of the government from developmental aspects to political aspects of the administration. Consequently, by 1946-47, the number of primary schools decreased to 172660 enrolling 130.4 lakh children, and that of secondary schools increased marginally to 18140 having enrolled 39.75 lakh children. The total number of colleges and universities was 594 and 21 respectively, which together enrolled 2.53 lakh students.

Table 1.1
Educational Development Before 1947

Year	Primary Education		Secondary Education		* College Education		** Universities Education	
	Number	Enrollment	Number	Enrollment	Number	Enrollment	Number	Enrollment
1855-56	3400	97000	290	33800	26	2250		NA
1865-66	14500	374000	2200	181050	27	1600	3	NA
1870-71	18600	1674500	3020	124800	42	3570	3	NA
1881-82	86270	2156240	4120	222100	85	7580	4	NA
1891-92	97110	2837600	4870	473300	141	16280	5	NA
1901-02	97850	3204340	5500	622770	191	23010	5	NA
1911-12	123580	4988140	6370	924370	186	36300	5	NA
1921-22	160100	6310400	8990	1239520	231	59600	14	NA
1931-32	201570	9454360	13740	229752	317	90400	16	9090
1941-42	181970	12018730	15200	2784790	400	156740	18	12530
1946-47	172660	13036250	18140	3974830	594	237200	21	16150

* Middle schools also included.
** Technical and Professional Colleges also included.

During the British period, the government never took education sector seriously. It was always pursued half-heartedly and haphazardly. This was because the basic objective of education was not to transform the Indian society for better living, rather, to serve education, not to talk of technical, professional or industrial education. The progress of education among girls was not satisfactory. In 1901-02, the enrollment of girls in primary schools was about 11% of the total enrollment, which increased to 19% in 1921-22, and then decreased to 13.8% in 1931-32. In secondary school, the enrollment of girls was only 7% in 1901-02, which increased to 10% in 1921-22, and then decreased to 8.7% in 1931-32. In higher education also, the progress was equally dismal. The total enrollment of girls was 9.5% in 1911-12, but came down to 2.3% in 1921-22.

In 1947, the enrollment in primary schools from class I to class V (age group 6-11 years) was about 10.5 million children receiving instruction in 141,000 primary schools. The number of upper primary (middle) schools for classes VI to VIII (age group 11-14 years) was 9,000 with a total enrollment of 1.60 million. Thus, total enrollment in elementary education for age-group 6-14 years was 12.10 million in 150,000 schools. The enrollment of girls was only about 3 million— about 25% of the total enrollment in elementary schools. In 1947-48, there were 20 universities, 500 colleges, and 2.15 lakhs students enrolled in them including 13,000 at post-graduate stage and 900 in research. The enrollment of girls was around 23,000 including 3,000 in professional courses. As a percentage of total enrollments it was only 9%, which increased marginally to 10.70% by 1949-50. The literacy rate among women was 8.30% as against 25% among men (1941). These figures, however, indicate only quantitative progress.

2

Educational Provisions in the Constitution

India achieved freedom from the British imperialism on August 15, 1947 after a prolonged struggle guided by Gandhiji's ideals of "Truth" and "Non-violence". It was, in fact, a new beginning of self-development and self-reliance. The society decided to uphold certain basic values to guide the functioning of the individual and social life. Based on these values and the philosophical traditions of India, the new Constitution was adopted on November 26, 1949. The basic values enshrined in the Constitution are Democracy, Socialism and Secularism. These values emphasize the following principles (Anand, 1983):

(i) Democratic principles such as freedom, equality, tolerance, readiness to see the other man's point of view, willingness to give and take, ability to adjust in and work with the groups;

(ii) Socialist principles such as respect for and commitment to equality in status and opportunity, maximizing production and wealth, and equitable distribution of wealth; and

(iii) Secular principles such as respect for all religions, freedom of worship, and readiness to see and manage civic affairs without reference to religion.

The Constitution declares India to be a Sovereign Socialist Secular Democratic Republic and stresses these values in the very Preamble, which states as follows:

> WE, THE PEOPLE OF INDIA, have solemnly resolved to constitute India into a SOVEREIGN SOCIALIST SECULAR DEMOCRATIC REPUBLIC and to secure to all its citizens:
> JUSTICE, social, economic, and political;
> LIBERTY of thought, expression, belief, faith, and worship;
> EQUALITY of status and of opportunity; and to promote among them all
> FRATERNITY assuring the dignity of the individual and the unity of the Nation;
> IN OUR CONSTITUENT ASSEMBLY this twenty-sixth day of November, 1949, do hereby adopt, enact, and give to ourselves this Constitution.

The Constitution, which came into force on January 26, 1950, has built-in provisions related to education. These provisions, implicitly or explicitly, refer to the basic values enshrined in the Constitution. Educational provisions may be described in terms of emphasis on various values, such as, those which emphasize— (i) democratic and socialistic values; (ii) equality and justice; and (iii) secularism, fraternity, and national unity.

DEMOCRATIC AND SOCIALISTIC VALUES

The Directive Principles of State Policy given in Part IV of the Constitution are meant for guiding the State in promoting social welfare. The provisions contained in this part of the Constitution, though not enforceable by the courts are fundamental in the governance of the country. It is the duty of the government to apply these principles while making laws. The Constitution directs the government to strive to promote the welfare of the people by securing and protecting, as effectively as it may, a social order in which justice — social, economic and political, shall inform all the institutions of social life (Article 38). The government policies shall also be directed to ensure equal rights for all the citizens in respect of means of livelihood, distribution of ownership and control of material resources and wealth for common good, equal pay for equal work for both the sexes, protection of women and children from unsuitable and forced labour and protection of children against the moral and material exploitation (Article 39). The government would provide for self-government through Panchayati Raj (Article 40) and right to work, to education, and to public assistance in cases of unemployment, old age, sickness and disablement, and other cases of unserved want (Article 41). The State is obliged to secure just and humane conditions of work, and provide for maternity relief (Article 42), work and living wages for all workers ensuring a decent standard of life and full employment by promoting cottage industries in rural areas (Article 43), and uniform civil code for the citizens throughout the territory of India (Article 44).

One of the most important constitutional provisions regarding education is incorporated in Article 45 of the Constitution, which states:

> The state shall endeavour to provide, within a period of ten years from the commencement of this Constitution, for free and compulsory education for all children until they complete the age of fourteen years.

This provision was made in the Constitution in view of the importance of universal elementary education for the proper development and success of Democracy. This provision has important implication for education.

EQUALITY AND JUSTICE

There are certain provisions in the Constitution, which are aimed at promoting equality and securing justice for all citizens. Equality before law or equal protection by laws is guaranteed to all (Article 14), and discrimination against any citizen on grounds of religion, race, caste, sex or place of birth is prohibited (Article 15). Though, Article 15 prohibits all kinds of discrimination on the ground of religion, sex, caste, race, place of birth or any of them, nothing in this Article shall prevent the state from making any special provision for the advancement of any socially or educationally backward classes of citizens, especially, women and children (Article 15-3), and Scheduled Castes and Scheduled Tribes (Article 15-4).

Reservation of seats in the Parliament and Legislative Assemblies of the states has been provided for in order to ensure political equity (Article 16). Similarly for women also, attempts are being made to reserve seats in the Parliament and state assemblies. The practice of untouchability, in any way, has been banned (Article 17) and made a punishable offence in order to secure social justice and equality. Special provisions have been made in the Constitution for the protection of the educational and economic interests of the under-privileged sections of the society. Article 46 states:

> The state shall promote, with special care, the educational and economic interests of the weaker sections of the people, and in particular, of the Scheduled Castes and Scheduled Tribes, and shall protect them from social injustice and all forms of exploitation.

The term "state" occurring in this article and others like Article 45, is defined in Article 12 to include 'the Government and Parliament of India, and the Government and the Legislature of each of the states and local or other authorities within the territory of India or under the control of the Government of India.' Article 46 empowers the government to provide reservations in educational institutions and government services for Scheduled Castes and Scheduled Tribes.

SECULARISM AND NATIONAL UNITY

As mentioned in the Preamble of the Constitution, India is a secular country, and therefore, does not provide for any kind of official support to any religion. However, the Constitution provides each citizen of the country a freedom to practice any religion. In view of this, the Constitution makes special provision regarding the status of religious instruction in the institutions funded by the state. The Constitution also provides special safeguards for the educational and cultural interests of minorities. The status of religious instruction in educational institutions is described in Article 28, which states:

(1) No religious instruction will be provided in any educational institution wholly maintained by the state funds.
(2) Nothing in clause (i) shall apply to any educational institution, which is administered by the state, but has been established under any endowment or trust, which requires that religious instructions shall be imparted in such institution.
(3) No person, attending any educational institution recognized by the state or receiving aid out of state funds, shall be required to take part in any religious instruction, that may be imparted in such institution or any premises attached thereto, unless such person or, if such person is a minor, his guardian has given his assent thereto.

The cultural interests of minorities are protected through Article 29, which states:

(1) Any section of citizens residing in the territory of India or any part thereof having a distinct language, script, or culture of its own shall have the right to conserve the same.
(2) No citizen shall be denied admission into any educational institution maintained by the state or receiving aid out of state funds on grounds only of religion, race, caste, language or any of them.

The educational interests of minorities are protected through Article 30, which states:

(1) All minorities, whether based on religion or language, shall have the right to establish and administer educational institutions of their choice.
(2) The state shall not, in granting aid to educational institutions, discriminate against any educational institution on the ground that it is under the management of a minority, whether based on religion or language.

It is clear that no institution established under Article 30 can refuse admission to any citizen of India (Article 29) on the ground of religion, race, caste, language or any one of them. It is to be noted that "sex" has not been mentioned among these grounds. Hence, it appears that admission on the ground of sex may be denied if such an act is not in violation of other provisions of the Constitution. In this connection it may be noted that Article 15(3) authorizes the state to make special provisions for women and children. Hence, separate educational institutions for women are constitutionally valid (Tope, 1989).

The Constitution does not provide any specific direction regarding medium of instruction. However, Article 350-A points out that 'it shall be the endeavour of every state or of every local authority within the state to provide adequate facilities for instructions in the mother tongue at the primary stage of education to children belonging to linguistic minority groups.' The Supreme Court of India has laid down rules regarding the medium of instruction in the institutions of higher education while deciding certain cases related to higher education. The law laid down by the Supreme Court becomes a kind of binding on the educational institutions. The Court has laid down that the universities cannot follow the regional language or languages as the sole medium of instruction.

EDUCATION, CONSTITUTION AND JUDICIARY

The discussion in the previous sections shows how Indian Constitution has provided directions to the government to facilitate social, political, economic, and educational advancement of all sections of the society with in-built "protective discrimination" in favour of weaker sections, namely, scheduled castes, scheduled tribes, minorities, women and children, and other backward sections. However, to some "law" means what they interpret it to mean. Consequently, there has been a lot of misinterpretation, wrong implementation, and in certain cases, misuse of the constitutional provisions. Many controversial matters have been taken to courts of law including the Supreme Court. Most of the cases settled by the Supreme Court have been related to Articles 15, 16, 28, 29 and 30. It would be out of context to refer to individual cases in this discussion. However, reference is being made to certain leading cases as and when considered relevant.

Articles 15 and 16 have several Clauses attached to them. Some of the measures adopted by the government to fulfil the obligation of promoting the educational and economic interests of the weaker sections (under Article 15) were declared unconstitutional by the Supreme Court considering them in violation of the provisions of fundamental rights. Hence the Parliament amended the Constitution and inserted a new clause 15(4), which states:

> Nothing in this Article (Art.15) or in clause (2) of Article 29 shall prevent the state from making any special provisions for the advancement of any socially or educationally backward classes of citizens or for the Scheduled Castes and the Scheduled Tribes.

This clause enables the government to provide reservations to weaker sections for admission to educational institutions. This became a useful and handy tool for political parties to increase their support base in the states, and hence, they started making indiscriminate reservations in the states ruled by them. Consequently, the Supreme Court, in one case (AIR 1962 SC 649, M.R. Balaji vs State of Mysore) ruled that such reservations could not be more than 50%. The much publicized and politicized Mandal Commission also laid down that maximum percentage of reservations could be only 50% (Tope, 1989). In another case (K.S. Jayshree vs State of Kerala, 1976, 3, SC 730), the Supreme Court ruled that the total number of seats reserved for weaker sections must be so allotted to students from these communities as to ensure that the benefits of reservations are really enjoyed by those who are under-privileged, even among the under-privileged classes. The Court also laid down the means-cum-caste/community criterion indicative of social and educational backwardness by which persons above a certain income level, otherwise qualified, are barred.

It was once again the Judiciary, which intervened, though to a limited extent, to stop the spate of indiscriminate reservations for weaker sections, launched after mandalisation of Indian politics and patronized by various casteist political parties as also, under compulsive electoral politics, by national parties like BJP and Congress; the latter even committing to 10% reservation of jobs for minorities as also for the affluent Jat community purely with the aim of capturing power. In a landmark majority (4-1) judgment, a

5-member bench of Supreme Court including Chief Justice Dr. A.S. Anand and others ruled (August 12, 1999) that competitive merit alone should be the criterion for admission to super specially medical courses as caste-based reservation at these levels would be against national interests. The judgment said that admission to the highest available medical courses in the country at super speciality levels, where even the facilities for training are limited, must be given on the basis of competitive merit. While the object of Article 15(4) of the Constitution is to advance the equality principle by providing protective discrimination in favour of weaker sections so that they may become stronger and be able to compete equally with others more fortune etc, one cannot ignore the wider interests of the society while devising such special provisions. The judgment further said that it would not be possible for the candidates belonging to weaker sections to fully benefit from the very limited and specialized PG training opportunities, which are designed to produce high calibre (CSR, Oct, 1999) well-trained professionals for the public. The Court also directed the Medical Council of India to examine whether minimum qualifying marks for quota candidates can be prescribed at the PG level.

The Indian Parliament, through the 82nd Constitutional Amendment (2000), altered the provisions of Article 335, which ensures the efficiency of administration, saying that nothing in this Article shall prevent the state from making any provisions in favour of the members of SC/ST for relaxation in qualifying marks with respect to examination/job/promotion. With this we are again back to square one. Once again the political expediency has prevailed over national interest.

Reservation or so called "protective discrimination" based on the logic of bringing about social and economic equality, and thereby establishing social justice, has been legitimized under the constitutional parameters. There are two strategies, which may be practised to carry out the reservation programmes. First, Article 15(4) can be used to make special provisions for the advancement of women and children, and socially and educationally backward classes or castes. This technique has been called "push technique" (Mitra, 1991). Second, under Article 16(4), provisions may be made for reservations in jobs and services for socially and economically disadvantaged groups or castes. This technique has been called "pull technique". Here also the constitutional provisions are not mandatory and have to be within the constitutional objective criteria of consistency with the maintenance of efficiency of administration. Thus, a dichotomy between "reservation" and "efficiency" is not to be presumed and any apparent conflict is to be resolved in a fashion so as to reconcile reservation with efficiency in administration. Article 15(4) embodies positive and corrective measure while Article 16(4) provides a short-term adjustment in the government services without anyway injuring the efficiency of administration. Which one to adopt and follow is a matter of serious consideration and choice of the political parties and the government.

There are a large number of cases related to Articles 28, 29, and 30, which provide the minorities a right to conserve their culture, language, and religion, and to establish and administer educational institutions of their choice. This right is conferred in absolute terms. However, the Supreme Court, in a series of judgments, has laid down that regulatory measures taken and enforced by the relevant authorities would be constitutional. In a historic judgment the Supreme Court has recently (TOI, Nov. 1, 2002) ruled that though minorities had an unfettered right to establish institutions of their own choice the right to administer them was not absolute. The state should apply regulatory measures for educational excellence even in the case of unaided minority institutions. However, the government should not interfere in the day-to-day administration of the unaided minority institutions, but in the case of disputes over employment a tribunal headed by a person of district judge rank should be set up.

On the basis of various judgments delivered by the Supreme Court, the following principles emerge, which may be taken as binding (Tope, 1989):

1. Right to administer is not a right to mal-administer. Hence, relevant/competent authority can lay down qualifications of teachers, courses, curricula, and conditions regarding the health of students.
2. Management must be efficient. The state can take regulatory measures to promote efficiency and excellence of educational standards and issue guidelines for the purpose of ensuring the security of service of teachers or other employees of the institution.
3. The Supreme Court, in a judgment laid down that even in case of minority institutions the teachers have a right

to approach Arbitration Tribunal in case of removal from service, dismissal or reduction of rank.

4. A minority institution cannot claim immunity from general laws of the land such as contract law, labour law or Industrial Disputes Act.
5. Minority institutions, which seek either recognition or aid from the state, are subject to regulatory provisions imposed by the state. Under such provisions, if the state is authorized to take over the management even of a minority institution, the state can do so.

In a case (AIR, 1987), filed by Frank Anthony School Employees Association, the Supreme Court ruled that conditions of service pertaining to minimum qualifications of teachers, their salaries, allowances, and other conditions of service which ensure security, contentment, and decent living standards to teachers and, which will consequently enable them to render better services to the institution and pupils, cannot be said to be violative of the fundamental rights guaranteed by Article 30 (1). The management of such an institution cannot be permitted, under the guise of fundamental rights, to oppress or exploit its employees any more than any other private employer. The Court, in another case, laid down that no linguistic minority can claim that the university, or an examining body, shall conduct its examination in the language or script which the institution has the right to adopt (Tope, 1988). A state aided minority institution cannot reserve seats for students of the minority community, because such reservation will violate provisions of Article 29(2) apart from the fact that they would be inconsistent with the provisions of equality under Article 14.

These provisions of the Constitution have functioned as effective guidelines for the government to promote social, economic, cultural, educational and political development of disadvantaged sections of the society including Scheduled Castes, Scheduled Tribes, women, minorities and other backward classes.

3

Social and Educational Systems of India

Education system cannot develop in isolation from the social realities of a nation. Socio-economic and political conditions determine not only the aims and objectives, but also, the direction and process of educational development. The development of education in India since independence can best be studied and analyzed with reference to social and cultural traditions, and natural and geographical conditions. After a prolonged foreign rule of over 750 years, political freedom came as a new life to the people of this land. From 1192 to 1947, the people saw many ups and downs having been exploited, oppressed, and tyrannized at the hands of the foreign rulers. The country with a very bright and rich past was consigned to a condition of acute poverty and hunger. The natural and material resources had been completely exhausted which threw an unprecedented challenge for survival. However, our cultural heritage remained intact because nobody could destroy it despite severe onslaught of foreign powers. After independence, we marched on the path of social reconstruction and considered education, and rightly so, as a powerful tool to achieve this goal. The development of education has been taken up on a priority basis, and during the last five decades, we have come a long way as far as educational development is concerned.

THE INDIAN SOCIAL ORDER

India is a vast country covering about 329 million hectares of land and providing shelter for a population of over 1,000 million. Since the total population of the world is a little more than 6,000 million, India has to support about 16% of the world's population on only 2.4% of land and 2% of the world's total income. As far as population is concerned, we are the largest democracy of the world. During the last 50 years our population has tripled. With the birth of 48000 children per day, 18 million are added every year to our teeming millions. This annual addition is more than the total population of Australia. It is reported that by 2001 census our population has risen to about 1027 million. Thus, the welfare of the people of India is the welfare of over one-sixth of mankind (Chauhan, 1990). The majority of this large population—about 73%, live in 579,000 rural habitations, meaning thereby that we are predominantly a rural society. According to the 2001 census about 65% of the people were literate. If the population aged 7 years and above is considered, the level of illiteracy was 35% with 46% among women.

Agriculture is the main source of living for the rural masses. Therefore, development and modernization of agriculture determine the degree of economic development of any particular region, and consequently, that of the nation as a whole. Gradually, with the population growth, forests are being converted into cultivable land in order to increase the production of foodgrains to feed the increasing number of mouths. According to the available scientific data, only about 15% of the land in India is under forest, and that too is slowly decreasing. This is a very unhealthy sign. India has 6000 kms of coastal belt, two large mountain ranges (Himalayas and Vindhyas), 14 major rivers whose ecology is to be protected to save the country from soil erosion, draughts and flash floods, not to speak of preserving underground water resources and country's rich flora and fauna (Sen, 1986).

Indian society is hierarchical, stratified, and deficient in vertical mobility. The social distance between different classes, particularly between the rich and the poor, the educated and the uneducated, is large and is tending to widen (Education Commission, 1964-66, para 1.07). Our people profess different religions. The followers of all the major religions of the world are found here. Four major religions were born in India—Hinduism, Buddhism, Jainism, and Sikhism. Majority of the population—about 82% profess Hinduism, about 12% profess Islam, about 2% profess Christianity, about 2% profess Sikhism, and the rest 2% follow other religions. Each religion has its own characteristics—customs, symbols, teachings and values, but there are some common threads, which keep them in harmony. At the same time, there are some points of conflict which, sometimes lead to social tensions. It is a fact that in our social history, we had riots, battles, and cold wars on religious and communal grounds (Ruhela, 1983). It is also a fact that, on the one hand, every religion has socialized millions of its followers and prevented them from being misguided, and on the other hand, it has played upon the emotions of its followers to make their social vision short-sighted, injected communal hatred, and promoted strange forms of exploitation of women, children, and poor men for centuries.

This multi-religious plural society in India has a further complexity based on a rigid traditional source of stratification, namely, caste system. The institution of caste is a very powerful, but undemocratic agency of social organization. Ironically, this undemocratic institution seems to have been legalized and legitimized under the constitutional and democratic processes. Constitutional discrimination based on caste, supposedly protective in nature, has legitimized caste as a social institution. It is virtually a backbone of the traditional Indian social structure. It is not that only Hindus have caste, even Muslims, Jains, Buddhists and Indian Christians are divided into castes and sub-castes. As a conservative estimate there are about 3600 castes and sub-castes in India. The system was originally based on the occupational grouping, but has been an important socially integrated unit in the society uniting its members by common bonds of history, culture, marital, and dining relations. However, recently it has taken a very dangerous and ugly shape and acted as a powerful divisive force having been used by the politicians for vote bank politics.

We created this structural organization centuries ago when the whole power was vested with the three upper castes—the Brahmins, who monopolized knowledge; the Kshatriyas, who monopolized political power; and the Vaishyas, who monopolized economic power. These three castes were described as twice born, their second birth being their initiation into the study of sacred texts to which they alone were entitled. This designation, therefore, showed what united these castes as well as what separated them from the vast masses of the people—the Shudras, who lived as slaves or workers, and the Antyajas or outcastes like the untouchables (Naik, 1982), who lived precariously on the social fringe. After independence, as education spread to the wider sections of the society and the forces claimed to be democratic and secular became increasingly stronger, the membership of the elite groups (upper castes) ceased to be based on the incidence of birth or caste, and a few members of the lower and disadvantaged groups (Shudras) were co-opted into the elite status through educational process, which acted as a screening device. Some of them were co-opted through the process of caste-based reservations in the educational institutions and government jobs. A large majority of people is still marginalized and deprived of all types of opportunities of development. The future educational strategies have to take care of the interests of this large majority.

Another characteristic of Indian society is that a major portion of the population suffers from acute poverty. According to the latest available data, about 36% of the people live below the poverty line some of them leading their lives under sub-human conditions. While the country as a whole is poor, the poverty is also unevenly distributed over the land. The higher percentages of poor people live in Bihar, Madhya Pradesh, Rajasthan and Uttar Pradesh. In these states, poverty is also accompanied by low level of literacy. A sizeable portion of national income is cornered by upper and upper middle classes, which constitute a small minority. Coupled with poverty, there is a large-scale unemployment. The school system is visualized as a channel for leading the students for university education and not for preparing them for the world of work. Sometimes, university education is blamed for large-scale unemployment, but the real problem is that our economy is not expanding rapidly enough to absorb the growing number of graduates and post-graduates with both general and professional education.

The socio-economic scenario is further polluted along with the political environment. The political situation is characterized by the inability of the successive governments to fulfil the tall promises made by them in election manifestoes and to be dictated by the policies of an elective multi-party system of democratic government. The electorate, despite the low levels of education, is mature enough to realize that no government can bring about sudden changes. So far, we have had more or less free and fair elections, though, the stability of our polity has been successively challenged by language based strife, sub-nationalist regional insurgencies, north-south regional consciousness, religion-based separatism and increasing criminalization of socio-economic and political life (Gore, 1991). Despite unprecedented development during the last fifty years, the Indian education has utterly failed in inculcating social, moral, and spiritual values in the youth so as to produce citizens of unquestionable integrity and sound character (Chauhan, 1991). Growing black-marketing, crimes, dowry deaths, communal strife, religious fanaticism, superstitions, and rampant corruption in the government and public life, all constitute an irrefutable testimony to the debasement of Indian value system. The politicians are impelled by lust of power and unquenchable greed, and often indulge in corrupt practices and even in physical violence to the point of murder. Our democracy lacks substance and vitality. The people have not yet developed the civic sense requisite for the effective functioning of the democratic institutions. The forces of disintegration propelled by parochialism (Sharma, 1990) and fuelled by regionalism, casteism, ethnic exclusiveness, sectarianism, and bigotry are on the ascendance. There has been a prolonged political instability and turmoil, which have had adverse impact on our economic development, social cohesion, and peaceful living.

THE EDUCATIONAL IMBALANCE

As soon as India became free, there was a pressing demand for education from all sections of the society as expected. The demand for education was more forceful from the disadvantaged classes than from the upper and upper-middle classes. Before independence, higher education was available only to a selected few belonging to the privileged classes mostly concentrated in the urban areas. With increased emphasis on industrialization, new employment opportunities emerged which were concomitant with the social, economic, scientific and technological advancement. The establishment of large-scale industries led to the expansion of administrative and managerial positions in the government and private sector undertakings. Right from the beginning, with roots in the freedom struggle, there has been a great concern for equity and social justice, balance among the geographical regions, linguistic groups, castes, tribes and sexes (Ahmad, 1991). Consequently, there was a rapid expansion of educational facilities at all levels with greater emphasis on higher education. These attempts were aimed at bringing about balance, and removing disparities to some extent. However, these efforts, somehow, could not solve the existing problems, rather, led to some new problems.

In order to serve the interests of pressure groups demanding equity, a one-dimensional approach of quantitative expansion was preferred and followed, and schools, colleges, and universities were opened largely in urban areas to begin with. In the long run, this linear expansion persisted over several decades with in-built urban bias. This urban bias resulted in the establishment of the best of the institutions in the country, only in metropolitan cities like Delhi, Bombay, Calcutta and Madras. With the result, the rural population had access only to the poor quality schools and colleges, which developed in them a lasting sense of deprivation and disadvantage. To overcome this problem partially, reservations in admissions to schools and colleges to the extent of 15% for Scheduled Castes and 7.5% for Scheduled Tribes have been provided under Article 46 of the Constitution. In some states, there is reservation for other backward classes also. Indeed, the total reservation at all levels, including professional and technical courses, sometimes reaches such a high level that no room is virtually left for meritorious students, who have been compelled to launch violent protests and have resorted to self-immolation. With the "mandalization" of politics, and consequently of the society, and upsurge of aggression among the "other backward castes" coupled with increased political awareness among them, last two decades have been the period of utmost political turmoil. Added to this, there is the problem of political expediency for which the successive governments at the Centre and states have been setting aside all norms to win over "vote banks". Our polity is so polluted that political expediency determines the priorities and urgencies of the government. The net result is that meritorious students are on the roads and the mediocre have managed to enter the quality education institutions through reservations. In future, situation is likely to be more explosive than ever before. The education system has to tackle these problems.

Unplanned and massive expansion resulting in fall in standards has shifted the emphasis from access to education to equality of opportunity in benefiting from it. A vast majority of the poor children living in villages are obliged to attend poor quality institutions and suffer from a variety of deficiencies, and hence, fail to qualify the tests organized for admission to quality institutions or for superior employment. Excellence seems to be the opponent of equity, as one has to be sacrificed for the other.

In addition to these problems, there are some other issues. There are disparities based on gender, geographical location, and physical environment. The scheduled tribe rural women are the most disadvantaged. There are many other social problems that the education system has to grapple with during the years ahead.

AIMS, OBJECTIVES AND PRIORITIES OF EDUCATION

There is a close link between education and society. Society can use education both as an agent to strengthen and perpetuate the status quo, and as an instrument of social transformation and development. How it would be used depends on our perception of the future society that we want to create. As our Constitution indicates, education in the post-independence India would be used as a powerful instrument of social reconstruction. The values enshrined in the Preamble of the Constitution determine the goals and objectives of education in free India, which have been properly worded by the Education Commission (1964-66, para 1.20) as follows:

> In our opinion, therefore, no reform is more important or more urgent than to transform education, to endeavour to relate it to life, needs and aspirations of the people, and thereby, make it a powerful instrument of social, economic and cultural transformation necessary for the realization of our national goals. This can be done if education:
>
> 1. Is related to productivity;
> 2. Strengthens social and national integration;
> 3. Consolidates democracy as a form of government and helps the country to adopt it as a way of life;

4. Hastens the process of modernization; and
5. Strives to build character by cultivating social, moral and spiritual values.

All these aspects are inter-related and in the complex process of social change, we cannot achieve even one without striving for all.

The Commission, therefore, laid emphasis on the need for a radical reconstruction of education, so as to increase productivity, achieve social and national integration, accelerate the process of modernization and, cultivate moral and spiritual values. The National Policy on Education (1968), which was based on the recommendations of the Education Commission (1964-66), also stated that the aim of education was to promote national progress, develop a sense of common citizenship and culture, and strengthen national integration, with increased stress on radical educational reconstruction, improvement of its quality with greater attention on science and technology, cultivation of moral values, and the relation between education and life of the people. According to the National Policy on Education (1986), as modified in 1992, 'education has an acculturating role. It refines sensitivities and perceptions that contribute to national cohesion, a scientific temper and independence of mind and spirit—thus, furthering the goals of socialism, secularism, and democracy as enshrined in the Constitution.

Broadly, the role of education may be visualized in terms of two functions of producing men of ability and character by:

(i) developing man-power for the growth of economy and enhancement of the pace of modernization to improve the quality of life of the people;
(ii) inculcating the moral and spiritual values in order to promote socialism, secularism, and national integration.

To achieve these goals, Education Commission (1964-66) visualized a National System of Education, which would (Naik, 1982):

(i) be based on a deep and widespread study of science and technology; cultivate a capacity and willingness to work hard and be closely related to productivity;

(ii) would strengthen social and national integration and help to create a more just and egalitarian social order;
(iii) would consolidate democracy as a form of the government and help us to adopt it as a way of life; and
(iv) would strive to build character by cultivating social, moral and spiritual values.

Reiterating that the Constitution embodies the principles on which the National System of Education is conceived of the National Policy of Education-1986 states that 'National System of Education implies that up to a given level, all students, irrespective of caste, creed, location, or sex have access to education of a comparable quality'. The policy document further stated that National System of Education envisages a "common educational structure" and would be based on a "national curriculum framework" containing a "common core" along with other components, which would be flexible. 'The common core would include the history of India's freedom movement the constitutional obligations, and other content essential to nurture national identity.' These elements would cut across subject areas and would be designed to 'promote values such as India's common cultural heritage, egalitarianism, democracy and secularism, equality of sexes, protection of environment, removal of social barriers, observance of small family norms, and inculcation of the scientific temper.' All educational programmes would be carried on in strict conformity with "secular values". Attempt would be made to foster among students understanding of the diverse cultural and social characteristics of the people living in different parts of the country. The minimum levels of learning (MLL) would be specified for each stage of education to ensure equality of educational opportunities and education of uniform and comparable quality. Attempts are to be made to provide for equal opportunities to all, not only in terms of access, but also in the conditions necessary for success. In the areas of research and development, and education in science and technology, special measures would be taken to establish network arrangement between different institutions in the country to ensure participation of the people in the process of national development. The policy calls on the nation as a whole, to assume the responsibility to provide necessary resource support to implement the programmes of educational transformation, universalization of elementary education, and liquidation of adult illiteracy, promoting equity, and scientific and technological research. Life-long education has to be the cherished goal of educational efforts and process with adequate facilities for continuing education followed by universal literacy. The nation proposed recently to launch a National Literacy Mission (NLM) in pursuance of the determination to liquidate illiteracy. In order to make education democratic and accessible to all, major thrust would be laid on distance education in future so as to incorporate flexibility and improve efficiency.

To fulfil the constitutional obligations certain programmes of education have to be taken on a priority basis. These programmes may also be taken as constitutional demands on education system of free India (Anand, 1983). In view of national goals of education and development, these programmes may be listed as follows:

(i) Universalization of elementary education for all children of the relevant age-group;
(ii) Eradication of illiteracy among adults;
(iii) Equalization of educational opportunities for all sections of the society irrespective of caste, creed, religion, sex and geographical location;
(iv) Adoption of Indian languages as media of instruction within specified time-frame;
(v) Adoption of a uniform pattern (common structure) of school and college education for the whole country;
(vi) Provision of education of adequate quality comparable to international standards at all stages of education;
(vii) Vocationalization of education at suitable levels to prepare the citizens for the world of work and become productive members of the society;
(viii) Development of education in science and technology to accelerate the pace of modernization and enhance productivity;
(ix) Generation of facilities for high level research in the university system and outside it; and
(x) Development and implementation of suitable programmes for inculcation of moral and spiritual values, and for strengthening national integration.

THE STRUCTURE OF EDUCATION IN INDIA

India, being a union of states, has accepted a uniform structure of school and college education popularly known as "10+2+3" pattern of school and college education. This pattern visualizes 10 years of general education including 8 years of Elementary followed by 2 years of Secondary education; 2 years of Senior Secondary followed by 3 years of College Education leading to the award of first degree. Until recently there existed several different patterns such as 8+3+3, 10+1+3, or 10+2+2. But, in pursuance of the recommendations of the Education Commission (1964-66) and the proposals of the National Policy of Education-1968, most of the states have adopted 10+2+3 pattern. The National Policy on Education (NPE)-1986 also reiterated the need for adopting a common pattern, namely, the 10+2+3 in the whole country. The NPE-1986 also proposed to adopt a common structure of elementary education consisting of 8 years of schooling—5 years of Primary and 3 years of Upper Primary education. Therefore, the present structure of school education can be represented as {(5+3)+2+2}. A child is admitted to class I, normally, at the age of 6 years and is supposed to complete primary education up to class V at the age of 11years, and elementary education up to class VIII, at the age of 14 years. Up to this stage the state is constitutionally obliged to provide for free and compulsory education to all children under Article 45.

Elementary education is followed by two years of secondary education popularly known as "High School". At this stage also there is no diversification of courses and there is common curriculum for all children. The main purpose of this stage is to build a strong foundation in the fundamental principles of all basic subjects. At the end of this stage, that is, after 10 years of general education, the first public examination is held. This stage is followed by two years of senior secondary education. The senior secondary or +2 stage consists of two streams, academic and vocational. These streams prepare students for different walks of life. The academic stream prepares them for higher academic/professional courses run in the universities and colleges and vocational stream prepares them for careers in agriculture, industry, government services and self-employment. The vocational courses are held either in the polytechnics or in vocational schools.

The higher education structure includes three years of general education in arts, sciences, and commerce as a part of 10+2+3 structure. These programmes lead to the award of the degrees of B.A., B.Sc. or B.Com. Alternatively, the students may go for first—degree courses in medicine, engineering, and other professional courses of first-degree level. After completing these courses, the students are awarded M.B.B.S. or other equivalent degrees in medicine, or B.E./B. Tech. or other equivalent degrees in engineering and technology.

The first degree courses in general education are followed by two years of post-graduate studies leading to Master's degrees in arts, sciences, and commerce. These degrees are abbreviated as M.A., M.Sc., and M.Com. respectively. Similarly, there exist postgraduate courses in professional and technical education leading to M.D./M.S. and M.E./M. Tech. degrees in medicine, and engineering and technology respectively. The professional courses in Law may also be pursued after the first degree in arts, science, and commerce, which leads to the award of the degree of LL.B., followed by LL.M. at the post-graduate level. Similarly, the professional courses in Education or Teaching may be pursued after the first degree courses in general education leading to the award of B. Ed. degree after undergoing a one-year course in the science of teaching. This is followed by a two-year post-graduate programme leading to the award of the degree of M.Ed. Up to this stage, a student has had studied for a period of about 17 years. After this, a selected group of students goes for Research Degree programmes leading to the degree of Ph.D. The minimum duration of research degree programmes is of 3 years; including 1 year of M. Phil. programme being offered in some universities. Research degree programmes are available in all streams including medicine, engineering, law and education.

In fact, the degrees in different courses, being awarded by universities in India bear different names. It is difficult to mention all of them. Recently, the UGC has listed 137 different degrees being awarded by the Indian universities and has asked all the universities to have such degrees listed as are not included in the list prepared by the UGC. Briefly, the structure of formal education in India consists of about 20 years from class I to the Research Degree—8 years up to elementary, 10 years up to secondary, 12 years up to senior secondary, and 20 years up to university education.

CURRICULUM AND EVALUATION

The concept of National System of Education is a part of the history of Indian freedom struggle. The idea first reflected in the scheme of Basic Education propounded by Mahatma Gandhi in the form of Wardha Scheme, which was an indigenous model of education rooted in the cultural and social traditions of India. The underlying philosophy emphasized the all-round development of the child—body, mind and soul. But the scheme could not be implemented in free India because of certain socio-political reasons. After independence, the University Education Commission (1948), headed by Dr. S. Radhakrishnan, held serious deliberations on the problems of school education having direct bearing on university education and recommended the implementation of a uniform pattern of school and college education. Soon after this, the Secondary Education Commission (1952-53), headed by Dr. A. L. Mudaliar, also considered the issues related to structure, curriculum and teaching methods of secondary education and made several useful recommendations. This commission strongly advocated the implementation of comprehensive and continuous internal evaluation at school stage and suggested doing away with external examinations in a phased manner.

In 1964, the Government appointed the Education Commission to study the system Indian education comprehensively in all its aspects. This commission submitted its report in 1966 under the title 'Education and National Development', which is the most comprehensive document on Indian education ever published. The Commission suggested a blue print of future Indian education covering all aspects right from primary to the university stage. This was an important landmark in the history of modern Indian education. The report of this Commission formed the basis for the formulation of the National Policy on Education (1968), which proposed to adopt the 10+2 pattern of school education in the entire country, with a common curriculum for all, during the first ten years of schooling. As a part of strategies for creating a National System of Education, efforts have been made, during the last three decades, to adopt a uniform/common curriculum at school and college levels. The first step in this direction, after independence, was taken in 1975 when the NCERT brought out the publication 'The Curriculum for the Ten-Year School—A Framework'. This document emphasized the teaching of environmental studies, mathematics and science as a part of the common curriculum up to class X. Soon after this, the NCERT published in 1976, another document titled 'Higher Secondary Education and its Vocationalization'. The National Policy on Education (1986), and its modified version (1992), also stressed the need of having a national system of education with a common structure and uniform curriculum.

Under the same project, the National Council of Educational Research and Training (NCERT), the apex body for school education at national level, brought out in December 1988 a National Curriculum Framework for Elementary and Secondary Education: A framework (NIEPA, 1988). The suggested scheme of curriculum for different stages of education under the national framework is presented below:

CURRICULUM FRAMEWORK FOR SCHOOL AND COLLEGE EDUCATION

SCHOOL EDUCATION

The present structure of school education in India is largely based on the National Curriculum for Primary and Secondary Education: A framework brought out by the NCERT in 1985 and another similar document published in 1988.

Pre-Primary Education

The Curriculum Framework (1985) suggested that the basic mode of upbringing of children at this stage should be through group activities and playway techniques, language games, number games, and activities directed to promote environmental awareness etc. These should be used to make the learning experiences joyful to the children. No formal teaching of 3 Rs is to be undertaken at this stage. The National Advisory Committee (1993) endorsed these views as follows:

> Despite official stipulations that no textbooks be used at this stage, pre-school teachers and parents in the urban centre are feeling compelled to burden the young child with the textbooks

and the formal learning they represent. The sense of compulsion comes from a widespread feeling that unless academic training of the child starts early, he or she cannot cope with the fast-paced pedagogy and the competitive ethos of the later school years. The pernicious grip of this false argument manifests itself in absurd, and of course deeply harmful, practices in pre-schools and primary schools, such as early emphasis on shapely drawing, writing, and memorizing information. Intrinsic motivation and child's natural abilities are being smothered at a scale so vast that it cannot be correctly estimated. Our national commitment to the development of human resource is daily challenged in our nurseries and primary schools.

Primary Stage

(i) One language—the mother tongue/ regional language,
(ii) Mathematics,
(iii) Environmental studies I and II,
(iv) Work experience,
(v) Art education,
(vi) Health and physical education.

Upper Primary Stage

(i) Three languages,
(ii) Mathematics,
(iii) Science,
(iv) Social sciences,
(v) Work experience,
(vi) Art education,
(vii) Health and physical education.

Secondary Stage

(i) Three languages,
(ii) Mathematics,
(iii) Science,
(iv) Social sciences,
(v) Contemporary India,
(vi) Work experience,
(vii) Art education,
(viii) Health and physical education.

As mentioned earlier, there is a provision for a general broad-based education for the first ten years of school education, all the curricular areas being compulsory without any bifurcation or streaming. The major thrust in primary education is on basic skills, literacy and numeracy, study of environment, development of productive skills, creative expression and habits of healthy living. At the upper primary stage, the curriculum is directed to the consolidation of knowledge, skills, attitudes, and values acquired at the primary stage and acquisition of wider knowledge base in the context of a broad-based general education. The curriculum areas are the same as those at primary stage, but a deeper study is required.

The objectives of curriculum at secondary stage are two-fold: to prepare the students to join the higher (senior) secondary stage followed by college, and to prepare them for the world of work. This stage is expected to be terminal for a large number of students who want to join the world of work.

Senior Secondary Stage

At this stage, diversified courses are introduced for preparing the students either to enter the university education for the first degree or to enter into the job market after undergoing the vocational training. The scheme of diversification is given below:

(A) The academic stream, which includes the study of elective courses chosen for in-depth study, consists of the following:
- *(i)* Science,
- *(ii)* Mathematics,
- *(iii)* Commerce,
- *(iv)* Social sciences,
- *(v)* Humanities.

(B) The vocational stream, which is designed to prepare students for careers in agriculture, industry, or government services as well as for self-employment, consists of the following:
- *(i)* One or two languages,
- *(ii)* General foundation courses,
- *(iii)* Elective subjects related to specific vocations, and designed to provide intensive training.

COLLEGE EDUCATION

This stage is also bifurcated into two streams, general and professional/technical courses, according to the following scheme:

(A) General education consists of under-graduate and post-graduate courses followed by research degree (doctorate) programmes in:
(i) Science,
(ii) Social Sciences and Humanities,
(iii) Commerce.

(B) Professional/Technical education courses leading to under-graduate and post-graduate qualifications followed by doctoral programmes in:
(i) Engineering and technology,
(ii) Medicine,
(iii) Law,
(iv) Agriculture, Veterinary Science and Forestry,
(v) Teaching, and
(vi) Management and Administration.

Evaluation

Evaluation is an inseparable component of the teaching-learning process. It is the process, which is carried out during or after the instructional programme to ensure that learning is proceeding in the desired direction. It ensures whether the objectives of the curriculums are being achieved or not. The information gathered through a systematic process of evaluation is used for taking important decisions, not only about the learner, but also about the entire instructional approach including objectives, curriculum, teaching strategies and techniques of evaluation. Examinations are also used for the purpose of certification. The completion of each stage of education is certified through a Certificate, or a Diploma, or a Degree awarded on the basis of evaluation carried out through tests or large-scale examinations. The process of evaluation involves both external and internal modes. As mentioned earlier, the first public examination is held after ten years of schooling at the end of class X. Another public examination is held at the end of Senior

Secondary Stage (class XII). After this, examinations are held every year and are conducted by the universities, but, the examinations, which are held at the end of the secondary and senior secondary school stages, are conducted by the School Education Boards, established for this purpose.

Perhaps, evaluation is the only component of educative process in which least change has taken place, though different commissions and committees have put largest number of suggestions forward in this regard. As early as in 1902, the Indian Universities Commission set up by Lord Curzon remarked that it was beyond doubt that teaching in India was subordinated to examination. The Calcutta University Commission (1917-19) also expressed similar views, and emphasized the need of establishing separate examination boards for conducting examinations for school stage. Hartog Committee (1929) also expresses concern about the dominance of examination over the entire system of education

During the post-independence period, the University Education Commission (1949) remarked, 'We are convinced that if we were to suggest any single reform in University education, it would be that of examination'. Expressing deep concern regarding the incredibility of examination system, the Commission called for immediate steps to be taken in order to introduce valid, reliable, and objective modes of evaluation. The Secondary Education Commission (1952-53), which was mainly concerned with secondary education, made significant recommendations for the improvement of external examination and introduction of internal evaluation so as to be able to made an all-round assessment of the pupil's personality. The Education Commission (1964-66) suggested that we should move in the direction of abolishing the external examinations by replacing them with a system of continuous internal evaluation. These recommendations of the Commission were incorporated in the National Policy on Education adopted by the Government in 1968. The Policy made the following proposals:

> A major goal of examination reforms should be to improve the reliability and validity of examinations and to make evaluation a continuous process aimed at helping the student to improve his level of achievement rather than at certifying the quality of his performance at a given movement of time.
> Thereafter, the National Policy on Education-1986 again made

certain important proposals for examination reforms the Policy document devoted the following three sections of its text to these proposals:

> **(8.23).** Assessment of performance is an integral part of any process of learning and teaching. As part of sound educational strategy, examinations should be employed to bring about qualitative improvement in education.
>
> **(8.24).** The objective will be to recast examination system so as to ensure a method of assessment that is a valid and reliable measure of student development, and a powerful instrument for improving teaching learning. In functional terms, this would mean:
>
> *(i)* The elimination of excessive element of chance and subjectivity;
> *(ii)* The de-emphasis of memorization;
> *(iii)* Continuous and comprehensive evaluation that incorporates both scholastic and non-scholastic aspects of education, spread over the total span of instructional time;
> *(iv)* Effective use of the evaluation process by teachers, students and parents;
> *(v)* Improvement in the conduct of examinations;
> *(vi)* The introduction of concomitant changes in instructional materials and methodology;
> *(vii)* Introduction of the semester system from the secondary stage in a phased manner; and
> *(viii)* The use of grades in place of marks.
>
> **(8.25).** The above goals are relevant both for external examinations and evaluation within the educational institutions. Evaluation at the institutional level will be streamlined and the predominance of external examinations reduced.

The present evaluation system suffers from several drawbacks. It lays undue emphasis on the measurement of cognitive aspects of behaviour, and non-cognitive aspects of personality are completely ignored. Here also, the scope of assessment is limited to the knowledge-related objectives only, and higher abilities like comprehension, analysis, synthesis, problem solving and creativity are left untouched. Only a small portion of total content area of the subject-matter is covered by examination, thus reducing its validity. This encourages students and teachers to limit their classroom interaction to only a few selected topics of the course supposedly important from the examination standpoint. The results are declared in terms of raw marks or percentages derived from them without applying the scaling technique to make the score comparable over different subjects, teachers/evaluators and years. These things give rise to certain serious malpractices in the conduct of examinations. Students suffer from severe stress and tension during the examination days, and sometimes, failure in an examination leads a few of them to extreme steps like suicide. Examination is such a component of educative process that brings the students under anxiety and stress.

RECENT DEVELOPMENTS

National Advisory Committee (1993)

During the last five decades since independence, we have mainly remained concentrated on the expansion and consolidation of the system of education that we borrowed from British rulers. Fortunately, our attention has recently centred on the problems of quality and quantity of learning. The National Advisory Committee (1993), headed by Professor Yashpal, was appointed by the Government for this purpose only. The Committee was concerned with one major flaw of our system of education, which, as the Committee said, might be identified briefly by saying, 'a lot is taught, but little is learnt or understood'. The problem manifests itself in a variety of ways, the most commonly observable being the size of the school bag that the children carry everyday from home to school and back to home. But, this is only one aspect of the problem, the physical load. Here, we are more concerned about the intellectual load that the children carry in terms of his daily routine, which leaves little time for play and enjoyment of childhood. The small children have go along a tight schedule of attending school, doing homework, attending tuition and coaching classes. The parents are party to this agony of their children because the aspirations of parents force the children to undergo this cycle of torture. The Committee made the following remarks on this subject:

> Both the teachers and the parents constantly reinforce the fear of examination and the need to prepare for it in the only manner that seems practical, namely, by memorizing the whole lot of information from he textbooks and guide-books. Educated parents who have themselves gone through examinations, and the uneducated parents whose knowledge of examination system is based on the social lore, share the belief that what really matters in education is the score one gets in the final examination.

The committee recommended that any kind of competitions through which individual achievement is rewarded need to be discouraged since they deprive children of joyful learning. Instead, the Committee suggested that the group activities and group achievements must be encouraged to give a boost to cooperative learning in schools. The responsibility of curriculum planning, and preparation of textbooks and other instructional material, should be left to the teachers. The process of planning and supervision of schools should be decentralized so as to involve the Village Education Committees specially constituted for this purpose. The committee was of the view that appropriate system should be evolved for establishment and maintenance of early childhood education institutions with proper mechanism to ensure quality. The Committee emphatically suggested, ' It should be ensured that these institutions do not perpetrate violence on young children by inflicting a heavy dose of "over-education" in the form of formal teaching of Reading, Writing and Numbers. The practice of holding tests and interviews for admission to nursery class be abolished.' Children should not be required to purchase books individually and carry them home everyday, rather, books should be the property of the school. The children should not be given homework. In addition, the Committee also made certain valuable recommendations for improvement of teacher education, secondary education and senior secondary education.

National Curriculum Framework for School Education (2000)

Recently, the NCERT has published a document entitled 'National Curriculum Framework for School Education', embodying a detailed scheme of the outlines of the proposed new curriculum for school education. As known to us, only two years ago (1998), the NCTE had brought out the 'National Curriculum Framework for Quality Teacher Education'. It is difficult to understand how the twin organizations, the NCERT and the NCTE, decided the order of publication of these documents. According to sound academic and pedagogical principles, teacher education programme/curriculum should be formulated in the light of the changes taking place in the school education. In fact, teacher education curriculum should be guided by the school education curriculum, and thus, the formulation of the former should always succeed that of the latter. But, somehow the events have gone in the reverse order, perhaps because the team of experts drafting the documents had common members on both the occasions, and it was the process of placement of the "same experts" in the two positions that had taken the reverse course. Moreover, this document was published in such a hurry that it was not even placed before the Central Advisory Board of Education (CABE) for consideration and approval. The CABE is the highest policy planning body of the government in the field of education and usually no educational policies are implemented unless approved by the CABE. But, something very unusual has happened this time. As usual, the Government also did not raise any questions about this lapse for the simple reason that education is not in their list of priorities. What happens in the educational circles does not make much difference for the Government and the bureaucracy, as it is the common man who pays the price. However, better late than never. A thorough study of this document also gives the impression that it has been prepared in a hurry. The press has highlighted many of its weaknesses during the last two years and sufficient debate has taken place. Therefore, there is no space here for repetition of those issues. But, the important point is that the Supreme Court of India had withheld the implementation of the syllabus proposed in the curriculum framework.

However, later on the Court, saying that nothing in it was found against the Constitution, upheld the National Curriculum

Framework for School Education-2000. It was argued that "education about religions" should be differentiated from "religious education" imparted in the minority institutions. Study of religion is not prohibited by the Constitution, as it is the fundamental right of students to know about religion. The education of religion could be imparted even in the state-funded and semi-aided schools. By a 2:1 majority the 3-member Bench of the Court held that non-consultation with the CABE is not a sufficient ground to declare the syllabus as unconstitutional. However, one of the members of the bench had some reservation about this view and opined that the CABE had been playing an important role in the framing of educational syllabus since 1935, and hence, a consensus between the Centre and the States on the syllabus could have been arrived at through discussions and consultation with this apex body.

The basic structure and elements of the new curriculum framework, proposed in this document, do not differ much from those of the one published by the NCERT in 1985 and another published in 1988. The stage-wise highlights of the main features of the proposed curriculum framework are presented below:

Early Childhood Education (2 Years)

(i) It is proposed that learning at this stage may be characterized by group activities, playway techniques, language games and the activities directed to promote socialization and environmental awareness among children.

(ii) The students at this stage should be provided more and more opportunities to use the language orally and listen to it in the natural interactive mode.

(iii) The children should be encouraged to interact with pets, knowing common birds, animals, plants and means of transport and some celestial bodies such as sun, moon and stars.

Elementary Stage (8 Years)

The document has visualized the elementary school stage as consisting of two sub-stages: *(i)* Primary Stage or Lower Primary Stage and *(ii)* Upper Primary Stage.

1. Primary stage of 5 years has further been visualized in two segments with an inherent continuity. The first segment comprises classes I and II, where children are just introduced to formal teaching and are at a stage of development which requires a smooth transition from informal and non-formal environment to a formal one (NCERT, 2000). The organization of the curriculum-content at this stage is almost the same as proposed in the 1985 and 1988 versions of the Curriculum Framework. The only visible difference is that three components of the earlier curriculum, namely Work Experience and SUPW, Art Education, and Health and Physical Education, have been combined into one entitled 'Art of Healthy and Productive Living'. However, one important component of "Environmental Education" has been excluded from the curriculum at this sub-stage. The curriculum of second segment comprising classes III to V includes Environmental Studies, in addition to all the components included in the curriculum for the first segment. These changes, though not significant, make the new curriculum look slightly different from those proposed in the 1985 and 1988 documents. Moreover these changes apparently attempt to address the questions raised by the National Advisory Committee headed by Professor Yashpal, which has been referred to earlier.
2. No change has been proposed in the curriculum structure of Upper Primary stage of 3 years. However in order to make the new proposals more attractive, a few changes in the nomenclature of the courses/components have been made. For example, the three languages to be taught at this stage have been specified in terms of the mother tongue/the regional language, modern Indian language and English. Similarly, the existing component "Science" has been given a more attractive and appealing name "Science and Technology". The other components are as these were in the 1985 and 1988 curriculum frameworks.

Secondary Stage (2 Years)

No significant changes have been proposed in the structure of curriculum at this stage also excepting minor shifts of emphasis here and there. Again, the component "Science" has been renamed as "Science and Technology" and the three languages to be taught have been specified in terms of the Three Language Formula. One noticeable change is that the component "Contemporary India", which was a part of the earlier curriculum, has been excluded this time; perhaps, it has been merged into social sciences. All other components are the same as in the earlier curriculum.

Senior/Higher Secondary Stage (2 Years)

No significant changes have been proposed in the basic structure of curriculum at this stage also. As per the recommendations of the Education Commission (1964-66), the curriculum at this stage is to be diversified into two streams—Academic and Vocational assuming that by now the students have acquired basic linguistic and mathematical skills essential for further learning. It is assumed that the students are now ready for making an in-depth study of differentiated and specialized courses in various branches of sciences, social sciences and humanities. The scheme of studies in the Academic Stream includes: (i) Foundation Courses, and (ii) Elective Courses. The foundation courses would consist of components of general education including language and literature, work education, and health and physical education, games and sports. The Elective Courses, on the other hand, will have to cater to the requirement of a large majority of those who, for some reasons, would like to undertake a job. In view of this, the course-contents would include certain emerging vocational fields such as computer science, biotechnology, genomics, yoga and environmental sciences, in addition to some interdisciplinary courses. The major emphasis to be placed on the subjects that have direct utility in their daily life activities. The areas like conservation education, consumer education, legal literacy, productivity education, population education, disaster management and family life education might find suitable place in the curriculum organization.

The main objective of the Vocational Stream is to develop among the youth skills and related knowledge required for specific occupations through diversified vocational and occupational programmes so as to prepare them for world of work. It is expected that after the completion of these courses the students would either get suitable jobs in the market or will be self-employed. The scheme of studies in this stream would include Language, General Foundation Course, Health and Physical Education and Vocational Electives. The vocational education would cover a wide variety of areas like agriculture, engineering and technology, business and commerce, home science, health and paramedical services and humanities.

Other Features of the Curriculum Framework

The Curriculum Framework (2000) was subjected to fierce debate, not only in the academic circles, but also among the major political parties. It was alleged that the proposed curriculum structure had in it a potential to bring about a major ideological shift in the entire system of school education. The matter was so vehemently politicized by some political formations including the Congress and the Leftists that the Supreme Court of India had to intervene by way of staying the implementation of the provisions embodied in the framework. It was also alleged that the framework was prepared in a hurry and the necessary procedure was not followed in its adoption. However, as mentioned earlier, the Supreme Court upheld the curriculum later on.

In addition to the proposed minor changes in the school curriculum organization, the framework has the following characteristics:

- *(i)* It reiterates the theme of "value education" proposed and emphasized by the Education Commission (1964-66) and stresses its need in the contemporary social environment.
- *(ii)* It advocates the shift of emphasis from "religious education" to "education about religions" thus trying to give a spiritual orientation to the school curriculum in order to integrate science with spirituality.
- *(iii)* It advocates the introduction of certain core subjects in the curriculum to strengthen "national identity" and inculcate the spirit of patriotism among children.
- *(iv)* It proposes the introduction of "Semester System" at senior secondary stage, to begin with, in order to ensure effective implementation of "comprehensive internal evaluation" to be undertaken by the teachers who teach.
- *(v)* As a part of semester system, it also proposes to

implement the concept of "credit accumulation" at the school stage. It is to be noted here that this concept is not being used even in universities in our country.

(vi) It also emphasizes the need of introducing Open Learning system at senior secondary stage for academic as well as vocational courses in order to extend educational opportunities to weaker and deprived sections of the society.

(vii) It proposes to bring about radical changes in the process of evaluation by way of introducing formative evaluation in the lower classes with greater role of teachers who teach the students. The use of written and summative tests should increase slowly with rise in the level of education.

(viii) It also proposes to introduce the system of awarding "grades" to indicate the level of achievement of children at different stages in order to avoid or reduce the psychological tension, which is generated by the idea of "failure" in the examination.

THREE CHANNELS OF EDUCATION

During the first three five-year plans, education system in India did not experience any structural changes and was based on only one channel of formal education, which insisted on a single point entry, sequential annual promotions, and full time attendance, by teachers and students. The Education Commission (1964-66) recognized that learning also takes place outside the formal school system through organized non-formal and self-study channels, and therefore, recommended the development of all the three channels of full-time, part-time, and own-time education, as a part of national system of education. The commission observed:

> One of the major weaknesses of the existing educational system is that it places an almost exhaustive reliance on full-time instruction and does not develop adequately the two alternative channels of part-time and private study or own-time education. It has to be remembered that reliance on full-time education as the sole channel of instruction often divides the life of an individual into three water-tight and sharply divided stages: a pre-school stage of non-formal education or

work, a school stage of full-time education, and a post-school stage of full-time work and no education. In a modernizing and rapidly changing society, education should be regarded, not as a terminal but as a life-long process. It should begin informally in the home itself; and thereafter, it should be the ultimate objective of the national policy to strive to bring every individual under the influence of the formal system of education as early as possible, and to keep him under it, directly or indirectly, throughout his life. Similarly, there should be no watertight separation between work and education at any stage of man's life, but only a relative shift of emphasis. An individual under full-time education should have some work-experience as an integral part of his education itself; and every full-time worker should have the inclination, leisure and means of continuing his education still further. In the same way, the transition from one stage to another should not be abrupt. If these objectives are to be attained, it is necessary to abandon the present policy of placing an almost exclusive reliance on full-time education, and the two alternative channels of part-time and own-time education should be developed on a large scale at every stage and in every sector of education and should be given the same status as full-time education. Secondly, adult and continuing education, which is almost totally neglected at present, should be emphasized to a very great extent. Taken together, these two reforms would:

(i) Enable those who have not completed a stage of education to complete it, and if they wish, to proceed to the next;
(ii) Help every educated person to have further education with or without formally enrolling himself in an educational institution;
(iii) Enable a worker to acquire knowledge, ability and vocational skill in order to be a better worker and to improve his chances of earning more; and
(iv) Help to refresh the knowledge of the educated person and enable him to keep pace with the new knowledge in the field of his interest.

In pursuance of this recommendation of the Commission, two additional modes of education have come up, and are fast developing. The non-formal system is being used not only as a supplementary channel, but also as an alternative to the formal schooling. Similarly, Distance Education, using recent advances in electronic media and communication technology, is being used as an effective alternative to conventional system. A network of open universities and open schools is fast emerging to make education more egalitarian, flexible and efficient. The details of these developments are discussed in the relevant chapters of this book.

4

Universalization of Elementary Education

One important characteristic of democracy is that it presupposes an educated and enlightened society. Democracy, both as a form of the government and as a way of life, cannot function when the society is uneducated and ignorant. When India acquired freedom in 1947, she accepted to have a democratic form of the government, not only as a result of the philosophical position taken during the freedom struggle, but also as an eventual necessity in view of the future model of the society sought to be created. In view of the future aspirations of the rapid development of science and technology in order to achieve self-sufficiency in all sectors of economy and polity, and a consequential modernization of traditional means of agricultural production and industrial growth, education of the masses was considered as a prerequisite. Education and modernization are the two wheels of the same cart. Both, when combined together, lead to a rapid socio-economic development of a nation. While study of advanced science and technology helps achieve modernization, the basic education helps the poor masses to take advantage of scientific and technological development, and hence, of modernization. It is, therefore, not by accident that the provision regarding education of the poor masses forms an integral part of the Constitution of India enforced on January 26, 1950. The Article 45 of the Constitution provides for free and compulsory education for all children in the age-group 6-14 years, up to a minimum level. The whole idea has been woven into the concept of universalization of elementary education. The level of compulsory education as envisaged in this Article corresponds to the elementary education of eight years' duration from class I to class VIII for the children aged 6-14 years.

HISTORICAL PERSPECTIVE

Historically, the demand for compulsory primary/elementary education in India emerged during the 18th century, which was a period of awareness and social change, and had considerably strengthened by the end of 19th century. By this time, on the one hand, the principle of compulsory education had been accepted in Britain, and on the other, Indians had become aware of the contribution of education in the development of other countries of the world. During the 18th century and earlier, there was a large network of indigenous schools providing instructions at elementary and higher levels mostly restricted to 3 Rs and religious education. The evidence available shows that there was a school for every 400 people in Bengal that time. The literacy rate was 6.1%, but education for women was completely non-existent (Saiyadain, 1966).

Perhaps, the first Indian to press the demand for compulsory primary education for the Indian masses was Dada Bhai Nauroji who pleaded before the Indian Education Commission (1882) that steps should be taken to provide primary education to all children. At the same time, Maharaja Shayaji Rao Gaekwad, the Ruler of Baroda State, who had introduced compulsory primary education in the Amaravati Division of his State in 1893, conducted a very significant experiment. Having obtained encouraging results, he extended the scheme to cover the entire state. This successful experiment gave further support to the demand for free and compulsory primary education. As a consequence of agitation by some enthusiastic Indians, the British Government appointed a committee to examine the feasibility of introducing compulsory education in Bombay (1906).

Unfortunately, the committee recommended that the time was not ripe for the purpose. In 1910, G. K. Gokhale moved a resolution in Central Legislature on compulsory education, which was withdrawn on the assurance from the government that it would examine the problem carefully. The next year (1911), Gokhale introduced a private bill related to compulsory education, which was opposed by the Indian states and the Central Government, and was subsequently turned down by a clear official majority. The bill came up again in 1912, and was again turned down, though it enjoyed the support of many prominent Indians in the Central Legislature (see chapter I). The repeated failure of Gokhale focussed public attention on the problem of compulsory education, and paved the path of complete success. In 1917, Vithal Bhai Patel moved a bill in the Bombay Legislative Council for the introduction of compulsory primary education in the municipal areas of the state. This became a law in 1918, which was popularly known as Patel Act. This success encouraged other states also to make attempts, and most of them soon placed a law in their statutes regarding compulsory education. The Government of India Act (1919) created provincial legislatures with a large representation of members elected by the people. In 1921, the Department of Education was transferred to an Indian minister responsible to legislature. By this time, the compulsory education had been introduced only in eight towns, but the progress continued slowly during the following years also.

An interesting example of Indian enterprise was reported by Hartog (1939). Mr. G. D. Birla and his family set up an educational scheme at Pilani, near Jaipur State. The Birla Trust controlled a Montessori school, a girl's school, some 150 village schools, a high school, and an intermediate college, all financed by the Trust. One of the features of the village schools was that crafts formed part of the curriculum. Reference was also made to the remarkable educational colony founded by Sir Anand Sarup at Dayal Bagh, near Agra.

The total enrollment of boys and girls at the primary stage increased from less than 6.5 million to over 9 million between 1917 and 1927. The enrollment of boys rose from 30.3% to 42.1% and that of girls from 6.7% to 10.45, taking the population of school going age children (6-11 years) as 14 %. By 1936 it had risen to 51% for boys and 17% for girls. In 1935-36, there were 197,858 primary schools, 165,240 for boys and 32,618 for girls, and the total enrollment by this time had increased to 14 million. However, the dropout rate from class I to class IV was about 74% (Hartog, 1939).

By 1936-37, compulsory education had been adopted in 167 urban areas out of total 2,703, and in 13,062 rural habitations out of 655,892 (Saiyadain, 1960). So in all, 2% of the total habitations were served by compulsory education, 6% urban and 1.99% rural. So, the Indian control over the period 1921-1947, which was only partial, led to a very steady progress in the field of compulsory elementary education. Consequently, in 1947, the enrollment in primary schools from class I to class V (age group 6-11 years) was about 10.5 million children receiving instruction in 141,000 primary schools. The number of upper primary (middle) schools for classes VI to VIII (age group 11-14 years) was 9,000 with a total enrollment of 1.60 million. Thus, total enrollment in elementary education for age-group 6-14 years was 12.10 million in 150,000 schools. The enrollment of girls was only about 3 million—about 25% of the total enrollment in elementary schools. The teacher-pupil ratio was approximately 1:35 (1948-49). The number of schools had increased to 220,000 with total enrollment of 17.39 million by 1948-49, which included 4.61 million girls (Chauhan, 1990). Thus, the enrollment of girls increased from 25% in 1947 to 26.10% in 1948-49.

The aforesaid analysis indicates that the progress of compulsory elementary education in India was slow and steady during the pre-independence period. In fact, it was true for education of any kind. Whatever little facilities were available served only a microscopic minority belonging to the elite groups, and the common masses were left completely deprived of all such facilities.

THE BASIC CONCEPTS

The concept of Universalization of Elementary Education (UEE), as guaranteed in the Constitution implies that:

(i) education from class I to class VIII would be free of cost for all children irrespective of their capacity to pay;
(ii) education at this stage would be made compulsory for all children between the age of 6 to 14 years, either by persuasion or by legislation or both;

(iii) the goal of providing free and compulsory elementary education for the children of the relevant age group would be achieved within ten years of the enforcement of the Constitution, i.e. by 1960;

(iv) the quality of education would be satisfactory, and comparable over all states, regions, types of schools, and modes of learning (full-time, part-time, and own-time).

In pursuance of the implementation of the constitutional provisions on the one hand, and social demand for education on the other, greater emphasis was laid on enrollment and expansion of facilities in the beginning. The periodic evaluation of the policies, programmes, and progress has led to considerable shift in the interpretation of the concept of universalization of elementary education. The methods and approaches followed in implementing the programmes of elementary education are determined by how the underlying concepts are defined. Since independence, we have been implementing the programmes mainly by—

(i) undertaking massive expansion of facilities in terms of number of primary and upper primary schools so as to make a school available and accessible to every child within a walking distance from his place of living;

(ii) trying to enroll maximum number of children of the relevant age group (6-14 years) in school so as to increase Gross Enrollment Ratio (GER) at primary and upper primary levels.

This is exclusively a statistical approach and ignores the qualitative aspects of education altogether, and hence, is totally unsatisfactory. Such practices have resulted in certain difficulties in the assessment of the progress of different schemes. The Committee for Review of NPE-1986, popularly called "Ramamurti Committee (1990)", has cited an instance of a micro-planning survey conducted in Tikamgarh District of the State of Madhya Pradesh, and pointed out that, in the rural areas, the number of children in the elementary school age group actually attending schools was 42.7% of those shown on the official records. Similarly, many instances are available when many children whose names were enrolled in the school register had, in fact, not attended school for more than a few days. It was also pointed out that since teachers were under pressure to show better enrollment targets, they kept the names of these children alive in their registers. This kind of situation creates an illusion about the actual achievements in terms of enrollment and reflects a gap between "claim" and "reality". The Committee had rightly pointed out that "enrollment" does not mean "retention", "retention" does not mean "participation", and "participation" does not mean "achievement". The logic can be further extended to say that "achievement" does not mean "learning", if it is assessed in terms of marks obtained.

The NPE-1986 as modified in 1992 has taken a more comprehensive view of universalization of elementary education. It stated:

> The new thrust in elementary education will emphasize three aspects: (i) universal access and enrollment, (ii) universal retention of children upto 14 years of age, and (iii) a substantial improvement in the quality of education to enable all children to achieve essential levels of learning.

The broader concept of "Education For All (EFA)", which has been accepted world wide, clubs "universal elementary education" with "adult education" and has led to a broad-based view. The World Conference on Education for All held in Jomtien (Thailand) in 1990 had set up an International Consultative Forum on Education for All to review the progress towards global EFA goals periodically. India hosted the second meeting of the Forum in September 1993, at New Delhi (Government of India, 1993). The four broad areas within the main theme—the quality of EFA, discussed at the meeting were:

(i) Early childhood education,
(ii) Improving schooling,
(iii) Improving non-formal education programmes, and
(iv) Financing quality education.

Against the background of demographic implications and complex ground realities of Indian scene, the Government of India (1993) has set up the following goals of EFA:

(i) Expansion of early childhood care and development activities including family and community, especially, for the poor, disadvantaged and children;

(ii) Universalization of elementary education (UEE) viewed as a composite programme of universal access to elementary education for all children up to 14 years of age, universal participation till they complete the elementary stage through formal or non-formal education programs, and universal achievement of at least minimum levels of learning;

(iii) Drastic reduction in illiteracy, particularly in the 15-35 age group, bringing the literacy level in this age group at least to 80% in each gender and for every identified disadvantaged group, ensuring that the levels of 3 Rs are relevant to the living and working conditions of the people;

(iv) Provision of opportunities to maintain, use, and upgrade their education, and provision of facilities for development of skills, to persons who are functionally literate and those who have received primary education through formal and non-formal channels;

(v) Creation of necessary structure and setting in motion processes which would empower women and make education an instrument of women's equality;

(vi) Improving the content and process of education to better relate it to the environment, people's culture and with their living and working conditions, thereby enhancing their ability to learn and cope with the problems of livelihood and environment.

POLICIES AND PROGRAMMES

Since the attainment of independence, considerable attempts have been made by the government to develop a national system of education rooted in the cherished traditions and fundamental values of the society and suited to the needs and aspirations of the people. Article 45 of the Constitution was taken as a major guideline for the development of elementary education to begin with. At the same time, the government decided to formulate and follow a policy of planned development and established the Planning Commission. The first five-year plan began on April 1, 1951 and ended on March 31,1956. Each plan consists of policies, programmes and strategies along with financial provisions for all sectors of economy including education. All the subsequent plans were also similarly formulated and implemented. The period of first three five-year plans was an era of quantitative expansion of schooling facilities in terms of number of schools, enrollment and recruitment of teachers. During this period, the Government of India accorded highest priority to the development of higher education, especially, the professional and technical. For this purpose, the government appointed the University Education Commission in 1948, with Dr. S. Radhakrishnan as its Chairman, which recommended massive expansion of higher education. Consequently, the progress of elementary education was slow during the period from 1951 to 1966.

In 1964, the government appointed the Education Commission headed by Dr. D.S. Kothari, the then Chairman of the University Grants Commission. The Resolution of the Government of India dated July 14, 1964, by which the Commission was instituted, stated:.

> It is desirable to survey the entire field of educational development as the various parts of the educational system strongly interact with and influence one another. It is not possible to have progressive and strong universities without efficient secondary schools and the quality of these schools is determined by the functioning of elementary schools. What is needed, therefore, is a synoptic survey and an imaginative look at education considered as a whole and not in fragmented parts and stages. In the past, several commissions and committees have examined limited sectors and specific aspects of education. It is now proposed to have a comprehensive review of the entire educational system.

The Commission recommended a model of National System of Education wherein it made significant recommendations for different aspects of education including compulsory and universal elementary education. The commission asserted (para 7.08) that:

> ...the fulfillment of the directive principle contained in Article 45 of the Constitution: that the state should strive to provide free and compulsory education for all children up to the age of 14 years. This should have been achieved by 1960. But in view of the immense difficulties involved, such as lack of

adequate resources, tremendous increase in population, resistance to the education of girls, large number of children of the backward classes, general poverty of the people, and the illiteracy and apathy of the parents, it was not possible to make adequate progress in primary education, and the Constitutional Directive has remained unfulfilled..., and we believe that the provision of free and compulsory education for every child is an educational objective of the highest priority, not only on grounds of social justice and democracy, but also for raising the competence of the average worker and for increasing national productivity.

The Commission further suggested that the best strategy for fulfilling the Constitutional Directive would be as follows:

(i) Each State and even each district, should prepare a perspective plan for the development of primary education taking into account the stage of development already reached and the local conditions and problems. The objective of the plan should be to fulfil the Constitutional Directive as early as possible;

(ii) Each State and the district should be assisted to go ahead at the best pace it can, and the progress in no area should be allowed to be held up merely for want of essential facilities or financial allocations; and

(iii) While the Constitutional Directives may be fulfilled in some places such as urban areas or advantaged States as early as in 1975-76, all the areas in the country should be able to provide five years of good and effective education to all the children by 1975-76 and seven years of such education by 1985-86.

This shows that the Commission had suggested a new target date and a fixed period for achieving the goal of UEE. Besides, the commission also suggested the strategies and programmes, which involved three stages of universal provision, universal enrollment, and universal retention with simultaneous implementation of a programme of qualitative improvement of education, because universal enrollment or retention depends largely on the attraction and holding power of the school. The Central Advisory Board of

Education (CABE) readily accepted this proposal of the Commission, along with other proposals, and the Committee of the Members of Parliament, which showed considerable interest in the proposals on UEE and Adult Education, and insisted on a shorter time span than the one recommended by the Commission.

Based on the recommendations of the Education Commission, the Government of India launched the National Policy on Education-1968, which made a specific proposal for UEE and stated:

> Strenuous efforts should be made for the early fulfillment of the Directive Principle under Article 45 of the Constitution seeking to provide free and compulsory education for all children up to the age of 14. Suitable programmes should be developed to reduce the prevailing wastage and stagnation in schools and to ensure that every child who is enrolled in school successfully completes the prescribed course.

This statement of the NPE-1968 is, in no way, different from the statement of Article 45 of the Constitution, as it does not point to suitable programmes and strategies to be followed to achieve the goal of UEE. This simply shows that the then government did not take the recommendations of the Education Commission seriously. Naik (1982 p 72) has put it in a very explicit way:

> It is our great experience that even in such non-controversial areas where we agreed on what is to be done but do not quite know-how to do it, most of the time available is spent on talking on the desirability of the programme, the significance of the Article 45, the lack of political great will to implement the programme, etc. While all such homilies on the subject are welcome, they do not help in solving the problem.

Although, the recommendations of Education Commission regarding UEE and other important aspects of education were incorporated in the NPE-1968 the follow-up programmes were not carried out seriously, perhaps because the overall socio-political environment was not conducive to it. The success of a programme, however good, depends on how sincerely and skillfully it is implemented. The Education Commission had apprised the government in advance regarding the desirability of favourable conditions for the implementation of the programmes suggested by them as follows (para 19.47):

A vigorous and sustained implementation of the recommendations made in the report demands a higher priority than that given so far to education in our national plans for development. A deliberate commitment about the crucial role of education in national development can alone provide the psychological motivation and energy needed for a massive programme of implementation. We realize that such environment will depend essentially on the extent to which education is effectively and demonstrably related to the life, needs and aspirations of the country. This is a task mainly for the educators, and it is the urgency of this that we have emphasized in the Report.

Naik (1982) has rightly pointed out that creation of a national system of education as proposed by the Commission, does need favourable political, economic and social conditions. The Commission had assumed strong and stable governments, both at the Centre and in the States, committed whole-heartedlv to the cause of education, a declining birth rate, a growth of national income at the rate of 6% per annum, a lessening of social tensions due to effective development, a strengthened and revitalized democracy, a committed and competent body of teachers, and a community of students dedicated to the pursuit of learning. However, the period from 1966 to 1986 was characterized by political instability with the weakening of the ruling Congress party in the general elections of 1967, and subsequent split in 1969, followed by proclamation of emergency in 1975 by then Prime Minister, Mrs. Indira Gandhi, after the invalidation of her parliamentary election by the Allahabad High Court. The excesses committed by the power brokers in the government and the bureaucracy led to the defeat of Congress party in the general elections of 1977. The Janata Party that subsequently came to power kept busy in consolidating itself but failed to keep its flock together, and split in 1979. The people in the general elections of 1980 rooted the Janata Party also out of power, with the Congress party emerging stronger and recapturing power at the Centre again. This shows that the period of 14 years from 1966 to 1980, when the National Policy on Education launched in 1968 was to be implemented, was a period of profound political uncertainty and instability. The country also had to fight a war against Pakistan in

1971. Nobody, either in the government or in the bureaucracy had time to think of education. Consequently, nothing substantial could be achieved, except something because of momentum in the direction of implementation of NPE -1968.

However, in the meantime, the Janata Party government (1977-80) formulated the Draft National Policy on Education in 1979, which could not be adopted by the Parliament, because the ruling party lost general elections in 1980. The draft NPE-1979 had also made significant proposals regarding all aspects of education. Regarding elementary education, the draft NPE-1979 stated:

> Highest priority must be given to free and compulsory education for all up to the age of 14 as laid down in the Directive Principles of the Constitution. Education up to this stage should be general and not specialized, and should give pupils a confident command of language and tool subjects, and inculcate a scientific attitude. Elementary education should be an integral stage.

The draft policy could not be approved by the Parliament, and hence, could not be implemented. As Mrs. Gandhi took over as Prime Minister again in 1980, the problems of terrorism took serious turn in Punjab and some other parts of the country, which detracted both the government attention and huge financial resources to the problem of controlling terrorism. Finally, in 1984, her own guards assassinated Mrs. Indira Gandhi. Therefore, along with political uncertainty, the economic growth of the country also slowed down. As a result of these circumstances, taken together, the educational progress during 1966-86 periods had been at a slow pace.

After Mrs. Gandhi, her son, Rajeev Gandhi, took over as Prime Minster of the then Congress government at the Centre, and in his first address to the nation he revealed his intentions to formulate and launch another National Policy on Education. In pursuance of this, the Government of India published a document entitled "Challenge of Education: A Policy Perspective" in 1985. This document, which reviewed the contemporary educational scenario in the country with reference to the preceding developments, was discussed nationwide in conferences and seminars. Finally, National Policy on Education (NPE)-1986 was launched in May 1986 followed by a Programme of Action (POA) published the same year. The NPE-1986 and POA-1986 visualized several ambitious proposals for the development of all aspects of education. Regarding elementary education, the NPE-1986 proposed to shift emphasis from mere enrollment to retention of children in schools and provide for education of adequate level of quality.

But, Congress party lost elections in 1990 and the next government headed by V.P. Singh as Prime Minister appointed a committee to review the NPE-1986 under the chairmanship of Acharya Ramamurti. This committee also expressed deep concern about the UEE and non-achievement of its goals for such a long time. The Committee specifically pointed out to the phenomena of non-enrollment and dropout rate, especially among girls. The Committee emphatically stated:

> In contrast, Universal Declaration of Human Rights declares that all individuals, irrespective of sex, caste, and economic status, have the "Right to Education". India rightly subscribed to this famous declaration. Now, time has come to recognize the Right to Education as one of the fundamental rights of the Indian citizens for which necessary amendments in the Constitution may have to be made and, more importantly, conditions be created in the society such that this right would become available to all children of India.

The Congress party regained power in 1991 and appointed another committee to review the recommendations of the Ramamurty Committee the same year under the chairmanship of Mr. Janardan Reddy, then Chief Minister of Andhra Pradesh. As the Central Advisory Board of Education appointed this committee, this is also known as the CABE committee. On the basis of the suggestions made by the Ramamurti Committee and the CABE Committee, the NPE-1986 was reviewed and the "Revised Version" was published in 1992. The modified NPE-1992 is now under the process of implementation. As mentioned earlier in this chapter, the goal of UEE was to be achieved by 1960 as stipulated by the Constitution. But the target date was revised first from 1960 to 1970, then to 1976 (Reddy and Kumaraswamy, 1990), and again to 1985-86 (Education Commission). The NPE-1986 also proposed to revise the target date further to 1995. It said:

> The New Education Policy will give highest priority to solving the problems of children dropping out of school and adopt an array of meticulously formulated strategies based on micro-planning, and applied at the grass roots level all over the country, to ensure children's retention at school. This effort will be fully coordinated with the network of non-formal education. It shall be ensured that all children who attain the age of about 11 years by 1990 will have had five years of schooling, or its equivalent through the non-formal stream. Likewise, by 1995, all children will be provided free and compulsory education up to 14 years of age.

After evaluating the progress of UEE achieved by 1990, the modified NPE-1992 further revised the target date for achieving the goal of UEE. Its statement reads as follows:

> It shall be ensured that free and compulsory education of satisfactory quality is provided to all children up to 14 years of age before we enter the twenty-first century. A national mission will be launched for the achievement of this goal.

SOME NEW PROGRAMMES

In view of the prevailing circumstances, the Government of India realized that formal system of education cannot serve the purpose of UEE, specially, under the contemporary phase of development, and some alternative strategies would have to be planned, not only for providing access to education, but also for improving its quality and checking the dropout rate. The NPE-1986 also proposed to strengthen and expand non-formal education scheme not only as a supplement but also as a substitute for formal schooling. Similarly, it was proposed that a massive programme called "operation blackboard" would be launched in order to improve physical facilities in schools.

Non-Formal Education (NFE)

Non-formal education, as defined in the documents of the Government of India, is only a complementary system to formal education (Singh, 1987). It is being planned, designed, and propagated by almost all government agencies as a sub-system of the formal system. Perhaps, the terms more commonly associated with non-formal education are cost effective need based, functional, flexible and dropouts etc. It is a strategy to provide education to those that did not attend school or dropped out of it due to some reasons. It is also meant for those to whom formal schools are either not available or not accessible. It is an organized and systematic educational activity carried out outside the framework of formal school system to provide selected type of learning to particular sub-groups in the population, adults as well as children.

The NFE programme originated in India through a Resolution of the Central Advisory Board of Education adopted in 1974 (Singh, 1987 p 5), which recommended that a radical reconstruction of the existing system should be carried out through the adoption of multiple-entry system and a large-scale programme of part-time education for those children who cannot attend school. The Ministry of Education, in 1977, asked nine educationally backward states to establish 500 NFE centres each. These states were: Andhra Pradesh, Assam, Bihar, Jammu & Kashmir, Madhya Pradesh, Orissa, Rajasthan, Uttar Pradesh, and West Bengal. Later on, the NFE was linked with the programme of adult literacy called National Adult Education Programme (NAEP) launched by the government in 1978. So, NFE was used to serve out-of-school children, unemployed youth, women and girls, and illiterate adults including neo-literate adults. The NFE programme was a major initiative to bring the dropouts and other non-enrolled children in the 9-14 age group to the learning stream launched in the nine educationally backward states in 1979. The NFE scheme is based on 50% Central Government sponsorship, the balance 50% to be provided by the states.

Till 1985-86, the number of children targeted for NFE enrolment was 5.68 million, but only 3.67 million were enrolled leaving a shortfall of 35.30%. Similarly, the number of NFE centres opened was 1.28 lakhs as against the proposed 1.70 lakhs recording a shortfall of 24.4% (Rajagopalan, 1987). The programme was extended to all the states and Union Territories from 1987 onwards (NIEPA, 1990). From 1985-86 to 1992-93, the number of NFE centres increased to 2.77 lakhs, and enrollment increased to 6.8 million (GOI, 1993). During this period, the NFE centres for girls also increased from 20,500 to 81,600. A proposal for revising and continuing NFE programmes under the eighth Plan (1992-97) became effective in October 1993, and a budget of Rs. 110.16 crore was set aside for the year 1993-94. The revised scheme called for an intensified project approach, greater decentralization in financial and administrative management, more effective training, development of teaching/learning material of high quality, and the introduction of semester system in NFE courses (GOI, 1994). In order to increase motivation, a cash incentive was also proposed to be introduced for instructors and a substantial increase in the expenditure was envisaged. Significantly, the number of NFE centres for girls as opposed to co-educational centres was to be increased from a ratio of 25:75 to 40:60. At present (1998-99), there are 2.97 lakhs NFE centres covering about 74.20 lakhs of children in 24 States and Union Territories. While 2.38 lakhs of centres have been sanctioned to States and Union Territories (of which 1.18 lakhs of centres are exclusively for girls), and 58788 centres are run by 816 voluntary organizations. Two Parliamentary Standing Committees have reviewed the performance of the scheme *inter alia*, one on human resource development, and second on the problem of dropouts. The Planning Commission has evaluated the performance of the scheme also. Based on their recommendations, action has been initiated to revise the scheme.

The performance of NFE programmes in India has been sluggish and unsatisfactory for which there are numerous reasons. These include failure to train instructors, delayed payment of remuneration to staff, abandoning or shifting NFE centres, non-supply or delayed supply of teaching material, and absence of proper monitoring and evaluation system. Due to these and other associated reasons, a large number of NFE centres had to be closed down in Orissa, Bihar, West Bengal, Jammu & Kashmir, and Uttar Pradesh. These inadequacies have to be removed, if NFE programme is to achieve success.

Operation Blackboard

Lack of physical facilities in our schools is one of the many serious problems of our education system. Although, in terms of number our school system has grown very large, yet the quality of education imparted in schools is not satisfactory. It is not that only the buildings of the schools are not satisfactory, even trained teachers are not there in adequate number. A large number of schools run without libraries, laboratories and playgrounds. Even drinking water facilities are not available in many schools. According to the Sixth All India Education Survey (NCERT, 1998), 16.27% of the primary schools in the country are without buildings. This means that these schools are functioning in kachcha buildings, thatched huts, and tents and open space. The situation of upper primary schools is slightly better as only about 10.70% of them are without building. Surprisingly, 10.59% primary schools have no instructional rooms and about 60% have one or two instructional rooms. Again, the situation of upper primary schools is a little better as 21.13% schools have zero to two instructional rooms. It was also reported that 44.23% primary schools have the drinking water facility, 18.93% have urinals and 8.66% have separate urinals for girls. Out of the total number of schools in the country, only 10.86% have lavatory, which include 5.12% schools having separate lavatories for girls. The situation in upper primary schools is a little better in this case also. Another serious matter is that 62.03% schools have one or two teachers in position in each of them. Most of the States and UTs have over 30% single teacher schools. The number of untrained teachers posted in these schools is also very large. The Government of India has taken a serious note of this situation and has initiated some programmes for the improvement of physical facilities in schools.

One of the key programmes proposed by the NPE-1986 was "Operation Blackboard", which was launched in 1987. The main purpose of this programme was to ensure minimum essential physical facilities in all elementary schools. As stated by the NPE-1986:

> Provision will be made of essential physical facilities in primary schools, including at least two reasonably large rooms that are usable in all weather, and the necessary toys, blackboards, maps, charts, and other learning material. At least two teachers, one of whom a woman should work in every school, the number increasing as early as possible to one teacher per class. A phased drive, symbolically called OPERATION BLACKBOARD will be undertaken with immediate effect to improve primary schools all over the country. Government, local bodies, voluntary agencies and individuals will be fully involved. Construction of school buildings will be the first charge on NERP and RLEGP funds.

The use of the term "Operation" implied that there was urgency in the programme, which had a predetermined timeframe about its implementation, and the term "Blackboard", symbolized physical facilities. Hence, the concept of 'Operation Blackboard' implied 'speedy creation of minimum essential physical facilities in schools both in terms of man and material'. The scheme had three interrelated components:

(i) provision of at least two large all weather rooms for all primary schools;
(ii) provision of at least two teachers in every school one being preferably a woman; and
(iii) provision of minimum essential teaching/learning material for every primary school.

To begin with, each state was supposed to conduct detailed surveys of blocks to be covered by the scheme, and implement the scheme in a need-based manner. The scheme was to be implemented in three phases beginning with 20% of the blocks and municipal areas in 1987-88, 30% in 1988-89, and the remaining 50% in 1989-90 (Ray, 1993). However, due to the resource crunch, it could not be implemented in all the blocks by 1989-90, and was therefore, continued in 1990-91 and 1991-92 also. The NPE-1986, as revised in 1992, proposed to enlarge the scope of the scheme to provide three reasonably large rooms and school library along with necessary teaching material. At least three teachers were to be provided to each school with the number reaching one teacher per class as early as possible. At least 50% of the teachers recruited in future would be women. As per revised NPE, the scheme would be extended to upper primary schools also, and construction of school buildings would be a priority charge of JRY funds.

By March 1992, the scheme had covered 4.14 lakhs (77%) schools in 5385 (84%) Community Development Blocks and 1142 (29%) municipal areas. About 70,000 teachers had been appointed as against 1.52 lakhs single teacher schools identified for coverage, and over 1 lakh classrooms had been constructed as against the target of 2.39 lakhs (NPE-POA, 1992). By March 1993, as many as 4.69 lakhs (87%) of primary schools had been covered in 5853 (91%) blocks. An amount of Rs. 179 crore was earmarked for the scheme during 1993-94 to cover 68,378 additional schools during the year. By 1993, 1.10 lakh teachers had been appointed against the target of over 1.31 lakhs, and 1.15 lakhs of rooms had been constructed against the target of 2.69 lakhs. West Bengal and Bihar accounted for about 70% of the total uncovered schools.

The first phase of implementation of the scheme was evaluated in 1994 by several agencies including the Ministry of Human Resource Development and the NCERT. It was found that even after several years of functioning of the scheme, many schools in several states were running with a single teacher. In some cases the post of the second teacher had been created but had not been filled up due to certain reasons. The expansion of the scheme, as proposed in the revised NPE-1992, is being taken up in those states where the initial scheme has been successful. In order to improve the quality of the scheme, the teachers are being trained in using the material provided under the scheme. While a limited number of schools will be covered under the extended scheme during the eighth Plan, all upper primary schools will be covered by the turn of the century depending on the availability of funds.

Since, the scheme involves huge investment, there are reports of misuse of funds in some states such as Bihar (the Hindustan Times, May 31,1993). The slow progress of the scheme is also due to mismanagement of the scheme at the hands of the administrative setup in the states, which were not ready to handle such a challenging task. Lack of commitment on the part of state governments, administrative machinery, and teachers has also been an important factor adversely influencing the progress of the scheme.

SOME ALTERNATIVE STRATEGIES

In addition to NFE, a few more alternative strategies to achieve UEE have been suggested. The NFE is often rated as a second grade alternative due to poor infrastructure facilities and low financial inputs (Rajput, 1994). While the quality of NFE centres and of education provided by them will have to be improved, there are a few more strategies, which can be used effectively. Some of them are cited below:

1. Shiksha Karmi Project of Rajasthan may be an effective alternative strategy. This project sought to solve the problem of teacher absenteeism in remote villages of Rajasthan. The regular school teachers posted in remote

areas indulging in prolonged absenteeism were replaced by young and willing youths. These substitute teachers were known as "shiksha karmis" and were selected by the local people. The scheme was assisted by the Swedish International Development Agency (SIDA) and involved a component of intensive training of shiksha karmis for 37 days. These local youth were supposed to hold classes at day centres and night centres. The Project aimed at covering about 1050 remote villages in 70 blocks of Rajasthan by 1994. The total outlay on the Project from June 1991 to June 1996 was Rs. 412.3 million (GOI, 1993). The evaluation of the scheme showed that the level of attainment of students is comparable to that of those attending formal schools. It has been estimated that by 2003, the project will cover 4100 villages/day schools, 7335 prehar pathshalas, 121 upper primary schools covering all districts of Rajasthan with an expected enrollment of over 3.25 lakhs of students.

2. Another innovative project was "Promoting Primary and Elementary Education (PROPEL)" undertaken by the Indian Institute of Education, Pune. PROPEL was an inter-disciplinary action research project which aimed at liberating the creative energies of the rural masses for an integrated local effort towards development based on micro planning. The Village Education Committees and Village Education Councils help streamline Panchayat action for conducting pre-school, non-formal education of different kinds, literacy activities, and women's development groups. Micro planning, community participation and the transparency of all educational operations are the characteristic features of the project. The PROPEL has been selected by the UNESCO as a "show case" project for Asia.

3 One more alternative may be the concept of the "Non-formalized School" proposed by the Ramamurti Committee (1990). All essential resources, both financial and intellectual, should be made available to the school to enable it to "reach out to" the children outside the school, at least two-thirds of whom are girls. 'The school should open up and non-formalize in creative ways'. According to Ramamurti Committee, this would be

preferable to building up an exclusive parallel system of non-formal education for the poor and working children. The school could be non-formalized by:

(i) shifting school timings to early morning hours, afternoons, or late evenings as per requirements of the community;
(ii) adjusting school calendar to agricultural activity and other local needs to maximize attendance;
(iii) holding classes twice in the day for written and oral traditions and using ungraded classrooms;
(iv) providing for flexible entry points for first generation learners and girls;
(v) providing freedom to question, inquire, explore, and enjoy through group learning and peer-teaching;
(vi) introducing environment-based content and formative evaluation, community participation, and internship model of teacher training.

The scheme proposed to empower the school headmaster to recruit "para- teachers" for early morning and late evening classes, on a respectable salary, and from the local community. A para-teacher may have even less than minimum qualifications, but interchangeable with regular school teachers and liable to be absorbed as regular teacher after gaining requisite experience and upgrading qualifications. The idea appears to be somewhat hazardous and impracticable (CABE Committee, 1992), but if modified properly to suit local conditions, it can work effectively.

Micro-Planning

The NPE-1986, also suggested the idea of micro-planning, which forms a strategy aimed at "a family-wise and child-wise design of action" to ensure that every child attends school or an NFE centre regularly, progresses at his own pace and completes at least five years of schooling or its equivalent at NFE centre. This implies area specific planning to be participative, decentralized and flexible, based on community mobilization and support. The basic to this approach is the role of Village Education Committee (VEC) formed by Panchayat. At block/taluka level also, there will be similar planning bodies or committees.

District Primary Education Programme

The District Primary Education Programme (DPEP) is a part of the micro-planning strategy. The Eighth Five-year Plan (1992-97) envisaged that "District" would be the unit of planning for UEE instead of the State. District specific plans would be developed by the state governments as "projects" with specific activities and targets depending on the specific needs and possibilities in the district. The overall goals of the project would be the reconstruction of primary education in selected districts in terms of reduction of existing disparities in educational access, provision of comparable standards of education for disadvantaged groups, improvement in physical facilities, and decentralization of planning and management (GOI, 1993). Under this scheme, districts are categorized into three groups:

(i) High literacy districts in which access and enrollment are almost universal, and need for education is high.

(ii) Districts in which total literacy campaigns have been successful leading to an enhanced demand for elementary education.

(iii) Low literacy districts in which educational facilities are unsatisfactory, and community awareness is also low.

These groups of districts will be approached by different strategies depending on their level of readiness for UEE drive in terms of environment building, awareness generation, and residual enrollment completion. The DPEP is the major strategy to execute the district based planning launched in 1993-94. The programme seeks to operationalize the strategies of district level planning. It is a "home grown" programme based on the assumption that in a country like India, planning must be contextual in nature. The target groups for DPEP include girls, working children, children from disadvantaged groups, and children from geographically isolated areas. It is supposed to take initiative in all areas, particularly, the Total Literacy Campaign (TLC) districts, where a demand for education is being raised by the population. It is aimed at the all-round development of education in selected areas rather than piecemeal implementation of educational schemes. It had been initiated in 42 districts by 1994 (GOI, 1994) spread over seven states, and the target for 1993-98 was to extend the programme to 110 districts. According to the latest reports, the DPEP has been extended to 43 more districts in Uttar Pradesh (The Hindustan Times, Oct. 14, 2000) and West Bengal with an aim to achieve universalization of primary education. The DPEP, by the end of 2000, covered 219 districts in 15 states.

Minimum Levels of Learning

According to NPE-1986, emphasis in UEE would shift from enrollment to retention, and providing education of comparable quality in all the schools. It would be ensured that every child acquires certain minimum levels of skills, knowledge, and competencies. The strategy aims at laying down learning outcomes expected from a basic education at a realistic, relevant and functional level to be achieved by all children completing a given stage of schooling. The learning outcomes define the Minimum Levels of Learning (MLL), which are common to both school and equivalent NFE programme. The main steps to be followed in introducing MLL in the schools include assessment of existing levels of learning achievement, definition of MLL for the area, reorientation of teaching practices to competency based teaching, introduction of continuous and comprehensive evaluation, review and revision of text-books, and provision of necessary inputs such as physical facilities, teacher training and evaluation. The main emphasis would be on monitoring, evaluation, and improvement of instruction to bring uniformity and reduce disparities.

PROGRESS AND ACHIEVEMENT

It has been mentioned elsewhere that at the time of independence in 1947, there were 150,000 elementary schools in India having enrolled 12.10 million children including 25% girls. By 1948-49, the number of schools increased to 220,000 and enrollment of children increased to 17.39 million including 4.61 million girls. As mentioned earlier, the First Five-year Plan (1951-56) began on April 1,1951. At the beginning of the First Plan in 1950-51, there were about 223,600 elementary schools — 210,000 primary and 13,600 upper primary (middle), which enrolled 22.30 million children — 19.20 million in primary and 3.10 million in upper primary schools. The total number of teachers working in these schools was 624,000, 538,000 at primary and 86,000 at upper primary stage, which included 16.80% female teachers.

Table 4.1
Growth of Recognized Elementary Schools since 1951

Year	*Primary Schools*	*Upper Primary Schools*	*Elementary Schools*
1950-51	209671	13596	223267
1955-56	278135	21730	299865
1960-61	330399	49663	380062
1965-66	391064	75798	466862
1970-71	408378	90621	498999
1975-76	454270	106571	560841
1980-81	494305	118571	612860
1985-86	528872	134846	663718
1990-91	560935	151456	712391
1995-96	590421	171216	761637
1999-2000	641695	198004	839699

Sources:

1. Government of India Ministry of Human Resource Development, Annual Reports 1999-2000 and 2000-2001.
2. Selected Educational Statistics—1997-98, 1999-2000, MHRD, Government of India.

As mentioned earlier, the progress of school education during the first three five-year plans was slow, though, there took place noticeable quantitative expansion in terms of number of schools, teachers, and enrollment. By 1965-66, when the Education Commission submitted its report, the number of primary schools had increased to over 391,000 and that of upper primary schools to about 75,800, thus raising the total number of elementary schools to 466,800. These schools had enrolled about 61.00 million children —50.50 million at primary stage and 10.50 million at upper primary stage (GOI, 1987). The enrollment of girls was 21.10 million, which constituted about 34.60% of the total enrollment. The number of teachers working in these schools had also increased to 15.70 lakhs —12.30 lakhs at primary and 3.20 lakhs at upper primary stage of which about 21.60% were women. The details of the numerical growth of schools, the children enrolled, and teachers working in them are given in Tables 4.1, 4.2 and 4.3 respectively.

The period between 1965-66 and 1985-86 had been a period of political uncertainty, and hence, the progress of education was slow and steady, as most of the proposals of the Education Commission could not be properly implemented.

Table 4.2
Enrollment by Sex and Type of School Since 1951 (in millions)

Year	*Primary Total*	*Female*	*Upper Primary Total*	*Female*	*Elementary Total*	*Female*
1950-51	19.2	5.4	3.1	0.5	22.3	5.9
1955-56	24.6	7.5	4.8	1.0	29.4	8.5
1960-61	35.0	11.4	6.7	1.6	41.7	13.0
1965-66	50.5	18.3	10.5	2.8	61.0	21.1
1970-71	57.0	21.3	13.3	3.9	70.3	25.2
1975-76	65.6	25.0	16.0	5.0	81.6	30.0
1980-81	73.8	28.5	20.7	6.8	94.5	35.3
1985-86	87.4	35.2	27.3	9.6	114.7	44.8
1990-91	97.4	40.4	34.0	12.5	131.4	52.9
1995-96	109.8	47.4	41.0	16.0	150.8	63.4
1999-2000	113.6	49.5	42.1	17.0	155.7	66.5

Sources: Same as for Table 4.1.

When the progress was reviewed in 1985-86, it was found that the number of elementary schools had increased to 662,000, including 528,000 primary and 134,000 upper primary schools. The total enrollment in these schools had also increased to 114.60 million—69.90 million boys and 44.70 million girls. The number of teachers working in these schools had increased to 2478 thousands—1757 thousands male and 721 thousands female. An interesting trend which can easily be observed is that enrollment of girls has grown at a higher rate than that of boys during the entire period from 1950-51 to 1985-86. The period from 1986 onwards has been the period of implementation of the NPE-1986. Therefore, it is expected that elementary education might have developed considerably, both quantitatively and qualitatively.

As per latest reports of the government of India (GOI, 2000-2001), by 1999-2000, the total number of elementary schools has gone up to 839,700, including about 641,700 primary and 198,000 upper primary schools. The total number of teachers posted in these schools also increased to 3217 thousands—1919 thousands at primary and 1298 thousands at upper primary stage. About 36% of the teachers were female. The number of children enrolled in these schools has also increased to 155.7 million in which 89.2

Table 4.3
Number of Teachers by Sex and Type of School (in 000s)

Year	*Primary Total*	*Female*	*Upper Primary Total*	*Female*	*Elementary Total*	*Female*
1950-51	538	82	86	13	624	95
1955-56	691	117	151	19	842	136
1960-61	742	127	345	83	1087	210
1965-66	944	180	528	139	1472	319
1970-71	1060	225	638	175	1698	400
1975-76	1248	283	778	224	2026	507
1980-81	1363	342	851	253	2214	595
1985-86	1496	402	968	305	2464	707
1990-91	1616	473	1073	356	2689	829
1995-96	1740	553	1165	409	2905	962
1999-2000	1919	687	1298	469	3217	1156

Sources: Same as for Table 4.1.

million are boys and 66.5 million girls. The progress of UEE in India may be analyzed in terms of three identifiable periods in history after independence:

(i) Before Education Commission (1947-1966);
(ii) Between Education Commission and the NPE-1986; and
(iii) After NPE-1986.

Table 4.4
Gross Enrollment Ratios by Sex and Type of School

Year	*Primary (I-V)*			*TotalElementary (I-VIII)*		
	Boys	*Girls*	*Total*	*Boys*	*Girls*	*Total*
1950-51	60.6	24.8	42.6	46.4	17.7	32.1
1960-61	82.6	41.4	62.4	65.2	30.9	48.7
1970-71	92.6	59.1	76.4	75.5	44.4	61.9
1980-81	95.8	64.1	80.5	82.0	52.1	67.5
1990-91	115.3	86.0	101.0	100.2	71.6	86.3
1995-96	114.5	93.3	104.3	101.8	79.3	90.9
1999-2000	104.08	85.18	94.90	90.14	72.02	81.32

Sources: Same as for Table 4.1.

If the whole situation is studied in terms of Annual Compound Growth Rates (ACGRs) given in Table 4.5, some very interesting trends may be observed. These are:

(i) The quantitative growth of enrollment has been faster in the case of girls than in the case of boys throughout the period of five decades, since the beginning of the first five-year Plan.

(ii) The enrollment of students has increased at a higher rate than the number of schools and teachers as may be observed in the table, which shows that the ACGR of enrollment for classes I-VIII is 6.8%, while those of the number of teachers and number of schools are 6.4 and 5.1 respectively, during the first phase.

(iii) The expansion of education had been the highest during the first phase, that is, from 1950-51 to 1965-66, and then slowed down successively as indicated by the ACGRs of enrollment, teachers and schools. This may be because of the increase in the base for computation of ACGRs. The ACGRs of all the three aspects in respect of elementary education, as a whole, are consistently higher than the corresponding ACGRs in respect of primary education alone over all the three phases. This shows that upper primary (middle) sector of education has developed at a higher rate than the primary sector.

(iv) One potential reason of the downfall in the quality and standards of school education during the recent decades may be the uneven growth of enrollment, number of teachers and number of schools, the enrollment growing faster than the other two. This is evident from the deteriorating Teacher Pupil Ratio (TPR), which was 1:24 at primary stage and 1:20 at upper primary stage in 1950-51. The corresponding ratios at present are about 1:58 and 1:32 respectively.

(v) As a conservative estimate, the population of children in the age group 6-14 years, at present, may be about 200 million of which about 160 million (2001-2002 estimate) might be attending elementary schools. This leads to the conclusion that about 40 million children are still out of school, which constitute about 20% of the relevant age

group. It is reported that 22% of the total out of school children of the world are in India.

(vi) As about 18 million children are added to our population every year, the total number of children to be enrolled within the next five years will be over 130 million. But, our formal system of schooling cannot accommodate more than 30 million. What will happen to the remaining 100 million?

(vii) Since, we can enroll only about 4.5 million children every year against the total 18 million of newly added ones, about 13.5 million are added to the backlog every year. With this pace of development, how long shall we take to achieve the UEE?

(viii) This leads to the conclusion that the formal system of education that we have created is not sufficient to fulfil our requirements. We should look for some effective efficient, flexible and cost-effective alternatives.

(ix) We should modernize the existing system so as to take advantage of the new developments in information technology, and expand alternatives like non-formal education so as to cover larger groups and wider areas.

Table 4.5
Annual Compound Growth Rates of Enrollment, Teachers and Schools By Sex and Phases

Phase	Enrollment			Teachers			Schools
	Boys	*Girls*	*All*	*Male*	*Female*	*All*	
PRIMARY (IV)							
(i)	5.8	8.5	6.7	4.2	6.1	4.6	4.2
(ii)	2.3	3.2	2.7	1.2	3.7	1.8	1.5
(iii)	2.3	3.7	2.9	1.2	2.5	1.5	1.0
ELEMENTARY (I-VIII)							
(i)	6.1	8.8	6.9	5.8	6.5	6.4	5.1
(ii)	2.8	3.8	3.1	1.8	3.9	2.1	1.7
(iii)	2.7	4.2	3.3	1.3	2.2	1.6	1.2

*Computed on the basis of Data given in Tables 4.1, 4.2 and 4.3.

PROBLEMS

As discussed in the previous sections, we have not been able to achieve the goal of the UEE as guaranteed in Article 45 of our Constitution. Though, there has been a massive expansion of schooling facilities during the last 50 years, the goal has moved farther with the number of out of schools children increasing. Moreover, there are glaring disparities in what has been achieved, which are based on caste, sex, religion, and rural-urban dichotomy. There are good reasons to believe that India will not be able to achieve this goal even by 2030 unless some effective and efficient alternative strategies are planned and implemented. There are a few hurdles, which retard our progress on this front. Some of these problems are socio-economic while others are academic, and still others are political. A few prominent problems are discussed below:

Population Explosion

It has been described elsewhere in this chapter that India is the second most populous country of the world accounting for about 16% of the total global population. As a conservative estimate, the population of India is more than 1045 million at present (2002-estimate), while total world's population is about 6200 million. About 78 million are added every year to the population of the world (Manorama Yearbook, 2002) to which India's contribution is 18 million. Our educational system, including formal and non-formal channels, cannot accommodate such a large section of the relevant age group. Therefore, on the one hand we should expand both the formal and non-formal modes of education in order to increase its enrolling capacity, and on the other hand, popularize the family welfare programmes in order to reduce birth rate.

Non-Enrollment of Children of Weaker Sections

Although, the enrollment of girls, and that of the children of Scheduled Castes (SCs) and Scheduled Tribes (STs) has increased at faster pace over the last five decades especially at the primary stage, yet girls account for only 43.2% enrollment at the primary and 39% at the upper primary stage. In fact, as educational facilities expand and reach out to the lower socio-economic status groups, the rate of enrollment slows down. This is known as the phenomenon of 'resistant-to-education groups'. Saraf (1985) has rightly pointed out that the phenomenon starts operating as soon as GER reaches 60 per cent. That is what happens in Indian context also. The 'resistant-to-education groups' constitute mostly of those who live below the poverty line. In India, girls also form a similar group due to social constraints. Due to this phenomenon it is very difficult to enroll the last 5-10% of children in the relevant age from such groups. In Indian conditions these groups are girls, SC and ST children, and children of educationally backward minorities. At present, of the 40 million out of school children aged 6-14 years, a large majority belongs to these groups. According to National Sample Survey (42nd round), participation in household/economic activities, lack of interest, other economic reasons, non-availability of schooling facilities, and some other socio-economic factors prevent the young children from being enrolled in school.

The Problem of Dropouts

It has been mentioned earlier that during the first three five-year Plans, more emphasis was placed on enrollment than on improvement of the quality of education. Consequently, the majority of those who were enrolled in class I left school after some time without completing eight years of schooling. This phenomenon is called 'Dropout'. Those who dropout include two categories of children:

(i) Those who are forced to leave the school due to socio-economic constraints of the family, and may be called 'pull-outs';

(ii) Those who leave the school because they do not find school environment joyful and satisfying, and may be called 'push-outs'

The out-of-school children include both 'dropouts' and 'left-outs', the latter category being of those who are never enrolled in school for one reason or the other. As per the latest available data for the year 1999-2000, the dropout rate up to class V was 40.20% and that up to class VIII was 54.5%. The dropout rate for girls has been consistently higher than that for boys throughout the last five decades. During the same year the dropout rate among girls was 42.3% up to class V and 58.00% up to class VIII. In 1960-61, the dropout rate was considerably higher. It has come down gradually. The details of the improvement in the dropout rate have been given in Table 4.6.

Table 4.6
Dropout Rates at School Stages by Sex since 1960-61 (percentages)

Year	*Primary Stage (I-V)*			*Elementary Stage (I-VIII)*		
	Boys	*Girls*	*Total*	*Boys*	*Girls*	*Total*
1960-61	61.7	70.9	64.9	75.0	85.0	78.3
1970-71	64.5	70.9	67.0	74.6	83.4	77.9
1980-81	56.2	62.5	58.7	68.0	79.4	72.7
1990-91	42.0	47.6	44.3	60.6	67.6	63.4
1995-96	37.9	41.3	39.4	55.0	61.7	57.8
1999-2000	38.7	42.3	40.2	51.7	58.0	54.5

Sources: 1. Selected Educational Statistics, Government of India, MHRD 1995-96.
2. Ministry of HRD, Annual Report, Department of Education. 1996-97, 1999-2000.

It has also been observed that dropout rate among children of SCs and STs has also been consistently higher than even the overall dropout rate among girls. In addition to this, there are regional variations even in this respect. In some of the states like Rajasthan dropout rates are higher than the national average. In Rajasthan, over 76% of the boys and 82% of the girls enrolled in class I dropped out before completing the elementary education. This is related to the data available for the academic year 1995-96. The dropout rate up to class V was even higher. Nearly half of the dropout occurs during the first two years. The inter-regional differences in dropout rate are significant (Rajput, 1994). The dropout rate for classes I-VIII for boys is only 18.37% in Kerala but 74.98% in Arunachal Pradesh. For girls the corresponding figures are 16.99% and 76.68%. Now, the situation has slightly improved along with overall improvement.

Poor availability of schools near habitations, low attendance, lack of suitable rural women who can be appointed as teachers etc.

account for the large incidence of dropout among girls. The rigid and stagnant curriculum and the load of the school bag are some of the factors hampering the progress of UEE. According to Ramamurti Committee (1990), about one-third to one-half of students find schools 'either boring or threatening'. In addition to this, about 40-50% of the children, who are enrolled, stay away from school.

School is not the only factor promoting dropout rates. There are social reasons also. In rural areas, education, particularly of girls, does not receive adequate attention due to social traditions such as child marriage, purdah system and negative attitude towards education of girls.

Non-availability of Schools within Easy Reach

Although, the number of elementary schools in India has increased from only 2.1 lakhs in 1950-51 to more than 8.40 lakhs in 1999-2000, schooling facilities are not available to all children within easy reach. According to Sixth All India Educational Survey (1998), 93.76% of the rural population is served by primary schools within a walking distance of 1 km from the place of living of every child and 85% of the rural population is served by an upper primary school within a distance of 3 kms. This means that there are about 15% of the people to whom an upper primary school is not available within easy reach from their residence. Not only this, even primary schools are not available to over 6% of the rural population. This proves to be a great hurdle, especially to the education of girls.

Poor Physical Facilities in Schools

The linear expansion of schooling facilities in numerical terms has resulted in poor physical facilities, and consequently, in poor quality of education being imparted by the schools. The Sixth All India Educational Survey (1998) published recently by the Government of India has revealed that in 1993, 7.22% of the primary schools were without building while another 9.05% were running in mud huts. About 10.70% upper primary schools also had unsatisfactory buildings. The percentage of primary schools having zero instructional rooms was found to be 10.59 and of those with not more than two rooms was over 60. Only 44.23% primary schools had the drinking water facilities, 18.93% schools had urinals and 8.66% had separate urinals for girls. Moreover, there were regional variations even in these inadequacies with the states identified as educationally backward having the least of these facilities.

Educational objectives cannot be achieved unless the schools have minimum essential facilities. In view of this, the NPE-1986 had proposed to launch a programme called "Operation Blackboard" for improving the physical facilities in schools. The details of this programme have been discussed earlier.

Illiteracy Among Parents

The large-scale illiteracy among parents, especially in rural areas, is another factor that retards the progress of UEE. Uneducated people do not appreciate the value of education, and hence, do not send their children to school. In this context, the education of women is of a special significance. A comprehensive study conducted by Usha Nayar of the NCERT has established that a strong correlation exists between rural underdevelopment and high dropout and low enrollment among girls. Also, enrollment of girls is strongly and positively correlated with women's education showing that an educated mother wants to educate her daughter also.

Poverty Related Factors

There is acute poverty, especially in rural areas, in some of the states such as Bihar, Orissa, Rajasthan, Uttar Pradesh and Madhya Pradesh. Because of this factor, women and girls have to work, for wages or in their own fields, in order to supplement the income of their families. When mothers go to work, their daughters have to look after their young siblings or domestic chores. They have to cook food for the family and fetch water, fuel and fodder. These economic constraints do not allow poor people to send their children, especially girls, to school.

Other Factors

There are certain other socio-economic factors that have adverse impact on the progress of UEE. Due to serious problems of unemployment and poverty, children of school going age have to work for wages. It is reported that there are about 40 million child-labourers in India working in the factories, mines, kilns, construction industry and agriculture. Most of them are of school going age. Cultural and linguistic diversity in India is also a potential factor having adverse impact on the progress of UEE. For example, in the case of tribal children, instructional material is not available in their own language, curriculum is not suitable to their environment, proper transportation facilities are not available, and tribal youths are not available in adequate number to be appointed as teachers.

Sometimes, those who are involved in the process of execution of government plans face serious financial difficulties. Most of the times, adequate funds are not allocated, and the amount sanctioned is not released in time. As a consequence of this, even very good and ambitious plans do not provide desirable results.

CAN WE REALLY DO IT?

The Government of India has now fixed up a new target date for achievement of the goal of UEE. As per published reports, a new programme known as Sarva Shiksha Abhiyan has been launched by the government recently in order to provide eight years of elementary education to all children in the 6-14 age group by 2010. Sarva Shiksha Abhiyan (SSA) has a central objective of mobilizing all resources—human, financial and institutional—necessary for achieving the goal of Universalization of Elementary Education. On the recommendations of the Conference of Education Ministers, a National Committee of State Education Ministers was constituted under the chairmanship of the Minister of Human Resource Development to develop the structure and outline of implementing Universal Elementary Education in a Mission Mode. It is a historic step taken to achieve the goal of UEE through a time bound integrated approach, in partnership with states, local bodies and the community. It aims at providing relevant and quality elementary education to all children. It is expected to cover the entire country by March 2002 with a special focus on educational needs of girls, scheduled castes and scheduled tribes and other children in difficult circumstances. It is a holistic and convergent approach to implement UEE in a mission mode with a clear district focus. The major objectives of SSA are (The Hindustan Times, Jan. 26, 2001):

(i) All children to be in schools, Education Guarantee Centres, alternative schools, or "Back to School" camps by 2003;
(ii) All children to complete five years of primary schooling by 2007; and
(iii) All children to complete eight years of schooling by 2010.

In addition to this, the Sarva Shiksha Abhiyan envisages providing:

- One teacher for every 40 children in elementary schools and at least two teachers in a primary school.
- School or alternative school within one kilometre of school-less habitations.
- New school buildings, classrooms and resource centres, one classroom for every teacher.
- Free textbooks for girls and SC/ST children up to Rs. 150 per child.
- Annual School grant of Rs. 2000 per school and Teacher Grant of Rs. 500 per teacher.
- Teaching learning equipment of Rs. 50,000 for uncovered schools.

According to the official data, the number of children enrolled in the primary schools were respectively 101.6, 105.4, 108.2, 109.0, 109.8, and 110.4 millions (Sahay, 1999) during the years 1991-92, 92-93, 93-94, 94-95, 95-96 and 96-97. During the years 1998-99 and 1999-2000 the corresponding figures have been 151.2 and 155.7 respectively. Thus, we find that enrollment in primary schools during these six years increased only by meagre 9 million, that is, at an average rate of 1.5 million per year. However, recently total annual enrollment has increased to about 4.5 million. But, the population growth rate suggests that we are adding about 18 million every year to our population. Thus, the reality is that only about 25% of the "additional" children are getting enrolled in primary schools and, the rest, 13.5 million are left to grow up without any formal education. In view of the above, is our target of achieving UEE by 2010 realistic?

Based on the recommendation of the Saikia Committee, a proposal to amend the Constitution of India to make education for children from 6 to 14 years of age a Fundamental Right was considered and approved by the Cabinet in May 1997. In pursuance of the decision of the Cabinet, the Constitution (Eighty-third Amendment) Bill, 1997 was introduced in the Rajya Sabha on 28 July, 1997. However, the Bill could not be passed due to certain political difficulties. It was decided that special assistance would be provided to the states for implementing the proposal to make Elementary Education a Fundamental Right. The scheme would be implemented as a part of the Sarva Shiksha Abhiyan.

On the night of November 28, 2001, the Lok Sabha unanimously passed the 93rd Constitutional Amendment Bill to make education for children in the age group of 6-14 years a fundamental right. Replying to the debate on the Bill, the Human Resource Development Minister Dr. Murli Manohar Joshi described the amendment as a "revolutionary" step as it would make it a duty of the parents to send their children to school, but would not penalize them for not doing so. Hitherto, Article 45 of the Directive Principles of state policy enshrined in the Constitution urged the state to provide free and compulsory education for children until they complete 14 years of age. Universal free and compulsory education should have been achieved in India by 1960—the Constitution said that the state should endeavour to provide this within 10 years of the commencement of the Constitution. To date, successive governments have failed to do so. Now, as a fundamental right, the provision of free and compulsory education has become legally enforceable (CSR, January 2002). It is believed that the provision will help the Government achieve the goal of UEE within a reasonable time during the years to come.

5

Adult Education and Eradication of Illiteracy

Education and development go together, each of them either promoting the other or throwing new demands on it. When India became free in 1947, the first question before the native government was how to increase the pace of economic development, as it was realized that modernization could not be achieved without reaching a proper stage of development. Therefore, higher education in science, technology, humanities and social sciences received highest priority among all sectors of education. This was, probably, done at the cost of elementary and adult education. Because of this, there was a rapid advancement in the field of science and technology, which in turn, enhanced industrial development. But, unfortunately, the benefits of scientific and technological advancement remained confined to the upper and upper-middle classes of the society, because only they constituted the educated and elite group, and hence, could take advantage of the situation. Modernization cannot be achieved unless masses or common people are able to benefit from scientific and technological advancement. For this, the prerequisite condition is that common people should be enlightened enough to take advantage of new discoveries and inventions.

Therefore, socio-economic development in the modern age requires two things:

(i) Rapid growth of science education and research leading to new technologies and modern means of living;
(ii) An enlightened society capable of making use of new scientific and technological development for the betterment of the quality of life.

For the first requirement, higher education in science and technology is needed, which we have been trying to develop since independence, and have succeeded in creating the third largest higher education system of the world. India ranks tenth in the list of industrialized countries of the world and third as producer of scientifically and technologically trained manpower. For the second requirement, again, two conditions are to be met one of providing universal elementary education for all children (Article 45 of the Constitution), and the other of liquidating illiteracy among adults. Unless these conditions are fulfilled no step towards modernization is possible. For about a long period of three decades (1947-1978), adult education had been neglected in India due to misplaced priorities. To put the discussion in a proper perspective, a brief historical review of adult education is in order.

HISTORICAL REVIEW

Steele and Taylor (1995) have rightly pointed out, 'Adult education in all societies is almost always a politically charged activity, but this has been particularly the case in India. Whether seen as a means of ensuring social control and cultural incorporation, or in sharply contrasting terms, as a potential agency of radical democratization and empowerment, adult education in India has always had a strong political dimension.' It is reported that 'literacy classes and night schools were established in India by the British during nineteenth century. William Adams in 1836-37 claimed only 6% literacy; in its last twenty-five years the East India Company tended to disregard indigenous system of education to promote knowledge of English literature and science.' During the late nineteenth century, say Steele and Taylor (1995), the British established adult education provision in most of the urban centres, but in rural areas little attempt was made. The Indian Education Commission (1882-83) reported that in Bombay there were 134 night schools with about 4000 students, and 223 in the southern division of the Presidency with about 5000 students. In addition, there were 1000 adult classes in Bengal, which rose to 1587 by 1896-97, and 312 in Madras. The level of education was so low that in late 1880s only one person in 3300 had experienced secondary education, and only one in 22,000 had experienced college or university education.

Under the compulsion of circumstances and freedom movement gaining ground, the Resolution on Education Policy adopted in 1913 emphasized the importance of vernaculars. After the introduction of "Diarchy" under the Government of India Act (1921), the situation changed, and with the sharing of power by natives, adult education became a significant part of educational provisions for the years to follow. The Provincial Governments were given freedom to plan programmes of educational expansion. The Government of Punjab made specific provisions for adult education in 1921-22, and by 1926-27, there were 3984 literacy schools attended by about 100,000 adults. Other states, such as Bombay and Bengal, also took similar initiatives.

During the period from late 1920s to late 1930s adult education faced a decline due to global recession. According to the census of 1931, only about 16 per cent of the male population and 3 per cent of the female population, over 5 years of age, could read and write in any language; and of 353 million included in the census only some three million and a half could speak English (Hartog, 1939). In 1937, with the formation of popular governments, adult education received a big boost under the banner of "Citizenship Education" and the Central Advisory Board of Education (CABE) appointed a committee in 1938 to consider the question of adult education. The committee submitted its report in 1940, which emphasized the need of developing mass education by putting in more central funds and involving voluntary organizations. Accepting these recommendations, the CABE examined the progress of provinces in adult education. It was found that considerable development had taken place in literacy work and library facilities. For example in 1939, Bengal had 10,000 literacy classes with an enrollment of 150,000. By 1942, the number of literacy classes had increased to 22,547 with an enrollment of 530,000. There were about 700 public libraries. Another significant development was that Indian Army started an adult education programme for soldiers in 1921, which expanded rapidly during the World War II years. This programme emphasized citizenship education as well as literacy among other things.

In 1938, the Indian Adult Education Association (IAEA) was created and the Indian Journal of Adult Education (IJAE) was started in 1940. During the decade 1931-41, literacy increased by 70%. The Post-War Plan of Educational Development of 1944, popularly known as Sargent Plan, stated that adult education should form an integral part of "mass education", with initial emphasis on liquidation of illiteracy. The contemporary concept of 'National System of Education' was also considerably loaded with emphasis on adult education.

When India became free in 1947, adult education had acquired considerable political appeal, and hence, had established itself as an important sector of education. After independence, the Congress Party came to power under the leadership of Pandit Nehru who had been influenced by western culture during the period of his education. British authors have recently written (Steele and Taylor, 1995, p 62):

> Nehru was from an Indian upper-class background and his British experiences reinforced rather than countered his indigenous surroundings. Nehru, and indeed most of the leading figures in the Congress party, never had any real, direct experience of the Indian masses. And in many respects they had little rapport with the ordinary people. The high culture and elitist liberalism of the British intellectual establishment was integrated with the attitudes of the Indian upper class from which Nehru came. As far as education was concerned, this led to the advocacy of a dualist structure. For the elite education should be wide-ranging, steeped in the civilization of the West, including mathematics and science but emphasizing the classics, literature and the arts. Above all, it should develop an inquiring, critical frame of mind. For the mass of ordinary people, on the other hand, education should aim at imparting virtues such as obedience, modesty, rule-governed behaviour and acceptance of one's station in the society.... Nehru was aiming for a society "based on modernization, industrialization and a scientific temper," with

> the initial emphasis placed upon the building of heavy industry for the production of capital goods as a base... and on the wide expansion of village industries for producing consumer goods as well as employment....True, university education expanded rapidly, but little was done to provide mass technological training for the envisaged new industrial society.... There was a continuation of the belief of the British Raj that the most important aspect of education was concerned with the small elite groups in the society, which could then "filter down" appropriate educational and ideological knowledge and perspectives to the masses... Educational policy under the Congress party in fact did little for elementary education and precious little for secondary or adult education. The main emphasis was upon the expansion of the university sector.

Some of the facts embedded in this statement may be true for the early years of Congress rule (1951-1966) until it was realized that education of the masses was as important as higher and professional education for a selected few. Immediately after independence, the traditional concept of adult education was replaced by a new and more appealing concept of "social education", which supposedly included generation of awareness about the social aspects of democracy. The Adult Education Committee of 1948, so as not to reduce its meaning to "literacy", emphasized this connotation of the term. The term "social education" was the brainchild of Maulana Abul Kalam Azad, the then Minister of Education.

POST-INDEPENDENCE POLICIES AND PROGRAMMES

With the beginning of the First Five-Year Plan (1951-56), the social education programme was run with the help of teachers in the village schools, community centres and youth clubs. Libraries were also introduced to give a boost to the programme, which was also integrated with the Community Development Projects. At the beginning of the Plan in 1950-51, the literacy rate in India was 16.67 per cent. The corresponding figures for male and female sub-populations were 24.95 and 7.93 respectively. By 1955, 83,000 community centres had been established, and 169,000 programmes had been organized. A large number of Youth Clubs, Mahila

Mandals and Vikas Mandals, were also organized. These programmes continued during the Second (1956-61) and Third (1961-66) Plans also.

According to 1961 census, the literacy rate by that time had increased to 24.02 per cent with corresponding figures for male and female sub-populations being 34.44 and 12.95 respectively. The main reason for slow progress was that it was thought that the country should concentrate on achieving UEE by 1960 as a more effective instrument of making the society literate. Consequently, during the first three plans, only a small-scale programme of adult literacy was carried out under the title of "social education", which was attached to the Community Development Schemes (Naik, 1982).

Education Commission (1964-66) recommended that very high priority should be given to the programmes of adult literacy in order to liquidate illiteracy by 1985-86. The Commission observed that India was more non-literate in 1961 than in 1951 with the addition of 36 million non-literate persons in 10 years. In 1966, it had 20 million more non-literate persons than in 1961, though, the percentage of literacy had risen from 16.67 in 1951 to 24.00 in 1961 and 28.6 in 1966. The National Policy on Education (1968) made the following proposals for improving literacy:

(a) The liquidation of mass illiteracy is necessary, not only for promoting participation in the working of democratic institutions and for accelerating programmes of production, especially in agriculture, but also for quickening the tempo for national development in general. Employees in large commercial, industrial, and other concerns should be made functionally literate as early as possible. A lead in this direction should come from the industrial undertakings in the public sector. Teachers and students should be actively involved in organizing literacy campaigns, especially as part of Social and National Service Programmes.

(b) Special emphasis should be given to the education of young practising farmers and to the training of youth for self-employment.

As clear from the above statement, the NPE-1968 did not propose any specific programme or strategy to be planned and implemented by the government. Consequently, the efforts in this field slowed down and the progress was stagnant for one full decade (1968-78). The net result was that literacy rate increased marginally from 24.02% in 1961 to 29.45% in 1971. For male and female sub-populations the literacy figures increased to 39.45% and 18.69% respectively. During this period, the number of adult education centres decreased from 220,000 in 1965-66 to 180,000 in 1975-76, and enrollment in these centres also came down from 16.38 lakhs to 4.39 lakhs (Sharma, 1985).

National Adult Education Programme (NAEP)

The situation was reviewed in 1978 and the government made a policy statement regarding organization of adult education programmes for about 100 million adults, mainly in the age-group 15-35 years. Consequently, a massive programme of adult education called National Adult Education Programme (NAEP) was launched in 1978-79, which emphasized correlation between working, living and learning. This programme also did not work to the expectations of the people. The NAEP perceived adult education as one of the minimum needs of the poorest sections of the society. The Union Government was motivated to launch such a huge programme by success of a similar programme known as the Gram Shikshan Mohim (meaning village education movement) being conducted in the State of Maharashtra, which led to the achievement of 100% literacy in the 14-50 age group in 1100 villages" during 1961-63. The NAEP was centred on three main components (Bordia, 1980):

(i) Literacy and numeracy to enable the learners to continue to learn in a self-reliant manner;
(ii) Functional development with emphasis on the role of an individual as a worker, a family member, and a citizen; and
(iii) Social awareness of laws, policies and need to organize, and press for common interests and rights.

It is worth noting here that the government of Janata Party, which came to power in 1977, reorganized the NAEP. This government accorded high priority to the programmes of UEE and

Adult Education. A draft National Policy on Education was formulated in 1977, which made special provisions for adult education. It stated:

> It is estimated that 230 millions of our adult population are illiterate. These form mostly the poorest and the most neglected sections of the nation. Their contribution to the national well being could be far greater than it is, if they received some education. Their condition is such that they are not able to take advantage of the benefits available to them under the development plans and continue to be exposed to exploitation and social disabilities. The nation should deem it its solemn duty to impart education to them. The National Adult Education Programme, which has been organized, should be implemented with urgency and sustained vigour. The immediate target should be to educate under this programme 100 millions in a period of five years so that universal literacy becomes a reality in our country within the shortest possible time.

But unfortunately, this government did not last longer and Congress regained power in 1980. With this political change, the priorities of the government also changed, and thus, the NAEP crashed before it could take off. Adult education, therefore, hardly received any significant push from the government from 1951 to 1981 when the next census report was published. According to 1981 census, the literacy rate had increased to 36.17%, the corresponding figures for male and female sub-populations being 46.74 and 24.88 per cent respectively.

With the end of Janata Party rule, the NAEP came in the hands of voluntary organizations, and the new government did not accord a high priority to adult education during the Sixth Plan period (1980-85). The government, during this period, funded 386 rural functional literacy programmes, assisted 380 voluntary agencies and 49 universities, to conduct adult education programmes in order to cover nearly 20 million illiterate adults. For this purpose a sum of Rs. 1280 million (5.07% of the total outlay for education) was allocated.

National Literacy Mission (NLM)

In 1985, when there was a change of government after general elections, it was declared that a new education policy would be launched soon. The NPE-1986 was subsequently launched in May 1986, which was modified in 1992. The NPE-1986, as modified in 1992, stated:

The whole nation has pledged itself, through the National Literacy Mission, to the eradication of illiteracy, particularly in the 15-35 age-group through various means with special emphasis on total literacy campaigns.... The National Literacy Mission will be geared to the national goals such as alleviation of poverty, national integration, environmental conservation, observance of small family norms, promotion of women's equality, universalization of primary education, basic health care etc.

The Government of India identified five areas of development, calling for urgent attention and action. These are immunization programme for infants, drinking water in rural areas, eradication of illiteracy, communication in rural areas, and production of edible oil. Each area was to be attacked through a "technology mission" The technology mission for the eradication of illiteracy was named the National Literacy Mission (NLM).

The NLM was formally launched, on 5th May 1988, by then Prime Minister of India Rajeev Gandhi. The basic idea underlying the NLM was that the problem of illiteracy would be tackled by pooling all possible resources, human and material, and by using scientific and technological knowledge so as to increase efficiency and obtain concrete results. It had a time bound target of imparting functional literacy to 80 million illiterate adults in the age group 15-35 years by 1995 (GOI, 1988) in two phases—30 million by 1990 and the remaining 50 million to be covered by 1995. The main emphasis of NLM would be on women and rural illiterate adults, as these constitute the bulk of illiterate population. As a technology mission, the NLM would harness and utilize the findings of scientific and technological researches for the benefit of the weaker sections of the society. While initial focus of NLM would be on rural areas and weaker sections, the facilities of literacy, continuing education and vocational training would be extended to other areas also by 1995. The NLM had the following characteristics:

(i) It recognized the role of motivation in learning and suggested ways and means of developing and sustaining motivation among the learners and instructors.

(ii) It envisaged people's participation along with mass mobilization by publishing special features of news items having bearing on adult education, and using leading newspapers to generate positive attitude towards adult education.

(iii) The NLM proposed to involve the voluntary agencies in literacy programmes, on a large scale, by providing additional financial inputs and incentives.

(iv) In addition to introduction and strengthening of the literacy programmes, the NLM proposed to promote continuing education programmes by establishing the "Jan Shikshan Nilayams (JSNs)" meaning people's learning centres. These JSNs were expected to provide for library and reading room facilities, training programmes for health and family welfare, and other cultural and recreational activities.

(v) It also proposed to make literacy a "people's movement" by involving teachers, students, trade unions, public sector undertakings and defence personnel in the programmes of literacy. Students would be involved in the Mass Programme of Functional Literacy (MPFL) in which a student volunteer would teach an adult for 150 hours spread over four months' period. It would be done under "Each One Teach One" campaign.

(vi) The NLM proposed to improve the quality of the programmes of adult education providing technological devices to improve efficiency and coverage, and to build environment for learning.

Total Literacy Campaigns (TLCs)

Under NLM, a strategy of mass mobilization of various agencies including government and non-government organizations, individuals, social groups and voluntary organizations, was adopted. This strategy was named "Total Literacy Campaign (TLC)" which required all concerned to join together for the common goal of achieving full literacy in a specified area within a specified time limit. Its distinctive characteristic was "mass mobilization on voluntary basis". The efficiency of this approach has been established beyond doubt and it has succeeded in transforming a fully government funded and government controlled, traditional, centre-based and honorarium-based programme into a mass campaign leading towards a people's movement (NPE-POA, 1992) for total literacy and awakening. The efficiency of this approach has confirmed in more than one sense that eradication of illiteracy is possible, feasible and achievable. The TLC approach has the following features:

(i) These campaigns are area-specific, time-bound, volunteer-based, cost-effective, and outcome-oriented.
(ii) These are implemented through district level committees represented by all sections of the society, registered under the Societies Registration Act and headed by the District Collector/Chief Secretary Zila Parishad.
(iii) These are based on grass roots level surveys and mass mobilization, targets being fixed from the grass roots levels. Voluntarism is the backbone of the scheme, meaning that people devote their time, energy, and resources on voluntary basis.
(iv) The management system works on the principle of participation and correction, and is outcome-oriented with achievement of certain predetermined levels of literacy and numeracy by the learners.
(v) It has an in-built monitoring and evaluation mechanism called "Improved Pace and Content of Learning (IPCL)" involving a multi-graded and integrated teaching-learning material.
(vi) Volunteers are trained by a participative and corrective approach.
(vii) The TLCs may be viewed as accelerators of the UEE and other welfare programmes such as immunization, propagation of small family norms, child and mother care, and national integration.

After NLM was established, the most significant development was the launching of TLC in Ernakulum district of Kerala on 26th January 1989, which in a period of one year, set a record by bringing together voluntary agencies and all sections of the society, and making the whole district literate by February 4, 1990. The Ernakulum experiment was the first success in the country and encouraged the Kerala Government to launch similar campaigns in other districts also. Consequently, other states also adopted the technique, and today, it has become a recognized approach of the government.

The literacy wave, which started from Ernakulum, spread to the entire southern region and finally reached all parts of the country. By the year 1996, the TLCs had been extended to 413 districts in the country of which 178 had entered post-literacy phase. An estimated 90 million learners had been enrolled in the programme and 56 million were reported to have become literate (GOI, 1996). As TLCs made significant progress in a given area, the post-literacy and continuing education programmes were launched. The objective was to cover 345 districts during the Eighth Plan (1992-97) and make 100 million people functionally literate. The net impact of the success of TLCs is that people become aware of the value of education and start demanding universalization of primary education. The major strength of the campaign is that women participate in the teaching-learning process in much larger numbers and with much greater enthusiasm than men do.

According to latest reports of the Government of India, over 448 districts (85%) had been covered by 1998, over 72 million non-literate people accessed and made literate. By 2000, 559 districts out of 588 districts in the country have been covered by NLM (Hindustan Times, Oct. 14, 2000), and 84 million people made literate by March 2000.

Jan Shikshan Nilayams (JSNs)

Jan Shikshan Nilayams or people's learning centres are meant for sustaining the literacy levels of those who have been made literate through TLCs or otherwise. These are part of the strategy of post-literacy and continuing education. They have been started in several TLC districts and are fully operational. Each JSN caters to the needs of five villages of about 5000 people and provides for a library, a reading room, a forum for discussion, evening classes for up-gradation of skills etc. These JSNs also offer simple and short-term training programmes in agriculture, animal husbandry and veterinary science, soil management and other similar fields (GOI, 1993). The main purpose is to prepare neo-literate individuals for self-employment. A centre covering 30-40 neo-literate persons functions under the supervision of 3-5 volunteers. These centres are serviced by rural libraries, which act as training and resource centres.

PROGRESS AND ACHIEVEMENT

At the time of Independence in 1947, the total population of India was 330 million (excluding that of Pakistan) of which only 46 million (14%) were literate. The progress of literacy in India has been presented in Table 5.1. It may be seen from the table that the literacy rate in India was only 5.35% in 1901. The female literacy rate was very low, only 0.6%. However, the total literacy rate had increased to 16.67% by 1951, the female literacy rate being 7.93%. After this, there was a steady progress in literacy and it increased to 24.02% by 1961, 29.45% by 1971, 36.67% by 1981 and 52.19% by 1991. The corresponding figures for female population are 12.95, 18.69, 24.88, and 39.19 respectively. However, male literacy rate increased from only 9.83% in 1901 to 24.95% in 1951 and to 64.20% in 1991.

Table 5.1
Demographic Characteristics of India's Population (1901-1991)

Year	*Population (Millions)*	*Literacy Rates (Percentages)*			*Population Density per Sq. Km.*	*Sex Ratio (Female per 1000 Male)*
		Male	*Female*	*Total*		
1901	238.40	9.83	0.60	5.35	77	972
1911	252.09	10.56	1.05	5.92	82	964
1921	251.32	12.21	1.81	7.16	81	955
1931	278.98	15.59	2.93	9.50	90	950
1941	318.66	24.90	7.30	16.10	103	945
1951	361.09	24.95	7.93	16.67	117	946
1961	439.23	34.44	12.95	24.02	142	941
1971	548.16	39.45	18.69	29.45	177	930
1981	685.18	46.74	24.88	36.67	216	933
1991	846.30	64.20	39.19	52.19	267	929
2001*	1027.01	75.85	54.16	65.38	324	933

* Provisional

Sources: *(i)* Manorama Yearbook 1988.

(ii) Census of India, 1981, 1991.

However, throughout the decades from 1901 to 1991, the total number of illiterate people has also increased along with the increase in the literacy rates, considering the total population as base. The total number of illiterate persons, which was only about 225 million in 1901 increased to over 300 million in 1951, 437 million in 1981 and about 491 million in 1991. This shows that India is more illiterate at present than in 1951.

It is worth noting here that till 1981 all literacy rates were computed with total population as base. From 1961 onwards, children below the age of 5 years were being treated as illiterate, and hence, were excluded from the numerator as it was considered that no child could be expected to be literate before that age. However, the denominator contained the entire population. The literacy rate was, therefore, somewhat depressed. But, in 1991 census, the population below 7 years of age was excluded from the calculations for obvious reasons (Premi, 1991). If the entire population is considered, the literacy rate for 1991 census works out to be a little more than 43%. However, it is reasonable to exclude the population below the age of 7 years from the calculations. According to the new method of calculation, the number of illiterate persons in 1991 census works out to be 320 million as against 491 million, as mentioned earlier. The 1991 census reveals one important point that the number of illiterate is less than the number of literate persons for the first time after independence. It may be observed from Table 5.2 that while number of male illiterate persons has increased marginally, there has been substantial rise in the number of female illiterate during the decade 1981-91. Similarly, the rural illiterate persons have recorded a higher increase than urban illiterate persons have.

Moreover, there are wide disparities/variations in literacy rates based on caste, religion, region, creed and sex. The literacy rate among Scheduled Castes is 37.40% and that among the Scheduled Tribes is 29.60%. There are sex differences even in these sections. The male and female literacy rates among the SCs are 49.90% and 23.80% respectively. The corresponding figures for STs are 40.70 and 18.2 respectively. While rural-urban differential in male literacy has declined between 1981 and 1991, the rural-urban difference in female literacy has increased from 34.60% in 1981 to 35.10% in 1991 (Ray, 1993).

Table 5.2
Number of Illiterate Persons in India in 1981 and 1991 (millions)

	1981			*1991*		
Population	*Male*	*Female*	*Total*	*Male*	*Female*	*Total*
Rural	104.80	154.79	259.59	106.69	165.12	271.81
Urban	16.16	26.31	42.47	18.08	30.52	48.60
Total	120.96	181.10	302.06	124.77	195.64	320.41

Source: Ray Ash Narain, The Hindustan Times, Dec. 13, 1993.

The literacy rate was 44% in rural areas and 75% in urban areas. There are visible regional disparities in literacy. It was highest in Kerala (81.56%) and lowest in Arunachal Pradesh (25.50%). The female literacy was also highest in Kerala (86.93%) but lowest in Rajasthan (20.84%). The states, which had more than 50% literacy, were: Goa, Gujarat, Himachal Pradesh, Maharashtra, Mizoram, Nagaland, Tamil Nadu and Tripura. The literacy levels in Andhra Pradesh, Arunachal Pradesh, Bihar, Jammu and Kashmir, Madhya Pradesh, Rajasthan, and Uttar Pradesh were between 30% and 40%.

It is clear from the above analysis that even after 50 years of planned development, literacy continues to be a matter of grave concern for India. According to the World Bank estimates, India will have the largest concentration of illiterate population in the world by 2000 AD, having 55% of the world's total illiterate population in the age-group 15-19 years. It is rightly realized by the Government of India that (GOI, 1985) neither democratization nor modernization is possible to be fully realized without literacy. If development is centered on people, the literacy for all must go hand in hand with development.

Recent Trends

According to the survey conducted by the National Sample Survey Organization (under the Department of Statistics) in 1999, for the National Literacy Mission, on the current literacy rate, Andaman & Nicobar Islands leads the tally with 97% literacy, Lakshadweep is second with 96% and Mizoram stands third with 95%. Kerala, which led the literacy rate since 1961, has been pushed down to the fourth position with 93%. Since the inception of NLM in 1988, 57.96 million people have been made literate under the Adult

Education Scheme. Total literacy campaigns have been launched for 157 million people in 448 districts and under Post Literacy Campaigns 230 districts have been covered. Approximately, 61% of the learners under the programme are women, over 22% are SCs and over 12% are STs. The target was to make 100 million people literate by 1998-99 and to bring about total literacy by 2005 (Manorama Yearbook 2000). Since the official assessment of the government is published in the census reports, the new results will be available only after March 2001. However, according to NSSO figures, literacy rates are growing at an annual rate of approximately 2 per cent. If this rate were maintained, India would reach a level between 66 and 68 per cent by the time of the decennial census of 2001.

But, the interim reports about the 2001 census recently published in some newspapers have said that literacy rate in India has gone up to 65.38%—75.85% for males and 54.16% for females. Assuming, as literacy experts hold, that full literacy for India means the sustainable threshold level of 75%. India would be expected to touch this level between 2004 and 2005. This would be far ahead of the previous expected target of 2011. To attain full literacy in 15-35 age group by 2005, Total Literacy Campaigns are in progress in 172 districts, and Post Literacy Programmes are ongoing in 292 districts.

PROBLEMS

Although, the Government of India has proposed to give the programmes of adult education an overriding priority, yet, there are some difficulties in successful implementation of the literacy schemes. It is rightly said that the success of any scheme depends on:

(i) The "commitment" on the part of those who are involved in the process of implementation, namely, learners, instructors, administrators and public in general;

(ii) The "competence" on the part of all concerned who are to play a key role in the process of implementation of various schemes formulated and launched by the government; and

(iii) The amount of "currency" or funds required making the necessary material and physical resources available to

those who have the required commitment and competence.

In the past, there has been a general lack of conviction on the part of those who have been directly or indirectly associated with the literacy programmes. The state governments have not been willing to provide the required resources and have been giving a step-motherly treatment to these programmes. There has been a general lack of faith among the functionaries and prospective beneficiaries. The NFE approach that was supposed to make a substantial contribution to the success of the programme has failed in its efforts. The management system has been deficient. The delay in the release of funds and honorarium of the instructors due to inherent corruption in the system has paralyzed the whole programme.

The quality of animators/instructors has not been satisfactory. These are recruited from the local people and are key persons in the implementation of the programme. According to a study conducted in Tamil Nadu (Rogers, 1989), it was found that the majority of supervisors in the state-run programmes possessed a B. Ed. degree while those in university-run programmes had an M. A. degree. For most of them it was a first job and they were employed on temporary basis for a period of 10 months without any assurance for re-employment after the expiry of their term. These conditions do not attract good animators. In a few cases a short-term training was also given. An interesting finding was that many of the animators were connected with political parties, trade unions and other similar bodies. Many of them worked in literacy programme for want of an alternative employment and dropped out as soon as they got it, or were married (as in the case of girls). The educational qualifications of the animators in the state-run programmes were low (below class ten). There was a mixed response about job satisfaction when they were asked to comment on.

A RESUME

The foregoing discussion of the progress of literacy in India leads us to certain questions, which every one of us, even remotely concerned with education, must seek to answer. How is it that the successive governments in India, even after independence, have attached less importance to adult education and literacy? If we include basic education also, the question becomes more comprehensive. Instead of giving a boost to elementary and adult education, the government shoed its first concern to higher education and appointed the University Education Commission in 1948. The second choice was the secondary education for which the Secondary Education Commission was appointed in 1952. In fact, for the first 15 years after independence, no government Central or State, ever seriously considered "education of the masses" as a constitutional responsibility, though it was an obligation under Article 45 of the Constitution. During this period, there was a single-party rule in the country and government was stable. Prior to 1976, education was a state subject, but no state attempted to make people literate on a priority basis. No separate allocation of funds for adult education was ever made prior to the Sixth Five-Year Plan (1980-85) in which the share of adult education was 9% of the total plan outlay. After this, this figure has been dwindling and has reached 3% in the Ninth Plan. Why have the successive governments been so indifferent to education of the masses? Perhaps the following remarks of Professor R. P. Singh (2001), a renowned educationist and President of the All India Association of Teacher Educators (AIATE), can explain the situation:

> We have never bothered to realize that in our society there are States whose ruling elite is so insensitive to the problems of its State that so long as they remain in power they would never ever permit their people to become literate. Illiteracy is a big help in administration. People thus can be denied the ability to grow beyond their superstitions and misery.... If this were not so, how is it that whereas the "Dispatch of 1813" permitted the then East India Company to spend one lakh rupees on education of the natives, they took 20 years to withdraw the first installment under the provision. In Independent India we have yet to fulfil our promised constitutional obligation even after more than half a century has elapsed. The simple answer is that whereas the successive governments realized the value of keeping the masses ignorant, the intellectual kept on believing in the sincerity of the rulers" promises and good intentions.

6

Secondary Education and 10+2+3 Pattern

The phrase "Ten plus Two plus Three" dominated educational discussions, formal as well as informal, for quite some time during the decade 1966-1976. Even common people on the roads and in the gardens talked about it, and rightly so, because it was not a simple arithmetical expression, rather, it referred to a major educational reform after independence. As mentioned in an earlier chapter, the structure of education in India is spread over a period of about 20 years divided into stages in a hierarchical order, and with increased degree of selectivity, as we move up the ladder from primary to the university. The first 15 years of education are represented as 10+2+3 indicating 10 years of general education for all who attend school, two years of diversified education preparing the students either for college education or for job market, and three years of college education leading to the award of the first degree. These stages indicate three terminal points giving the students opportunities at each point to decide the next course of action and make proper educational choice depending on their interests, abilities and aptitudes. The curriculum framework for each stage of education has been presented in an earlier chapter.

The expression 10+2+3 attracted wide attention because that time there were varying patterns of education being followed in different states in the country. With a view to bringing about uniformity, a common pattern proposed by the National Policy on Education-1968 was being implemented. The state governments were being asked to implement the pattern as early as possible. Therefore, it was a very hot issue for discussion those days. To put the matter in proper perspective, a historical review of the new pattern is desirable.

HISTORICAL REVIEW

It has been mentioned in Chapter 1 that till the end of 19th century the schools were under the control of the universities, and the matriculation examination, which was the first public examination for a student, was conducted by the universities. It was Calcutta University Commission (1917-19), which suggested the establishment of Intermediate Colleges to prepare students for college education and detachment of two years from college education to form a separate Intermediate stage. In the opinion of the Commission, there were following three main reasons for this reform:

- *(i)* The Intermediate stage, which earlier formed a part of college education, forced the young and immature adolescents (aged 15-17) to study through the methods appropriate for college education, which was not psychologically sound, and therefore, the Intermediate stage (after class ten) should form a part of school stage;
- *(ii)* Under the existing system, the first degree stage consisted of four years for students in the age-group (16-19) years, which kept a heavy burden of conducting examinations on the university, as a consequence, no curricular reforms for upgradation of quality were possible; and
- *(iii)* The standards of curriculum and teaching had to be kept at a lower level in order to accommodate the wide range of ability of students, thus making the college education of a lower standard than the comparable stages in the advanced countries.

In view of the above, the commission recommended that the duration of school education be increased by two years by shifting the first two college years to school stage. Simultaneously, the duration of education up to first degree level be increased from 14 years to 15 years, thus making a new structure of education 10+2+3 to replace the existing 10+2+2 or 8+3+3. The important difference would be that the middle two years should form a part of school education. For conducting examination at matriculation and intermediate stages, Boards of High School and Intermediate Examination be established in each state, thus freeing the universities from the burden of holding large-scale examinations for school education.

Although, these recommendations were widely accepted, yet could not be implemented due to political and financial difficulties. However, U.P. implemented the scheme partially by shifting two years of Intermediate stage from college education to school education, but not following the other part of the scheme, viz., increasing the duration of first degree stage by one year, thus keeping the total duration of 14 years intact. Moreover, no steps were taken to vocationalize the Intermediate stage as recommended by the Commission.

The Sargent Committee (1944) proposed the implementation of higher secondary pattern of 8+3+3, that is, an elementary stage of eight years (5 years of primary education and 3 years of middle school education), higher secondary stage of 3 years followed by 3 years of first degree courses. This pattern was implemented in the Union Territory of Delhi, which till that time was following the 10+2+2 pattern of Punjab (Naik, 1982, p 84).

The matter came up again for consideration of the University Education Commission (1948-49) headed by Dr. Radhakrishnan, which was appointed by the government to study and recommend the possibilities of expansion of university education in free India. Eventually, the Commission considered the status of secondary education in relation to college education, and recommended that it was necessary to adopt a uniform pattern of 10+2+3 for school and college classes, in order to vocationalize secondary education, so as to divert the students (after secondary stage) to different walks of life. This would help reduce the pressure of admissions on the university as well as improve standard of higher education with the addition of one year to degree course. However, no steps were taken to implement these recommendations.

The Secondary Education Commission (1952-53), under the Chairmanship of Dr. A. L. Mudaliar, again considered the issue and favoured the higher secondary pattern of Delhi, namely, 8+3+3. At that time, most of the states were following uniform pattern of 10+2+2, and hence, the Secondary Education Commission created a state of confusion. In effect, the Commission recommended the revival of the scheme proposed in the Sargent Plan (1944). Since, it was the first commission on secondary education after independence, the government showed enthusiasm to it and effected immediate implementation. The implementation of this scheme implied breaking up of intermediate stage into two parts and shifting one year to school and another year to college education. So, the conflicting recommendations of two commissions, made within a short period of four years from 1949 to 1953, created a lot of confusion and complication. Some states, where it was easy, implemented the scheme readily, but some others either refused to implement or expressed reluctance. As a consequence, four different patterns of education, which were being followed in different states, had emerged by 1964. These patterns may be described as follows (Hasan, 1975):

(i) Kerala was the only state where the pattern of 10+2+3 had been adopted with two-year intermediate stage being located in junior colleges;

(ii) The pattern of 10+2+2 prevailed only in Uttar Pradesh where a ten-year high school programme was followed by a two-year intermediate course, and then by a two-year degree course;

(iii) The pattern 11+3 prevailed in Delhi and Madhya Pradesh where an 11-year higher secondary school was followed by a three-year course for the first degree; and

(iv) The pattern of 10 (or 11 or even 12 in some cases)+1+3 was followed in other states, which had a school stage of 10 or 11 or 12 years, followed by a one-year pre-university (added to school in some cases) course and a three-year course for the first degree.

At this stage, the Government of India appointed the Education Commission (1964-66) to look at the entire spectrum of education comprehensively at all stages and in all its aspects. The Commission examined the issue of the structure of education thoroughly and stated:

> As far back as in 1919, the Calcutta University Commission proposed that the dividing line between the university and the secondary school should be drawn at the intermediate examination, which came after 12 years of education. Similarly, the University Education Commission (1948) recommended that students should be admitted to the university after the completion of twelve years of study, and that the first degree course should be of three years' duration. According to the Committee on Emotional Integration (1962), the 11-year period of school education was inadequate preparation for entrance to the university, and the lengthening of the course by one year was deemed necessary. At the Conference of the State Education Ministers held in 1964, it was resolved that a 12-year course of schooling before admission to the degree course was the goal towards which the country must work. We are in full agreement with these recommendations.

The Commission was, therefore, of the opinion that, on sound academic considerations, it would be highly desirable to adopt the uniform pattern of 10+2+3 for school and college classes in all parts of the country. The Commission was of the strong view that school education should consist of twelve years—a secondary stage of 10 years and a senior secondary stage of 2 years. The senior (or higher) secondary stage should be vocationalized so as to divert, in the long run, 50% of the enrollment at this stage to the vocational stream. These recommendations of the commission were discussed by the Central Advisory Board of Education and were approved with minor modifications to reduce cost and facilitate implementation.

The National Policy on Education-1968 made a statement on the subject, which is reproduced below:

> It will be advantageous to have a broadly uniform educational structure in all parts of the country. The ultimate objective should be to adopt the 10+2+3 pattern, the higher secondary stage of two years being located in schools, colleges or both according to local conditions.

This statement shows that two-fold relaxation was given during the process of discussions in the CABE and other bodies, namely, the freedom to attach intermediate stage of two years to school or college according to local conditions, and an option to divide three years of degree course into a pass course of two years and a honours course of one year, or to keep it as an integrated course of three years.

IMPLEMENTATION

By now, it has become evident that the new pattern required modification or change in three ways:

(i) One year was to be added to the school stage in the states where 11+3 system was in operation;
(ii) One year was to be added to the first degree stage in the states where 10+2+2 system existed; and
(iii) A minor reorganization was required in the states where total duration up to first degree was 15 years.

Obviously, the implementation was easiest in the last case because no increase was needed in the total duration. Andhra Pradesh was the first state to come forward to implement the scheme because there were two different systems in operation in that state, which were inherited as a result of reorganization of states from the old Andhra and Hyderabad States. For similar reasons, Karnataka and Maharashtra also joined the queue. These states already had a total duration of 15 years up to first degree, that is 11+1+3, and therefore, readily implemented the 10+2+3 by making minor reshuffle. Gujarat and West Bengal also took steps to implement the new pattern. Some other states also agreed to implement the scheme 'in principle' and set up committees to consider the matter. However, no noticeable changes could be made for some time because the progress was slow. By 1972, the states having 15-year pattern had initiated the process of changeover, but the states having 14-year pattern were reluctant and showed indifference due to financial and other kinds of difficulties involved in the process of change.

Professor S. Noorul Hasan, then Minister of Education, took note of the situation and realized that some positive action by the

Central Government should be initiated to implement the reforms. He planned to achieve this objective through a three-fold strategy:

(i) By implementing the reforms in the Centrally Administered Union Territories including Delhi, and in schools affiliated to the Central Board of Secondary Education to begin with;
(ii) By pursuing the matter with the states having 15-year pattern to implement the scheme, because in these states, the change was relatively easy; and
(iii) By persuading, and if necessary, by pressing the states having 14-year pattern to initiate the process of changeover in a phased manner.

He succeeded in the first two parts of his strategy, but could do nothing about the third part because the 14-year states took no steps to implement the reform.

In 1972, the Conference of Education Secretaries and Directors of Public Instruction resolved that the uniform pattern of education of 15 years' duration leading to the first degree be adopted by all states (Singhal, 1992). The resolution was endorsed by the CABE, and the government of India appointed a National Committee to suggest practical steps necessary for implementation of the new pattern in all the States and Union Territories.

Eventually, the 10+2 pattern was implemented in all the schools, affiliated to the CBSE, in India and abroad. These schools included the schools situated in Union Territories, Kendriya Vdyalayas and some reputed convent schools. With this started the hectic activities, because the task was very challenging. This involved important decision regarding addition of one year to 11-year pattern by categorizing the existing schools into two categories. Secondary schools were to be created by reducing one year (11th class) from some schools, and senior secondary schools were to be created by increasing one year (12th class) in certain others. The existing higher secondary course of three years was to be redesigned into two separate subgroups, viz., secondary (classes IX and X), and senior Secondary (classes XI and XII). It was to be decided as to which higher secondary schools were to be designated as secondary schools, and which others as senior secondary schools.

This exercise was taken up by the CBSE in collaboration with the NCERT, Kendriya Vidyalaya Sangathan, State Institutes of

Education and State Directorates of Education. New curricula were developed, textbooks were written, teachers were trained and reoriented, and the entire machinery was revamped to cope with the change. The schools upgraded to senior secondary level were provided with additional staff, laboratories, workshops and enriched libraries. The change was introduced gradually beginning with class IX and then moving up one class every year. Under the new pattern, the first public examination for class X was held in 1977 and for class XII in 1979. This forced the state governments to take necessary action to cope with the situation. The State Boards of Secondary Education devised plans to implement the new pattern and organized seminars and workshops to design strategies and approaches.

In the meantime, there happened to be a change in the government at the Centre in 1977. The Janata Party government, which took over the regime, proposed to launch a National Policy on Education of its own. In spite of the reservations of the party leaders, including the Prime Minister, Mr. Morarji Desai, the then Minister of Education, Dr. P. C. Chunder felt that it would not be wise to reverse the process in view of the huge investment that had been incurred and the positive results achieved. Consequently, the draft National Policy on Education-1979 stated:

> The educational structure will broadly comprise elementary, secondary, and undergraduate stages of education. School education shall be of 12 years' duration and will comprise the elementary and secondary stages. There will be a publ c examination at the end of the secondary education. The undergraduate stage of education may be of three years' duration. However, where a university desires, it can have two years' pass and three years' honours course.

By 1986, the situation had improved a little more and the National Policy on Education, 1986 felt that 'the most noticeable development had been the acceptance of a common structure of education throughout the country and the introduction of 10+2+3 system by most states.' However, there were a few states, which had implemented the scheme partially by keeping the senior secondary stage a part of college education. In view of this, the NPE-1986 (as modified in 1992) has stated:

The National System of Education envisages a common educational structure. The 10+2+3 structure has now been accepted in all parts of the country. Regarding the further break-up of the first 10 years, efforts will be made to move towards an elementary system comprising 5 years of primary education and 3 years of upper primary, followed by 2 years of high school. Efforts will be made to have the +2 stage accepted as a part of school education throughout the country.

CHARACTERISTICS OF 10+2+3

The new structure of education, which was recommended by various committees and commissions, had certain characteristic features, which made it advantageous over the earlier patterns, and hence, made it acceptable to all in the long run. The salient features of the new pattern are listed below:

(i) It lengthened the total duration of education up to first degree level by one year, which improved the standards of both school and college education by giving an opportunity to improve curricula.

(ii) Before the introduction of 10+2+3, a student entered college education at the age of 15 or 16 years. This was an inappropriate time for a child to be forced to follow the teaching methods practised in college education. In all the advanced countries, the age of entering the college is 18 years. The new pattern solved his problem by shifting one year to school education from college education.

(iii) The university education is characterized by increasing amount of self-study, which can be effectively done after attaining adequate level of maturity in terms of age. The twelve years of schooling would prepare the young children better for university education. This would improve not only the level of achievement of the individual students, but also the general standard of university education.

(iv) The new pattern has envisaged the vocationalization of secondary education so as to make it terminal for a large majority of students, who would enter the word of work instead of lining up at the college gate for admission for

want of any other alternative. This would reduce pressure of enrollment on the university system.

(v) The 10+2+3 pattern proposed general education to be imparted during the first 10 years of schooling without any diversification to ensure that every child learns all subjects up to a minimum essential level. It enabled science and mathematics to be introduced as compulsory subjects up to class ten. This would provide every child with a solid foundation for further studies.

(vi) It proposed to introduce work experience at secondary level, partly to prepare the students for vocational stream at +2 stage, but mainly to develop in them a respect and favourable attitude to manual work.

(vii) The 10+2+3 was not simply a mathematical expression to represent structure and duration of education, rather, it implied a comprehensive improvement in curricula at all stages so as to enhance overall quality of education.

(viii) The +2 stage was supposed to be divided into two streams —an academic and a vocational, the former to prepare the students for higher studies in the university, and the latter to prepare the students for identified vocations.

(ix) A student's decision to choose the stream of study, and consequently, his future carrier after class X was tentative, because there was a provision to switch over from one stream to another at the appropriate time.

(x) Education at senior secondary stage would be cheaper when given as a part of school education than when given as a part of college education, thus making education at this stage cost-effective. This would benefit both, the students and the government.

(xi) The addition of one year would enable the universities to improve undergraduate curricula in order to raise academic standards so as to make the quality of education comparable to international standards.

SECONDARY EDUCATION AND ITS VOCATIONALIZATION

As referred to earlier in this chapter, the Education Commission (1964-66) had proposed vocationalization of secondary education, both at lower secondary (classes IX and X) and senior secondary (classes XI and XII) levels, so as to make secondary education terminal for a sizeable number of students, in order to reduce pressure of admissions on higher education as well as to train middle level manpower for growing industry. The Commission expected that about 20% of the students in lower secondary, 50% in higher secondary, and 30% of those in higher education would be enrolled in vocational and professional courses of all categories. It also made several important recommendations regarding the organization of these courses and for establishing closer relations between education and industry (Naik, 1982). The commission was very emphatic in stating that:

> Secondary education should be vocationalized in a large measure and enrollment in vocational courses raised to 20% of the total enrollment at the lower secondary stage and 50% of the total enrollment at the higher secondary stage by 1986.

Emphasizing the need to inculcate the dignity of labour, and the concept of social and national service, the Commission recommended that work experience and social or national service should form essential and integral component of education at all stages. All concerned accepted this recommendation of the Commission, and eventually, the NPE-1968 incorporated the following provisions:

(i) The school and the community should be brought closer through suitable programmes of mutual service and support. Work experience and national service, including participation in meaningful and challenging programmes of community service and national reconstruction, should accordingly become integral parts of education. Emphasis in these programmes should be on self-help, character formation, and on developing a sense of social commitment.

(ii) There is need to increase facilities for technical and vocational education at this (secondary) stage. Provision of facilities for secondary and vocational education should conform broadly to the requirements of the developing economy and real employment opportunities. Such linkage is necessary to make technical and vocational

education at the secondary stage effectively technical. Facilities for technical and vocational education should be suitably diversified to cover a large number of fields such as agriculture, industry, trade and commerce, medicine and public health, home management, arts and crafts, secretarial training etc.

Work Experience

The concept of "work experience" put forward by the Commission was an adaptation of Gandhian idea of "basic craft" to the new situation without any change in the basic purpose, that is, inculcation of dignity of labour and manual work. The Commission opined that work experience would emphasize the use of science and technology and modern methods of production as opposed to the idea of training in a basic craft, which revived traditional outlook. Secondly, it would include actual participation in the productive process by working in the factories instead of working in the simulated environment of school premises, as was the case with craft training in "basic education". However, the concept of work experience was not acceptable to the leaders of the Janata Party which ruled the nation during the period 1977-80, and a committee headed by Ishwarbhai Patel was appointed (1977) to review the programmes in the curriculum of classes I–X. This committee suggested the concept of 'socially useful productive work' or SUPW as a combination of "work experience" and "craft training". Consequently, the draft National Policy on Education-1979 formulated by the Janata Party government proposed to diversify school curriculum to include, among other things, the SUPW and "social service" to help students acquire the knowledge and skills, attitudes and values essential to democratic, secular and socialist society, with Gandhian values of life. This policy was, however, never implemented.

Diversification of Secondary Education

It was Wood's Education Despatch (1854) that first talked of providing the great masses of the people a "useful and practical knowledge" and establishing the institutions of 'professional and technical education' in India. A little later, the Indian Education

Commission (1882) proposed to introduce "practical subjects" in primary schools and bifurcate secondary education into "two streams", one leading to the entrance examination of the university and the other of a "more practical character". After this, the Calcutta University Commission (1917-19), the University Education Commission (1948-49), and Education Commission (1964-66) all made similar recommendations about diversification of secondary education (especially the senior secondary) into academic and vocational streams.

During the pre-independence period, various alternative vocational courses in agriculture, commerce, engineering, medicine, fine arts, forestry, teacher training and veterinary science were provided at secondary level. But, no noticeable progress had been made in these efforts by 1947. At the time of independence the total enrollment in all the vocational courses put together was even less than 10% (Naik, 1982) of the total enrollment at secondary school stage. Due to rapid development of agriculture and industry, and a consequential fast urbanization, new job opportunities opened up, especially at middle level. Therefore, between 1950 and 1965 the enrollment in secondary vocational courses was almost three times the earlier enrollment. But, during the same period, the enrollment in the academic stream of higher secondary increased even more rapidly so that the ratio of enrollment in vocational stream to the total enrollment at senior secondary stage remained unchanged.

When 10+2+3 was implemented in the CBSE and other schools under the Central Government, the NCERT and the CBSE undertook the exercise of curriculum development for the new pattern. In 1975 the NCERT published the 'Ten-Year School—A Framework', which was a document embodying the outlines of new curriculum for classes I–X under 10+2+3 pattern. A similar document for classes XI and XII was also published in 1976.

Lower Secondary Stage

The introduction of vocational education at lower secondary and senior secondary stages required a drastic change in the curriculum. The NCERT curriculum, developed with the help of the expert groups, included science and mathematics as compulsory subjects for all children up to class X. In the earlier scheme, the students had a choice between social studies and sciences, which deprived over 50% of the students, of the study of science, which was so essential for daily life activities. Work experience was an integral part of the new curriculum.

The new curriculum, thus, provided for a "broad-based" general education with adequate vocational bias, for all children up to class VIII. As discussed earlier, the concept of work experience was later replaced by that of SUPW as recommended by Ishwarbhai Patel Committee in 1977. The old curriculum on the other hand, required the students to make a decision about the choice of their future career at the age of 14, which was obviously too premature an age to take such a crucial decision.

The Education Commission (1964-66) attached considerable significance to vocational education at lower secondary stage and proposed several alternatives of full-time and part-time education in both the streams. The Commission also recommended 'part-time and non-formal courses of general and vocational education to smoothen the transition from full-time education to full-time work by interposing a period of part-time education and part-time work between the two.' The Commission had clarified that vocational courses might not necessarily be a part of lower secondary education as such, to be conducted only in secondary schools, rather, the Commission proposed separate courses of vocational nature whose duration might be of one to three years (Naik, 1982). This implied opening of more Industrial Training Institutes (ITIs) or institutions of similar nature for those who completed elementary education. Therefore, as originally visualized by the Commission, the vocational courses were to be conducted both in lower secondary schools and specialized technical and vocational schools for 14-16 age group.

Senior Secondary Stage

In the curriculum for senior secondary stage, the main emphasis was on diversification and flexibility, bifurcation of the course into academic and vocational streams, and upgradation of the course content in view of addition of one year. The senior secondary stage was to be terminal for some students, and preparatory for some others for higher or tertiary education.

The academic stream was to provide the students with freedom to choose subjects cutting across different areas of arts, sciences and commerce, but in practice, different State Boards divided the academic stream into sub-streams of arts, sciences and commerce for convenience. However, the CBSE provided open choice and promoted interdisciplinary approach to teaching learning process.

The vocational stream was to provide job-oriented courses of two or three years' duration for those who would discontinue their studies after +2. This required some of the existing higher secondary schools to be upgraded as senior secondary schools. All the vocational course were not to be provided for as part of senior secondary school programme, rather, some of them were to be conducted in special institutions like polytechnics. This means that vocationalization at senior secondary stage implied the introduction of diploma level courses with a duration of one to three years for those who passed class X and were in the age-group 16-18 years. Of course, some of these courses could be provided in the senior secondary schools along with academic stream. The Commission also recommended the introduction of a large number of part-time courses (vocational as well as academic) for those who would discontinue formal schooling after class X, but would like to continue studies while in job or at work.

The Janata Party government appointed a committee headed by Dr. Malcolm S. Adiseshiah (1977) to consider the re-organization of vocational curriculum at +2 stage. The recommendations of this committee are summarized below:

(i) The academic stream should include the study of one language, socially useful productive work, and three electives from humanities, sciences and social sciences with the following scheme of allocation of time:

One Language:	15%,
SUPW:	15%,
Three Electives:	70%.

(ii) The vocational stream should include the study of one language, a general foundation course, and vocational electives with the following scheme of time allocation:

One Language:	15%,
General Foundation Course:	15%,
Vocational Electives:	70%.

(iii) The general and vocational streams should not be completely isolated and there should be several points of crossover from one stream to another. If necessary, bridge courses may be planned for this purpose.

(iv) The vocational courses should be planned to suit the requirements of the employment market. Frequent surveys should be conducted, at local level, to study the available employment opportunities.

(v) Necessary steps should be taken to create required physical facilities for vocational stream such as workshops, textbooks and trained teachers.

(vi) The recruitment policy of the government should be modified so as to suit the requirements of students passing out from vocational schools with proper opportunities for vertical mobility, so that vocational education may be popularized.

THE PRESENT SCENARIO

It has been pointed out elsewhere that linear expansion of educational system inherited from the British was the first priority of the government immediately after independence. Along with development of elementary education, there has been corresponding development of the secondary education. The details of the development of secondary education are given in Table 6.1 below:

Table 6.1
Development of Secondary Education (1951-2000)

Year	*Schools (units)*	*Enrollment (lakhs)*			*Teachers (000s)*		
		Male	*Female*	*Total*	*Male*	*Female*	*Total*
1950-51	7416	13	2	15	107	20	127
1960-61	17329	27	7	34	234	62	296
1970-71	37051	49	17	66	474	155	629
1980-81	51624	76	32	108	658	254	912
1990-91	78619	140	69	209	857	416	1273
1992-93	84086	150	77	227	908	445	1353
1995-96	98134	161	88	249	982	511	1493
1999-2000	116820	172	110	282	1142	578	1720

Sources: (i) Selected Educational Statistics, Ministry of Human Resource Development, Government of India, 1996-97, 1999-2000.
(ii) Ministry of Human Resource Development, Government of India, Annual Report, 1996-97, 2000-2001.

A careful study of the Table 6.1 reveals the following facts about the development of secondary education in India:

(i) The total number of secondary schools (for classes IX-XII) have increased from only 7416 in 1950-51 to over 116,820 in 1999-2000, registering an annual compound growth rate (ACGR) of 5.6%. These figures include high schools, higher secondary schools, intermediate colleges, junior colleges, community colleges and PUC sections wherever they exist.

(ii) The total enrollment at this stage has increased from only 15 lakhs in 1950-51 to about 28.2 million in 1999-2000, recording an ACGR of 6.7%. The enrollment of girls has increased at a faster rate (8.2%) than that of boys (5.9%) during the same period.

(iii) The total number of teachers has also increased from only 12,700 in 1950-51, to 17.20 lakhs in 1999-2000. The ACGR being 5.8%. The number of female teachers has also increased from 20,000 to 5.78 lakhs during the same period recording an ACGR of 7.6% as against 5.2% of the male teachers.

(iv) It is, therefore, clear that enrollment at this stage also has grown at a faster rate than institutions and teachers. Moreover, the growth rate of the female enrollment has been faster than the male enrollment. Similarly, the growth rate of female teachers has been faster than that of the male teachers.

(v) In 1950-51, girls constituted only 13% of the total enrollment at secondary school stage. This figure had increased to about 37.8% by 1998-99. Similarly, female teachers have increased from 15.7% to over 32.6% of the total number of teachers during the same period.

(vi) In 1950-51, there were 30 elementary schools for every secondary/higher secondary school. This ratio has now become 7:1. This is a remarkable development.

Since 1976, when the NCERT published national curriculum for higher secondary education, the growth of vocational schools has been slow. By the year 1985-86, the programme of vocationalization of education had been implemented in 10 States and 5 Union Territories. In 1985-86, the intake in the vocational stream was of the order of 72000, only about 2.5% of the students entering senior/higher secondary stage. Obviously, it was not a satisfactory coverage. The government made several efforts to improve the situation by conducting evaluation studies in most of the states making the findings available to the states for feedback. But, no noticeable headway was made between 1975-76 and 1985-86. The National Policy on Education-1986 stated:

> It is proposed that vocational courses cover 10% of higher secondary students by 1990 and 25% by 1995. Steps will be taken to see that a substantial majority of the products of vocational courses are employed or become self-employed. Review of the courses offered would be regularly undertaken. Government will also review its recruitment policy to encourage diversification at secondary level.

When the NPE-1986 was revised in 1992, the target dates were again revised with a proposal to cover 10% of higher secondary students by 1995 and 25% by 2000 AD. The progress of vocationalization of secondary education made since 1950-51 has been presented in the following table:

Table 6.2

Progress of Vocationalization of Secondary Education in India

Item	*1987-88*	*1988-89*	*1989-90*	*1990-91*	*1992-93*	*1998-99*
Number of States covered	18	23	23	27	28	28
Number of schools covered	1080	1552	163	1046	5701	6486
Vocational sections approved	3167	4237	484	2428	16450	18719
Amount spent (Rs. in crores)	32.36	49.73	43.97	74.00	NA	NA

Sources: 1. Singhal R. P., Journal of Educational Planning and Admn. NIEPA, Vol IV, No 3,1992.

2. Development of Education in India, 1993-94, MHRD, Government of India, 1994.

3. Ministry of HRD, Government of India, New Delhi, 2000

A substantially funded and centrally sponsored scheme for vocationalization of secondary education was started with effect from February 1988. The scheme was implemented in all the States and Union Territories excepting a few smaller ones. At the end of 1991-92, 12543 vocational sections were approved in 4400 schools, thereby creating facilities for diversion of about 6.27 lakh students at the +2 stage. This amounts to 9.3% of the students enrolled at this stage (NPE-POA, 1992). By the year 1992-93, facilities for vocational education had been created in 5701 schools to enroll 8.22 lakh students. The total number of sections for vocational education created during 1988-93 was 16450. In quantitative terms this appears to be a substantial improvement over the previous years, but qualitatively, much is supposed to be done. According to the latest reports of the government, by 1998-99, 18,719 vocational sections had been sanctioned in 6,486 schools all over the country thereby creating capacity for diversion of about 9.35 lakh students to the vocational stream, which is 11% of enrollment at the +2 stage.

SOME NEW DEVELOPMENTS

In order to achieve the targets fixed in the NPE-1986 as revised in 1992, an elaborate and time bound programme is being launched. This task has been entrusted to the Joint Council of Vocational Education (JCVE), which has been established at national level to lay down the policy guidelines. The supervision of work has been entrusted to a standing committee. The Joint Councils have also been set up at state levels (Mishra, 1994) as education is in the Concurrent List and it needs the support of state governments to make a time bound planning for a change in reality. The other function of the JCVEs is to coordinate with the agencies pursuing vocational education programmes.

In addition to vocational courses at +2 stage from 1993-94, pre-vocational courses were also centrally sponsored and introduced at the lower secondary stage. This scheme aimed at covering 1000 schools during the Eighth Plan. Non-formal vocational education and training programmes are also being introduced through non-governmental organizations (NGOs), which receive financial assistance for innovative projects, especially in backward rural areas, and those intended for girls in the 14-18 age group.

Central Institute of Vocational Education (CIVE)

Pandit Sunderlal Sharma Central Institute of Vocational Education (PSSCIVE) was set up at Bhopal (MP) on July 1, 1993 to serve as the research and development institute for vocational education in the country. Currently, the CIVE is deeply involved in review and standardization of curriculum, textbooks and instructional material. It is also reviewing the teacher training programmes and the inter-state relations to facilitate and share information and experiences related to vocational education. The CIVE has been identified as the focal point in India for UNESCO's International Project on Technical and Vocational Education (GOI, 1994).

The NCERT has developed 82 competency-based curricula for six identifiable subject-areas in vocational education at secondary and senior secondary levels. These curricula will serve as guidelines for States and Union Territories, which may adopt them as they are or may adapt them according to the local needs. However, the overall framework is simple and practical. General Education and Foundation Courses as well as language development will form 30% of the teaching/learning requirements in addition to vocational theory and on-the-job training, which accounts for 70% of the course time. It may be seen that these guidelines are in line with the recommendations of Adiseshiah Committee (1977).

However, real enrollment and utilization of facilities was expected to be somewhat lower. Efforts are now being made to improve quality and efficiency of education, rather than undertaking further expansion. Besides, the Department of Personnel and Training has also been pursuing different departments and ministries, to keep provision for absorbing the vocational pass-outs against the future vacancies. Linkages are being established with private industry, insurance companies, and the banking sector to extend training facilities for students and teachers from the vocational stream; create apprenticeship training opportunities after course completion; and in order to encourage industry to contribute actively to developing curricula and learning materials for vocational studies.

Jawahar Navodaya Vidyalayas

As early as in 1882, the Indian Education Commission had suggested the selective development of institutions, and setting up of pace-setting schools. It had recommended that the government should establish and maintain "model" institutions, a school in every District and a college in every Province, as mark of standards of quality, and leave the rest of the field open to the private enterprise. The institutions established by private bodies would strive to attain the standards of excellence set by the government institutions. This process would continue till all the institutions attained a reasonably high standard of quality. The idea was considered at later stages, prior to independence also in different forms, but was never accepted by the Indian public. The critics generally gave the following arguments in support of their points of view:

1. The Government cannot and should not monopolize the establishment and maintenance of quality institutions, and thereby, deny the opportunity of doing so to the private enterprise.
2. There were many private institutions that imparted education of a superior quality than that imparted by the government institutions, and thus, the claim of the government alone to provide quality education was not justified.
3. Many of the government schools, despite heavy investment in them, could not perform the role of pace-setting "model" schools as expected, rather, they became what they should not have become.
4. The establishment and maintenance of such schools involved very heavy investment, which made the repetition of such experiments extremely difficult. They were like Qutab Minars and Taj Mahals, which have their own importance, but cannot be repeated.
5. The "model" schools, in the long run, would tend to become elitists and would be out of reach for the common people, thus contributing to the widening gulf between the rich and the poor.

The idea was once again revived by the Education Commission (1964-66), which expressed grave concern over the quality of education at all stages. It held the view that educational standards should be maintained and continually improved so as to be comparable with the international norms. For this purpose, the Commission suggested the approach of selective development of institutions and establishment of pace-setting ones at all stages. In the opinion of the Commission, such institutions would generate excellence, which could be extended to other institutions also. This means that the Commission was in favour of identifying and developing existing institutions quality institutions, and at the same time, establishing new ones capable of generating excellence in the first instance. It hoped that by the time the entire system absorbed and internalized this excellence, the pace-setting institutions would have climbed to a still higher level of excellence and set in motion another wave for spreading excellence of a higher order; and so on. The Commission described this process of selective development of institutions as the seed-farm technology and opined that existence of high quality and pace-setting institutions at every stage and in every sector was an essential characteristic of the national system of education (Naik, 1982).

Taking due care of the previous experiences and criticism, the Commission recommended a programme of improving the quality of every school to a certain minimum level and creation of a few pace-setting schools. The remarks of the Commission on this subject are given below:

> The highest priority in the programme should be given to the creation of a minimum proportion of 'quality' schools at every stage, which would serve as pace-setting institutions. The number of really good schools in the present system is pitifully small, and in order to obtain good results in the shortest time, it is necessary to concentrate available resources in a few centres. As a first step towards improving all schools, therefore, we should strive to improve, during the next 10 years, at least 10 per cent of the schools at the primary stage to an optimum level. At the secondary stage, we should have one quality school in every community development block.

The Committee of the Members of Parliament, which was appointed by the Government to discuss its recommendations, rejected this proposal of the Commission outright. They opined that better results could be obtained if all the schools were developed to a minimum level of quality, and special assistance was provided to those institutions, which showed some superior performance and promise. Consequently, these proposals were not even referred to in the National Policy on Education-1968.

The concept of pace-setting schools was again highlighted in the National Policy on Education-1986. On this subject the policy stated:

> 5.14 It is universally accepted that children with special talent or aptitudes should be provided opportunities to proceed at a faster pace, by making good quality education available to them, irrespective of their capacity to pay for it.
>
> 5.15 Pace-setting schools intended to serve this purpose will be established in various parts of the country on a given pattern, but with full scope for innovation and experimentation. Their broad aims will be to serve the objective of excellence, coupled with equity and social justice (with reservation for SCs ad STs), to promote national integration by providing opportunities to talented children largely rural, from different parts of the country to live and learn together, to develop their full potential, and, most importantly, to become catalysts of a nation-wide programme of school improvement. The schools will be residential and free of charge.

In pursuance of these proposals of the NPE-1986, the Government of India launched the scheme of establishing, on an average, one Navodaya Vidyalaya (NV) in each district in the country with the following objectives (GOI, 1999-2000):

(i) To provide good quality modern education including a strong component of culture, values, environmental awareness and physical education to all talented children in rural areas without regard to their family's socio-economic condition.

(ii) To ensure attainment of three-language formula by all students.

(iii) To serve all districts, as focal points, for improvement in the quality of school education through sharing of experiences and facilities.

The Navodaya Vidyalaya Samiti, an autonomous organization under the Ministry of Human Resource Development, Department of Education, manages these institutions. The Minister of Human Resource Development as Chairman heads this body. The Navodaya Vidyalayas are fully residential and co-educational institutions providing free education up to senior secondary stage. The total expenditure of education including boarding and lodging, textbooks uniform etc. in these schools is borne by the Government.

The scheme, which started with two experimental schools in 1985-86, has now grown to 430 schools in 430 districts with a total enrollment of 1.27 lakh students. Every year, about 25,000 new students are enrolled in these schools (GOI, 2000-01). Admissions in these schools are made at class VI level through a test conducted in each district. All those students who have passed class V of a recognized school in the concerned district are eligible to appear in the admission test. The admission tests are designed and conducted by the Central Board of Secondary Education, New Delhi.

It has been observed that this scheme is working well in identifying and nurturing rural talent as 75% of the seats are meant for children belonging to rural areas. Seats are reserved for SC/ST children as usual, and attempts are made to see that about one-third of the students admitted are girls. In fact, there was a pressing need of such institutions because the Government had already set up Central Schools to take care of the urban children. These institutions are showing very good results in the examinations conducted by the CBSE. In the year 2000, the pass-percentages of students of these schools appearing in the class X and class XII examinations were 87.0 and 83.3 respectively.

PROBLEMS

The implementation of the 10+2+3 programme is facing some problems from the very beginning. These problems are being summarized below:

(i) One of the major problems faced by the new pattern was that some of the states, at the first instance, did not take the reform programmes seriously. The main reason for this was that by 1976 education was a state subject and the states thought that they might have their own way in this matter. Consequently, different states

implemented the programme differently, some of them making only the structural changes. Some of the reformatory programmes, which were basic to 10+2+3 system, were, therefore, ignored.

(ii) Education was introduced in the Concurrent List of the Constitution in 1976 through 42nd Constitutional Amendment, which paved the way for universal acceptance and implementation of the new pattern. But, the change of government at the Centre in 1977, gave a serious jolt to the programme, because the new leadership questioned the very basic philosophy of the programme. So, the pace of implementation of the programme slowed down till it regained momentum during the 1980s.

(iii) Amrik Singh (1990) has rightly said that having evolved for a century and a half in a certain manner people have got accustomed to functioning in a certain way, and therefore, they do not wish to change. In view of this tendency the reform was either opposed or resisted by teachers and parents. The teachers who resisted the change were mainly those who wanted to follow the beaten path and were scared of change, as it would involve additional work under improved curriculum. The parents who resisted the change were mainly those, whose children were being affected because of addition of one extra year to school education.

(iv) Introduction of science and mathematics as compulsory subjects created the problem of physical facilities. Some of the schools were not teaching science and mathematics in classes IX and X before the introduction of 10+2+3. Moreover, some people believed that study of science and mathematics was meant for only brighter children, and especially, mathematics was meant for boys only because, they thought, that it was beyond the comprehension of girls. This belief was later on proved to be wrong when it was found that girls excelled boys in all the subjects including mathematics.

(v) The problem of location of +2 stage in school or college dominated all the discussions preceding the implementation of the scheme. States tackled this problem in their own way. Consequently, the +2 stage

found a place in school, college, or both depending on the line of action taken by different states. However, the states were allowed to do so for the time being with final and ultimate objective to make +2 a part of school education.

(vi) Traditionally, the university degree has been taken as a mark of social status and prestige in our society. Therefore, the vocational courses at +2 stage did not receive the expected acceptance among the public. So far, because the secondary and higher education have been accessible only to upper and middle classes of the society whose children have always preferred to go for university degree than to join the vocational courses, the vocational component has not been attractive for students, and hence, the growth of enrollment in vocational stream has been very slow.

(vii) The Education Commission (1964-66) had suggested that vocationalization of secondary education should be linked to manpower planning and the recruitment policy of the government should also take care of the employment opportunities for the vocational pass-outs. But unfortunately, this has never been possible. In our model of development, there are hardly any linkages between education and economy. Consequently, the vocational pass-outs do not find jobs in the employment market. A committee set up by the government of Karnataka (1991) reviewed the progress of vocationalization of education (Singhal, 1992) in the State and observed that vocational education programme of the State had not been effective. It was found that only 20 to 25 per cent of the students trained in vocational stream could find gainful employment. The success of the programme cannot be judged in terms of percentage of students diverted to the vocational stream, rather, in terms of percentage of those who get gainful employment.

(viii) The vocationalization of secondary education was a well-considered but poorly implemented programme. No adequate preparation was made before the programme was implemented. It required huge plants and

workshops in order to provide training in practical skills, which in turn, involved huge investment. When we want that 20% of the students be diverted to the vocational stream, we should also set aside 20% of the funds allocated to secondary education for the vocational stream. But this generally does not happen.

(ix) Due to poor infrastructure, inadequate training of teachers and highly theoretical nature of vocational courses, and the quality of vocational pass-outs remains poor. Therefore, they are not acceptable in the job market in preference to those trained in other technical and vocational schools such as ITIs and polytechnics. There is a need for a rigorous apprenticeship training of the vocational pass-outs by attaching the students to working industrial units for sufficiently large period.

(x) The examination reform has been advocated for as a basic requirement for the improvement of educational standards in India. However, the progress on this front has been the slowest.

To summarize the discussion, the 10+2+3 pattern proposed by various committees and commissions, was an important and inevitable reform, which was long overdue. It was not simply meant for a structural change in the system of education, rather, implied a radical reconstruction of various aspects of education. This is satisfying that after over 20 years of sustained efforts the 10+2+3 pattern has been implemented in all the States and Union Territories of India. However, in a few states the +2 stage continues to be a part of college education the examinations being conducted by the State Boards of Secondary Education. It is expected that these states will also take necessary steps to make it a part of school education. The 10+2+3 is a long-term educational reform programme having far-reaching implications.

7

Higher Education

Even before the establishment of universities in Europe, India had a long history of higher education. There had been a tradition of enlightenment and scholarship in various fields since ancient times. The older universities of Europe came into existence during the medieval period. Even during Vedic-Upanishadic period, India had enlightened the world through famous seats of higher learning. It is on record (Radhakrishnan Commission, 1948-49) that the university of Takshashila flourished up to the end of fifth century AD and that of Nalanda survived up to the 12th century AD. The curriculum in these universities included the study of Vedas in addition to Upanishads, religious scriptures, philosophy and logic. Nalanda was basically a Buddhist centre of learning, but its working resembled the contemporary Hindu centres of learning such as those located at Vallabhi, Vikramshila, Banaras, Nadia, Ujjain and Kanchi. The purpose of education in these institutions was not utilitarian; rather, learners acquired knowledge for its own sake. The philosophical and religious systems dominated the foundations of education with "idealism" occupying the prominent position and without any place for "materialism" and physical aspects of life.

The organization of these institutions resembled more to the modern concept of "non-formal" education than the traditional "formal" system. The teachers maintained themselves on "guru dakshina" received in the form of presents from the students, and there was no formal arrangement for payment of salaries. No fee was charged in the ancient Indian system of education, but at a later stage, during the Buddhist period, Takshashila and Nalanda started charging fees from rich students for maintaining the institution. There was no formal system of state funding of universities, however, kings provided endowments in terms of land and building, scholarships for poor and needy students and prizes for meritorious students. Since there was no state funding, there was no state interference in the academic or financial matters of the institutions. The greatest motivation for the teachers was the respect and status in the society, which they enjoyed. Higher education was, however, not accessible to all and was available only to the upper and ruling classes of the society. Education was the territory of Brahmins who were responsible for teaching. Shudras, the lowest of the caste hierarchy or Varna Vyavastha, were not allowed to study the sacred scriptures.

The foreign invaders destroyed these great seats of learning during the medieval period, which was a period of conquest, destruction and loot. However, Mohammad Ghauri, who was the first Muslim ruler to start a "madarsah" at Aimer, encouraged higher education. Some more schools (maktabs) and colleges (madarsahs) were set up by some other Muslim rulers at Lahore, Delhi, Rampur, Bidar, Lucknow, Allahabad, Jaunpur, Ajmer Fatehpur Sikri and Agra. The curriculum in these institutions included seven liberal arts in line with the contemporary European institutions. The medium of instruction was either Arabic or Persian or both.

BEGINNING OF MODERN HIGHER EDUCATION

The East India Company, which came to India in 1600, paid no attention to education till 1813 when British Parliament directed the Company 'to accept the responsibility of education of Indians and to spend not less than Rs. 100,000 a year for this purpose.' But, the Company had been reluctant to make any attempts in this direction, because the officers of the Company suspected that western education might encourage growth of nationalism among the people of India. Therefore, they adopted a policy of encouraging the indigenous system of education and opened Calcutta Madarsah in 1781 to encourage and develop education in Persian and Arabic. This was done to appease the Muslims of Bengal. Similarly, in order to appease the Hindus and to encourage the study of Sanskrit, they also opened Benaras Sanskrit College in 1791.

The western higher education began with the establishment of Hindu College at Calcutta (1817) by Raja Rammohun Roy and his friend David Hare (Rao, 1991) with the objective to provide a channel by which 'real knowledge may be transferred from European sources to the intellect of Hindustan.' The British East India Company founded another Sanskrit College at Calcutta (1825), which was protested against by Raja Rammohun Roy on the ground that Hindus should have received education in European languages and science. By this time, the Christian missionaries had started establishing colleges at other places, with the objective of spreading Christianity through teaching of English and western science. Elphinstone College was founded at Bombay (1834), and Madras Christian College (1837) at Madras, to prepare natives for public employment. In the same succession, colleges were set up at Masulipatanam (1841), Nagpur (1844), and Agra (1853). Upto this time, the number of colleges had risen to 25 in all, in the whole country.

Birth of Modern Universities in India

One interesting fact about Indian higher education is that colleges were established even before the birth of universities. Some of these colleges were established and managed by the government while some others were private aided by the government. As mentioned earlier, on the recommendation of Wood's Education Despatch (1854), the first three modern universities were established at Calcutta, Bombay and Madras in 1857. The function of these universities was to conduct examinations and award degrees, and teaching work was done in the approved and affiliated colleges. This was, in fact, an adoption of London University model. The only exception was that the pupils admissible to the matriculation examination were pupils from schools that had been recognized by the universities. This means that universities had their grip not only over the colleges affiliated to them, but also, over the secondary schools situated within the area of their jurisdiction. With the rapid rise in enrollment after the establishment of these three universities, the University of Punjab at Lahore (1882) and the University of Allahabad (1887), were also established. The University of Allahabad was given teaching powers but did not use them for many years. After this, no new university was set up in the Nineteenth Century. By 1902, there were 5 universities and 191 affiliated colleges with a total enrolment of 17,650 students.

The Indian Universities Commission (1902), appointed by Lord Curzon as Viceroy, resulted in the Universities Act of 1904, under which it was resolved that universities should also be teaching universities, and that stringent rules should be framed for affiliation and disaffiliation of colleges. This led to a rapid rise in the student enrollment during the next decade. The Government of India Resolution on Educational Policy (1913) stressed the need of separating teaching and examining functions of the universities and emphasized the need for having both teaching and examining universities. The Calcutta University was the first to set up its own teaching departments under the leadership of Sir Ashutosh Mukherji, following the Universities Act of 1904. With this development, universities became the primary organizations and colleges became secondary, though reverse was true before 1857. In 1917, the Calcutta University had 58 affiliated colleges and 26,000 students, out of a total for the whole India of 58,000—a large number compared to the literate population (Hartog, 1939). This shows that with the rapid rise in the enrollment, the quality of education had gone down.

In the meantime, the National Freedom Movement had gathered momentum and some enlightened Indians took keen interest in education. Consequently, six new universities came into existence between 1913 and 1921. These included Banaras Hindu University (1916), Patna University (1917) split from Calcutta University, Osmania University (1918), Lucknow University split from Allahabad (1920), and Aligarh Muslim University (1920), which were established by Acts of Central Legislature. These were all Central Universities that time. Prior to this, erstwhile MAO College, Aligarh and Central Hindu College at Benaras were both affiliated to the University of Allahabad. The Osmania University at Hyderabad used Urdu as a medium of instruction, though English was a compulsory subject.

With the establishment of Delhi, split from Punjab (1922), Nagpur, split from Allahabad (1923), Andhra, split from Madras (1926), Agra, split from Allahabad (1927), and Annamalai (1929) universities, the total number of universities became 16 by 1930. This sudden spurt in the number of universities was due to favourable recommendations of Calcutta University Commission (1917-19). Most of these universities were teaching universities. At the same time, during the period of Non-Cooperation Movement, Gandhiji founded Gujarat Vidyapeeth, Kashi Vidyapeeth, Tilak Maharashtra Vidyapeeth, Bihar Vidyapeeth and Jamia Millia Islamia to provide strength to the National Freedom Movement.

However, during 1929-47, the official effort to develop higher education was slow due to some political problems related to freedom struggle and breakout of the Second World War in 1939. Therefore, only 3 more universities could be set up during this period — Kerala (1937), Utkal (1943) and Sagar (1946). In this way, the number of universities established before independence was 19. Rajasthan University Jaipur and Punjab University Chandigarh were set up in 1947, because Punjab University Lahore was transferred to Pakistan during partition. Thus, the total number of universities set up by 1947-48 became 20 with about 500 affiliated colleges and 2.15 lakhs of students.

Post-Independence Efforts

As India achieved freedom in 1947, the Department of Education created in 1945 was converted into full-fledged Ministry of Education. Higher education was the first sector of education to attract the attention of the Union Government. As a first step, the University Education Commission (1948-49) was appointed, which recommended rapid expansion of higher education in India on a priority basis. The Commission also made several other recommendations having bearing on future development of the country. During a period of three years from 1947 to 1950, 7 new universities were created raising the total number to 27. The number of affiliated colleges also increased very fast. In 1950-51, there were 695 colleges. The total enrollment in higher education was 174,000 (excluding those enrolled in PUC). The total number of teachers working in these institutions was a little more than 21000.

After 1950-51, the growth of higher education has been

phenomenal. According to the latest reports of the UGC (1999-2000), the total number of universities at present is 256 and that of affiliated colleges is 11,831 and the total enrollment is over 77.34 lakhs. During the last 50 years, the total number of teachers in the universities and colleges has also increased to more than 3.51 lakhs. The growth rate of higher education was as high as 13-14% during the 1950s and 1960s, but declined to about 5.3% during 1970s. During 1980s and early 1990s the overall growth rate had been about 4.2%. However, at present the growth rate is around 5% per annum. Of all the university level institutions, 199 are traditional universities or institutions of specialized studies, 45 are deemed to be universities, and 12 are institutions of National Importance. These include 17 medical institutions and 10 open universities also.

The affiliated colleges have a very important role in higher education in India with most of the undergraduate and postgraduate teaching being done in them. During the last one-decade or so, the affiliated colleges have been enrolling about 87.8% of the undergraduate, 56.5% of the postgraduate and 15% of the total research students. Therefore, the quality of colleges has a very significant bearing on the quality of higher education in India.

Table 7.1
Development of Higher Education in India (1951-2000)

Year	*Universities (Numbers)*	*Colleges (Numbers)*	*Enrollment (in 000s)*	*Teachers (in 000s)*	*Growth (AGCR)*
1950-51	27	695	174	21.3	-
1955-56	33	1,025	295	33.2	11.10
1960-61	47	1,542	557	55.5	13.60
1965-66	75	2,572	1,067	84.7	13.90
1970-71	100	3,604	1,954	128.8	12.80
1975-76	120	4,395	2,426	167.6	4.40
1980-81	144	4,722	2,792	193.3	2.80
1985-86	164	5,816	3,571	227.0	5.10
1990-91	180	7,346	4,425	263.1	4.10
1995-96	226	9,252	6,426	300.6	2.50
1998-99	256	11,831	7,737	351.0	2.50

Sources:
1. Chauhan, C. P. S., Higher Education in India, Ashish Publishing House, New Delhi, 1990.
2. UGC Annual Reports, 1993-94, 1995-96, 1998-99,1999-2000.
3. Ministry of Human Resource Development, Govt. of India, Annual Report, 1996-97, 2000-2001.

Of the total enrollment in the universities and colleges, 88.05% students are enrolled in the undergraduate classes, 9.8% in the postgraduate classes and only 0.88% at the research degree level. The pattern of faculty-wise enrollment shows that:

(i) About 81.5% enrollment is in general education—40.5% in arts, 19.1% in science and 21.9% in commerce;

(ii) The remaining 18.5% enrollment is in professional and technical education—5.03% in Engineering and Technology, 3.5% in Medicine, 5.2% in Law, 2.3% in Education, 1.05% in Agriculture, 0.3% in Veterinary Science and 1.07% in other professional courses;

(iii) The total enrollment of girls has increased from only 9.3% in 1947 to 35.45% in 1999-2000. In 1947, there were only 14 women for every 100 men, but in 1999-2000, there were 55 women for every 100 men students. The majority of women are enrolled in Arts (54.4%), followed by Science (20.1%), Commerce (14.1%), Education (3.9%), Law (1.8%) Engineering and Technology (1.2%), and other faculties (4.5%); and

(iv) The major portion of girls is enrolled in general education (88.5%) and those enrolled in professional courses are 11.5% only.

With phenomenal expansion during the post-independence period, the higher education system in India has become one of the largest in the world. If the progress continues at the same pace, we may surpass even USA and Russia within a decade or so.

MAJOR POLICIES AND PROGRAMMES

On the recommendations of the University Education Commission, the Government of India reviewed the University Grants Committee constituted in 1945 and set up the University Grants Commission (UGC) in 1953, which became a statutory body in 1956 by an Act of Parliament. Similar bodies were also constituted for Agriculture education and education in Engineering and Technology. The Indian Council of Agricultural Research (ICAR) was established and became an autonomous body in mid-sixties. The All India Council of Technical Education (AICTE), which had been set up in 1945, became a statutory body in 1988 by an Act of Parliament.

Education Commission (1964-66) highlighted the role of higher education in the development of Indian society and expressed a grave concern over the deteriorating quality of higher education. Some important recommendations of the Commission were:

(i) Introduction of the policy of selective admissions in colleges and universities on the basis of merit;
(ii) Use of regional languages as media of instruction at the university stage;
(iii) Adoption of 10+2+3 pattern of school and college education;
(iv) Establishment of major universities; and
(v) Establishment of autonomous colleges.

As stated by Naik (1982) the post-independence period may be described literally as the 'Era of Higher Education' in Indian educational history. The elite group that came to power in 1947 longed for more higher education and better higher education, of which it had starved in the pre-independence period and, which alone could give it what it desired most. For about 15 years, from 1950-51 to 1965-66, the policy of open door admissions had created many problems. Therefore, the Education Commission (1964-66) recommended selective admissions and regulation of enrollments. This proposal was rejected, and therefore, the system expanded in an unplanned manner. The national policy on education, 1968 made the following proposals for higher education:

(i) The number of whole time students to be admitted to a college or a university department should be determined with reference to the laboratory, library, and other physical facilities, and to the strength of the staff;
(ii) Due care is needed to be taken in establishing new universities. These should be started only after an adequate provision of funds has been made for the purpose and due care has been taken to ensure proper standards;
(iii) Special attention should be given to the organization of

courses and to the improvement of standards of teaching and research at all levels;

(iv) Centers of Advanced Study (CAS) should be strengthened and a small number of "clusters of centers" aiming at the highest possible standards in research and training should be established; and

(v) There is need to give increased support to research in universities generally. The institutions of research should, as far as possible, function within the fold of the universities or in intimate association with them.

The draft National Policy on Education, 1979 also made some important proposals for development of higher education. The major proposals include:

(i) to devise measures to relieve pressure on higher education through vocationalization of secondary education, reformulation of recruitment policy of the government and de-linking jobs from the requirement of degrees;

(ii) to introduce the policy of selective admissions in institutions of higher learning with adequate safeguards for first generation learners, weaker sections, and women, and provision of part-time and own-time studies through correspondence courses;

(iii) to introduce three-year undergraduate courses under 10+2+3 and restructure courses to make them interdisciplinary with adequate provision of socially useful productive work (SUPW);

(iv) to encourage fundamental and applied research, especially, in science and technology by improving the quality of postgraduate education and research;

(v) to make 'extension' the third important function of universities in addition to teaching and research; and

(vi) to promote the quality of "centers of excellence" to make their standards comparable with the best in the world.

It must be clear by now that the NPE-1968 and the draft NPE-1979 drew most of their proposals from the Report of the Education Commission (1964-66). On the lines of these proposals, the higher education made considerable progress during the period from 1966 to 1986. It was during this period that the maximum development took place in other sectors of education also. The number of universities/university level institutions increased from only 75 in 1965-66 to 164 in 1985-86, the number of colleges increased from 2572 to 5816 during the same period. The student enrollment increased from 10.67 lakhs to 35.71 lakhs, recording over two-fold growth. However, the Annual Compound Growth rate (ACGR) of enrollment during the same period slowed down form 13.90% to 5.10%, the lowest of it being 2.80% during the period 1976-81. This was probably due to the larger denominator.

The National Policy on Education, 1986 also made important proposals for the quantitative and qualitative development of higher education in India. The NPE-1986 as revised in 1992 proposed:

- *(i)* to lay more emphasis, in future, on consolidation and expansion of the facilities of existing institutions;
- *(ii)* to take urgent steps to prevent the system from degeneration;
- *(iii)* to develop autonomous colleges in large numbers until the affiliating system is replaced by a freer and more creative association of universities with colleges;
- *(iv)* to develop, on similar lines, the autonomous departments in the universities, on a selective basis, with freedom being accompanied by accountability;
- *(v)* to redesign courses and programs to meet the demands of specialization better, and to enhance linguistic competence and flexibility in combination of courses;
- *(vi)* to develop planning and coordination mechanism at state levels through State Councils of Higher Education (SCHEs), which would function in close association with the UGC;
- *(vii)* to provide for minimum essential facilities and regulate admissions according to capacity, transform teaching methods by introducing electronic media, and develop science and technology curricula;
- *(viii)* to introduce in-service teacher orientation and continuing refresher programmes in order to improve the quality of teaching, and to systematically assess teacher performance and to fill all posts on the basis of merit;

(ix) to provide enhanced support to research, especially in science and technology, by setting up suitable coordination mechanisms and national research facilities within the university system having proper autonomous management;

(x) to establish autonomous commission to foster and improve teaching and research in Sanskrit and other classical languages, and to support interdisciplinary research in social sciences and humanities;

(xi) to set up a national body covering higher education in general, agriculture, medical, technical, legal, and other professional fields for sharing of facilities and developing interdisciplinary research; and

(xii) to strengthen Indira Gandhi National Open University (IGNOU) established in 1985 to democratize education through flexibility and innovative programmes of open learning system and to support establishment of open universities in the states.

Autonomous Colleges

The NPE-1986 called for effective and speedy implementation of its proposals in order to achieve desirable results. Though, one of the proposals was to lay more emphasis on consolidation of facilities, yet the unplanned proliferation of colleges and universities continues unabated. On the average, 5-6 universities and 250-400 colleges are established every year in different parts of the country. Consequently, the quality of education is deteriorating everyday, in spite of the claim that efforts would be made to prevent the system from degradation. The Education Commission (1964-66) had recommended the concept of autonomous colleges with a view to providing academic freedom to potential colleges, especially in designing curricula, evolving new methods of teaching, research and learning, framing own rules for admission, prescribing own courses of study and conducting examination. Under this scheme, a college declared autonomous by its affiliating university is fully accountable for the content and quality of education it imparts. The scheme of conferring autonomy on colleges has since been revised to develop adequate criteria for selection of colleges for autonomous status. The new guidelines issued by the UGC provide for financial assistance of Rs. 4-6 lakhs per annum to undergraduate colleges, and Rs. 8 lakhs to colleges offering both undergraduate and postgraduate courses. Under these guidelines, 123 colleges had been awarded autonomous status by the UGC by 1998-99, the number increasing to 131 by 1999-2000. However, most of these colleges are located in the southern states. Tamil Nadu has 49 autonomous colleges, Madhya Pradesh 40, Andhra pradesh 19, Himachal Pradesh 5, Orissa 11, Maharashtra and Uttar Pradesh 3 each, and Gujarat had 1 autonomous college. These autonomous colleges are independent in conducing examination and setting their own question papers, and recommending to the university concerned the names of candidates for the award of degrees. The NPE-1986 had envisaged the establishment of 500 autonomous colleges in the Seventh Plan. The progress in this direction, therefore, is not satisfactory. The allied proposal of creating autonomous departments has not yet taken off.

The scheme of redesigning curricula, as suggested in the NPE-1986, has been partially implemented by the UGC through establishing 27 Curriculum Development Centers (CDCs) to prepare model curricula in Sciences, Humanities, and Social Sciences during the 7th Plan. By the end of 7th Plan, 9 universities and 290 colleges had restructured their undergraduate courses in accordance with these guidelines. This shows that the programme is going slow. Still there are many universities and colleges, which are yet to take decision regarding their courses. This situation arises because the UGC lacks a monitoring and evaluation mechanism and keeps away from exercising its powers of withholding grants to non-performing institutions.

The NPE-1986 had also envisaged establishment of the State Councils of Higher Education, one in each state, to coordinate the state level planning and to maintain proper linkages with the UGC for maintenance of standards. But, so far, only a few states have set up SCHEs. Some states are reluctant to pursue the proposal because of certain apprehensions about new power structure. Under the programme of providing information technology to the universities, a large number of universities and colleges have been provided with computer facilities. Universities are being increasingly encouraged to start programmes in computer applications.

In pursuance of the proposals regarding improvement of status and quality of teachers, several steps are to be taken. Prominent among them is creation of avenues for career advancement linked with performance and incentives for research in teaching. For organizing orientation programmes for newly appointed teachers, the UGC formulated a scheme of Academic Staff Colleges (ASCs) in 1987-88. Under this scheme 48 ASCs were started of which 45 were operational for some time. At present, the Total number of ASCs has increased to 50. In 1991, this scheme was reviewed by an expert committee, which recommended its continuation with improved design. Besides, there are 154 Staff Centers located in different universities to provide refresher courses to update knowledge and skills of teachers. The IGNOU has also started a Post-graduate Diploma in Higher Education (PGDHE), which is very popular and has been recognized by the UGC.

The NPE-1986 also envisaged the establishment of a national apex body to coordinate the activities of various other bodies in different fields of knowledge. Due to certain difficulties, such a body has not been set up so far. However, in March 1992 the UGC resolved to set up a National Assessment and Accreditation Council (NAAC) as an autonomous body for the appraisal and accreditation of institutional performance.

Based on the proposals of the NPE-1986, the UGC has started to conduct the National Eligibility Test (NET) to certify the eligibility of candidates for the award of research scholarships and appointment as lecturers in the universities and affiliated colleges. The idea, though innovative and good, could not receive wide acceptance, partly because of the interference of vested interests, and partly because of frequent relaxation and changes made by the UGC, probably under pressure of vested interests.

UNIVERSITY GRANTS COMMISSION (UGC)

The University Grants Commission (UGC) was originally created by an executive order of the Government of India in 1953, and became a statutory body in 1956 by an Act of Parliament. The UGC Act, 1956 entrusted this body with the responsibility of promotion and coordination of university education and of determination and maintenance of standards of teaching, examination and research. As a statutory body, it is responsible to the Parliament. Initially, it was to have nine members including the Chairman three of whom were to be the Vice Chancellors, two from among the officers of the government and three educationists of repute. The Chairman was to be the whole time salaried person and not an officer of the Central or State governments.

The composition of the UGC was changed by the government through a Constitutional Amendment in 1972 to increase the total number of members from nine to twelve. The amendment also increased the powers of the UGC. The new composition includes the Chairman, Vice Chairman and ten members. The term of the Chairman is five years and that of the Vice-Chairman and other members, is three years. No member including the Chairman and the Vice-Chairman can hold office for more than two terms. The Constitutional Amendment of 1976 placing education in the concurrent list widened the scope of the activities of the UGC. The UGC performs two main functions:

(i) Disbursement of grants to eligible universities and colleges according to requirements; and
(ii) Determination and maintenance of standards in higher education.

Under function (i), the UGC has to identify the financial requirements of individual universities before disbursing grants. For this purpose, the UGC is empowered to make inquiries and conduct surveys if deemed necessary. All the eligible universities, central state or deemed to be, are entitled for development grant, but maintenance grant is provided only to central universities, and in special cases, to institutions deemed to be universities. Under function (ii), it has both recommendatory and advisory roles. It can make specific recommendations to the universities for improvement of teaching and research. In pursuance of this, the UGC has already issued guidelines to the universities regarding research activities, minimum workload of teachers and examination reforms, and qualifications of teachers. The UGC can also issue guidelines to the universities regarding implementation of government policies.

The UGC can also conduct an inspection in a university, if thought necessary, and recommend measures for improvement. It can withhold grant of a university in case of non-compliance of the guidelines issued by it or failure to maintain adequate standards of teaching, examination and research. Although, the

UGC has been given the responsibility of determining and maintaining standards, it has limited powers for having its guidelines implemented by the universities. However, to carry out its functions of determination and maintenance of standards of education, it has formulated several important programmes and issued guidelines for their implementation.

Special Assistance Programme (SAP)

Promotion of research in the universities is one of the important functions of the UGC, which it carries out through three programmes—SAP, COSIST and COSIP/COHSSIP. Under these programmes the UGC provides financial assistance, on selective basis, to such departments that have shown potential to conduct quality research in specific areas or are reputed centers of learning in them. It is expected that in the course of time such departments would develop into centers of excellence comparable to other leading institutions of the world. Under Special Assistance Programme (SAP), the UGC provides support to selected university departments in sciences, humanities and social sciences, and engineering and technology, at three levels:

(i) Centers of Advanced Study (CAS);
(ii) Department of Special Assistance (DSA); and
(iii) Departmental Research Support (DRS).

The Center of Advanced Study programme was initiated by the UGC on the recommendations of Education Commission (1964-66) for "encouraging the pursuit of excellence in certain specific fields and raising the level and quality of academic achievement at the post-graduate and research levels." A few centers have been selected on the basis of their work, existing facilities and potentialities to function as Centers of Advanced Study (CAS) in specific disciplines. The chief functions of a CAS include organization of refresher courses for teachers, seminars, symposia and conferences on specialized topics to bring out research publications. According to the latest available UGC report (1999-2000), there are 13 CAS in humanities and social sciences and 39 in sciences, engineering and technology (Table 7.2).

Table 7.2
Development of SAP (CAS/DSA/DRS) since 1990-91

Year	*Humanities & Social Sciences*			*Science & Technology*		
	CAS	*DSA*	*DRS*	*CAS*	*DSA*	*DRS*
1991-92	16	101	22	41	109	47
1992-93	16	102	20	41	111	44
1993-94	16	110	40	41	115	81
1994-95	16	108	47	41	115	87
1995-96	16	109	45	40	118	77
1996-97	19	99	44	39	116	75
1997-98	14	98	40	39	115	71
1998-99	13	89	52	40	110	83
1999-2000	13	86	53	39	108	73

Source: UGC Annual Reports from 1991-92 to 1999-2000.

Similarly, the UGC provides special assistance to selected university departments for undertaking academic programmes in "specific fields". Such a department is identified on the basis of recommendations of a Visiting Committee appointed by the UGC. By 1999-2000, there were 86 DSAs in humanities and social sciences, and 108 in sciences, engineering and technology. Besides, the UGC also provides assistance to selected university departments for undertaking research. By 1998-99, there were 53 DRSs in humanities and social sciences, and 73 in sciences, engineering and technology.

The SAP was reviewed by the UGC in 1992-93 and the ceiling of assistance was raised for science subjects (including mathematics and statistics) to Rs. 60 lakh, 50 lakh and 35 lakh for CAS, DSA, and DRS respectively. For humanities and social sciences, the level of assistance provided is about half the above amounts extendable in special cases. The performance of SAP departments is evaluated regularly through continuous monitoring on the basis of which it is determined whether the assistance to a department be allowed to continue at the same level, be upgraded to the next higher level or be discontinued. During the year 1998-99, the UGC took a decision to induct 25 departments in SAP at the level of DRS every year.

Strengthening of Infrastructure in Science and Technology

The UGC assists, on selective basis, a few Science and Technology Departments in the universities/institutions of higher learning for acquiring highly sophisticated equipment to enable them to become internationally competitive in frontier areas of teaching and research. These departments are selected on the basis of norms fixed by a Standing Committee and advice taken from experts in the concerned fields. The COSIST departments enjoy financial autonomy, and 5% of the cost of the equipment is also provided for the maintenance of the equipment. By the year 1998-99, 195 departments had been provided support under the COSIST programme. After a review in 1992-93, the COSIST programme has been integrated with SAP schemes.

Curriculum Development

The UGC set up 27 Curriculum Development Centers (CDCs), 10 in sciences and 17 in humanities and social sciences to review the existing syllabi in different disciplines at various levels (UGC Report 1993-94). These centers have been functioning since 1986 and have developed model curricula in different subjects. These model curricula are available as printed documents at subsidized rates to institutions and individual teachers.

The UGC also initiated a scheme of restructuring of courses at first-degree level during the 5th Plan, to make them employment oriented and relevant to developmental needs. The structured courses consist of the following components:

(i) A "foundation course" aiming at creating awareness among the youth about Indian history, culture, freedom movement, role of science and technology in India, culture of Asia and Africa, Gandhian thought etc.;

(ii) A "core course" to help the students acquire broad familiarity with chosen disciplines, including study of one and more in depth; and

(iii) An "application oriented component" intended to expose students to the world of work.

A college or a university is provided with an assistance of Rs. 7.5 lakh for five years by the UGC for introducing structured courses.

Improvement of Colleges

The UGC launched the College Science Improvement Programme (COSIP) in 1971 for the improvement of science teaching in affiliated colleges by bringing about qualitative improvement in all aspects of teaching science such as subject matter, teaching methods, curricula and syllabi, laboratory work, library, workshops and teaching materials. This programme was being implemented in 314 colleges as on 31.3.1994. A similar programme known as "College Humanities and Social Sciences Improvement Programme (COHSSIP)" was launched by the UGC in 1974-75, for improving quality of teaching humanities and social sciences in affiliated colleges. By March 1994, 784 colleges (including 50 teachers' training colleges) had been assisted under this scheme.

A programme was also launched to initiate interaction between the faculties of selected departments of universities with similar departments of colleges affiliated to it. The main purpose was to enhance professional competence of college teachers. This programme was called university leadership program (ULP). This program was discontinued after evaluation in 1992-93.

Some Other Programmes of the UGC

In order to provide avenues to the vocational pass-outs of +2 stage, the UGC appointed a Core Committee to devise a plan and course design to introduce vocational courses at first-degree level. The Committee recommended 35 vocational subjects to be introduced at undergraduate level covering all faculties along with requirement of infrastructure and implementation strategy. The report of the Core Committee was approved by the UGC and it was proposed that these programs would be implemented soon. The universities were immediately asked to send their proposals to the UGC.

The UGC has also constituted Subject Panels in 27 subjects to advise the Commission on several matters regarding improvement of quality of teaching and research in individual subjects. These panels are very useful to the UGC. The UGC has also made arrangement with the Doordarshan for allocation of transmission time for Countrywide Classroom Programme (CCP) of the UGC, between 1:00 P.M. to 2:00 P.M. for six days in a week, and between 6:00 A.M. to 7:00 A.M. on four days in a week. This programme has taken higher education to remote areas of the country. Similar programmes are also telecast in Hindi. These programmes are produced by Educational Media Research Centers (EMRCs) and Audio-Visual Research Centers (AVRCs) located at selected universities.

For optimum utilization of sophisticated equipment in teaching and research, the UGC has introduced the idea of "common pool". The UGC has set up University Science Instrumentation Centers (USICs) in selected universities. By 1997, the UGC had provided assistance to 75 universities for setting up USICs. The UGC has also initiated schemes for human resource development in teaching and research. Under this scheme, grants are available for organizing seminars and workshops at national and international levels. For outstanding teachers, the scheme of National Fellowships, Visiting Associateships, Guest or Part-time Teachers, Visiting Professorships, and Teacher Fellowships have been in operation for various purposes.

For encouraging research activities, the UGC provides grants for Major and Minor Research Projects to be undertaken by teachers in science, engineering and technology, humanities and social sciences Financial assistance is also available for writing quality books, monographs, and reference materials for use in universities and colleges. Similarly, partial Travel Grants are also provided to attend international conferences. The schemes of Career Awards for young teachers to pursue independent research and Emeritus Professorships for qualified retired teachers are also in operation.

SOME RECENT DEVELOPMENTS

Towards New Educational Management

The UGC had appointed a committee, headed by Prof. A. Gnanam, Vice-chancellor Bharathidasam University, Tiruchirapalli, to study the existing management patterns of the universities and recommend "Alternative Models of Management". The Committee submitted its report in January 1990, to the Chairman UGC. The Committee made wide-ranging recommendations relating to issues for improving efficiency in the management of the universities, which can be grouped in the following broad categories:

(*i*) Relationship of universities with central/state governments, UGC and State Councils of Higher Education;
(*ii*) Delegation of powers and decentralization of university management;
(*iii*) 'Autonomy' in the universities; and
(*iv*) Role of teachers, students, and society in management of universities.

The report of the Committee was placed before the Central Advisory Board of Education (CABE) at its meeting held on 8th and 9th March 1991(UGC Report, 1992-93). In view of the far-reaching implications of the recommendations contained in the Report, a CABE committee was formed under the chairmanship of the then Chief Minister of Gujarat. The terms of reference of the committee were:

(*i*) To consider the recommendations of the committee taking into account views of the state governments and the UGC in the light of the NPE-1986, and other developments since the formulation of the policy; and
(*ii*) To suggest the modalities of the implementation of the recommendations.

The deliberations, and consequently, the recommendations of the Gnanam Committee were based on the four basic principles of autonomy, participation, decentralization, and accountability (Gnanam, 1990). The Committee made 144 recommendations in a bulky report running into 400 pages. A few important recommendations are summarized below:

(*i*) University autonomy should be considered an essential pre-requisite for ensuring academic excellence and development. Therefore, autonomy of the universities, faculties within universities, departments of studies and the individual teachers should be ensured.
(*ii*) In order to ensure increased participation of all sections of the university community — students, teachers, and non-teaching staff in the governance of the university, clear policies should be laid down regarding election and nomination of members in different governing bodies. For

nomination of teachers, seniority and rotation, and for that of students academic excellence and participation in curricular and extracurricular activities, should receive due consideration. The role of elections should be minimized.

(iii) The power structure in the university system should be decentralized with delegation of powers to Deans, and Heads of the Departments of Studies with Central Registry to play a coordinating role. In the case of affiliating universities, move should be initiated towards granting academic autonomy to colleges with ultimate objective of making all colleges autonomous within a specified time frame.

(iv) There should be both individual accountability and institutional accountability. Individual accountability of teachers should be ensured through participative and objective performance appraisal based on sound quantifiable norms. The institutional performance should be evaluated every five years by autonomous bodies established for the purpose.

(v) The Central Government/Parliament should enact core laws to be followed by the states, regarding university governance. Similarly, universities, both central and state, should formulate fresh regulations for election/nomination of members to various governing bodies. A Council of Central Universities should be formed to play a coordinating role.

(vi) The UGC should have more powers and involvement in the development of higher education. It should establish Regional Centers to decentralize work. New universities should be opened only with prior concurrence of the UGC as obligatory.

(vii) State governments should constitute State Councils of Higher Education (SCHEs) for coordination of functions of the universities and for effective liaison with the state government and the UGC. It should be obligatory for the state universities also to follow the regulations framed by the UGC.

(viii) The universities should redesign the structure of their governing bodies and their functions so as to incorporate the recommendations of the Committee. The changes made, in this regard, be communicated to the State Council of Higher Education and the concerned State government.

Committee on Funding of Higher Education

The UGC had appointed, in November 1992, a high powered committee "to examine the present financial position in regard to Central Universities, institutions deemed to be universities, colleges of Delhi and technical institutions funded by the government of India, and to make recommendations about their financial needs and systems for the future." Justice (Dr) K. Punnayya headed the Committee.

The Committee made a thorough study of the existing pattern of funding of Central Universities, institutions deemed universities, and colleges affiliated to University of Delhi and Banaras Hindu University, in consultation with the UGC, the authorities of concerned universities/institutions and came across many weaknesses and anomalies. In view of academic, political, and social aspects of the problems and issues involved, the committee made the following recommendations:

(i) The income generated by a university in a given financial year, should not be deducted from the block grant and be kept in a separate fund for future utilization. The UGC may provide a matching additional grant as an incentive. There should be 100% tax concession on endowments, donations and other contributions, to the donors.

(ii) The Central/State governments should continue to fund the universities for essential development and maintenance requirements. However, the universities should try to recover a large portion of costs of education through fees, mainly from those who can afford to pay.

(iii) The Central universities should adopt a mix of input funding and student funding, the student funding being based on merit-cum-means criteria. The funding pattern should be standardized over comparable courses of study.

(iv) The unit cost system should determine eligibility for grants instead of existing incremental system. From Ninth Plan onwards grants should be provided on unit cost basis.

(v) The government grants must cover the wage bill of universities including periodic increases, and the subsidy on the student services such as electricity, transport, water supply, etc. should be reduced to the minimum.

(vi) The annual maintenance grant should be released in instalments—20% in April-May, 60% in September-October, and 20% in December. The development grants should be linked to an academic audit system and performance indicator. The central universities must avoid offering conventional courses unless they are specially needed.

(vii) The UGC should constitute a standing advisory committee to evaluate the perspective plans of central universities. The UGC should have special provision of funds in the plan for new courses and research in areas identified by the UGC.

(viii) The academic cost (the expenditure incurred directly on teaching and research) should be 60-65%, academic administration cost 10-12% and other costs (such as on auxiliary services) 20-25%, of the total maintenance grant.

(ix) The student-teacher ratio should be 1 : 12 and teaching-non-teaching staff ratio should be 1 : 3, and employees like gardeners, safaiwalas, watchwards etc. should be engaged on contract basis to the extent possible.

(x) The minimum workload of all categories of teachers should be 40 hours a week with adequate allocation to actual teaching, tutorials, research, study, supervision and consultation, examination and administrative work. The academic audit system should be introduced to monitor performance.

(xi) While UGC/government may continue to be the major funding agency, the universities must generate internal resources by upward revision of tuition and hostel fees, library, laboratory and sports fees. The income so generated be utilized for scholarships and fellowships programmes for weaker sections, the universities may let out their playgrounds and auditoriums for public functions to generate funds. The resources generated should rise to at least 15% of the total recurring expenditure within five years, and to 25 % within 10 years.

(xii) The income generated by the university and the matching grants provided by the UGC may be used for development of infrastructure, scholarships and for other support services.

(xiii) The UGC may introduce a broad-based scheme of scholarships and free-ships to postgraduate students to cover 20% of them including meritorious students belonging to weaker sections. The soft loan scheme may be introduced for needy and disadvantaged students.

(xiv) The colleges affiliated to central universities should also follow similar strategies of income generation and management of expenditure.

National Assessment and Accreditation Council (NAAC)

Earlier, higher education was not accessible to all; rather, it was available only to a privileged few, who could afford to send their children for higher studies to expensive big cities. This was so because the institutions of higher education were small in number, and located only in big cities. Consequently, higher education was not available in abundance. There was no other choice except to educate children in the institutions, which were available. But now, we have so many institutions of higher learning, and the prospective students are free to make choices keeping in view the quality of education imparted in these institutions. Therefore, even if we do not assess and accredit the institutions of higher learning, people have already graded them according to their quality. For instance, IITs are preferred by the public to other institutions of engineering and technology for engineering courses. This may be termed as "social accreditation". But, institutions do not worry about it so long as funds are made available by the government without reference to the quality of education provided by them. The cost of higher education is so high that we cannot afford to finance all the institutions indiscriminately irrespective of their quality, because then, we would be doing injustice to poor masses that finance them through indirect taxes. Therefore, assessment of performance of institutions of higher education and grading them according to quality is essential. It has the following main advantages:

(i) It will help students and parents make right decision regarding choice of educational institution so that they

might receive proper return of the investment incurred on education.

(ii) It will help the government and the UGC monitor the functioning of universities and colleges and allocate funds accordingly in order to avoid wastage of public money.

(iii) When funding will be linked to performance, the institutions of higher learning will strive hard to improve their quality for attracting increased funds during the succeeding year. It will also act as a check against the proliferation of substandard colleges.

(iv) In the process, the environment of universities/colleges will be de-politicized, and a work-culture, which has been missing for the last five decades, will be developed.

The system of higher education in India has grown so large that the entire financial input available is used up in keeping the system going, rather than, initiating new schemes. Even though the financial inputs in higher education have increased almost ten times during the last 50 years, there is always a resource crunch. Under section 12 of the UGC Act 1956, the UGC has to take all such steps as it may deem fit for the "coordination and promotion of higher education and for determination and maintenance of standards of teaching examination and research" in the institutions of higher education. The NPE-1986 and subsequent POA-1986, also stated that "excellence of institutions of higher education is a function of many aspect; self-evaluation and self-improvement are important if a mechanism is set up, which will encourage self-assessment in institutions and also assessment and accreditation by a council..... the quality, process, participation, achievement etc., will be constantly monitored and improved."

In pursuance of above recommendations, the UGC, in July 1994, constituted a committee to finalize rules and regulations, and finally, in September 1994, the National Assessment and Accreditation Council (NAAC) came into existence with its headquarters at Bangalore (NAAC Document, 1995). In order to achieve its objectives, the NAAC will:

(i) devise and establish mechanisms for periodic assessment and accreditation of institutions of higher education, or units thereof, or specific academic programmes;

(ii) initiate research studies on the process of assessment and accreditation so as to evolve appropriate criteria, their application to various institutes of higher education, and to understand the interdependence of socio-demographic factors;

(iii) create an Information and Data Base in Higher Education (IDBHE) to keep abreast with the latest developments in higher education, particularly, in the area of assessment and accreditation;

(iv) establish financial relationship with the UGC for sharing of information in all such matters as are related to assessment and accreditation of higher education institutions. The NAAC may recommend, from time to time, to the UGC measures necessary for improvement of teaching and research in higher education; and

(v) publicize its results to the students, teaching community, funding agency, employees and public in general.

The NAAC is a founder member of the International Network for Quality Assurance Agencies in Higher Education (INQAAHE), which has 120 international agencies as members that are engaged in quality assessment, accreditation, and academic audit. It is an external Quality Assurance Agency like the Higher Education Quality Control Council of UK.

The NAAC would be assessing and accrediting either an isolated teaching programme or a group of activities or an institution as a whole, through a participatory process. The process involves the preparation of a self-study report by the institution, which is validated by a three to four-member peer team consisting of vice-chancellors, college principals, dean and senior teachers, and other educationists. The reports of self-assessment, on-site visits arranged by NAAC and in-house analysis of information are examined by the executive committee of NAAC, which takes a final decision about the assessment and accreditation on the basis of recommendations of visiting teams and self-assessment reports. The report of the visiting team would be confidential and would be made available only to the institution concerned or to the UGC. However, the final decision on accreditation would be released to the public.

Quality assurance in higher education has, in fact, become a global issue with many countries calling for international standards. This aspect is particularly relevant in India (Powar, 2000) where the quality of institutions is variable, ranging from the excellent to poor, with a long tail of mediocrity. In view of the increased student mobility, and the need to provide international experience to both faculty and students, quality assurance should be a priority concern. All institutions must reach a certain minimum standard, and even the best must strive for continuous improvement. Therefore, in the initial years of twenty-first century, all academic institutions will have to develop internal mechanisms for monitoring activities, identify lacunae and shortcomings, and undertake effective measures to improve quality. There is a need for all academic institutions to undergo evaluation by an external agency for overall performance. In India, the agencies established for this purpose are the National Assessment and Accreditation Council (NAAC) under the UGC and the National Board of Accreditation (NBA) under the AICTE. It is in the context of institutional performance and accountability that UGC has set up such bodies. After considerable research and experimentation, NAAC has standardized a comprehensive model to measure the quality and relevance of the educational process in colleges and universities. As of now, accreditation is voluntary. But it is reported that the UGC has decided to make accreditation mandatory for institutions to receive their funds. In most of the western countries, accreditation is mandatory for institutions to receive public funds. An institution seeking accreditation will have to submit a Self-Study Report based on seven parameters (Kurup, 2000), each of which has been assigned a weight, as discussed below:

(i) *Curricular Aspects:* It deals with the comparability of the ongoing programme in the institution with its goals and objectives and carries a weight of 10 points out of 100.

(ii) *Teaching, Learning and Evaluation:* This is the most important parameter dealing with the quality of students' intake, the standard achieved by the students, the mode of teaching and learning, use of new technologies in teaching, variety of bridge and remedial courses, innovations in examinations, recruitment of staff, faculty development programmes, work

satisfaction of the faculty, and research output. This h. been assigned a weight of 40 points

(iii) *Research Consultancy and Extension:* This parameter related to the research efforts and output of the facult and students, and its social relevance. The weigh assigned to it is 5 point (in the case of a college).

(iv) *Infrastructure and Learning Resources:* It is related to th physical facilities such as library, laboratory, compute center, hostels, health and sports services, and thei optimum utilization. The weight assigned to it is 15.

(v) *Student Support and Progression:* This parameter deal with students' performance and employabilit (including self-employment), their feedback for teachers performance, and grievance redressing mechanism. Th weight assigned to it is 10 points.

(vi) *Organization and Management:* This is related to the governing mechanism, management of teaching-learning process, participation of different groups in the decision making, generation and utilization of funds, and future plans. Its weightage is 10.

(vii) *Healthy Practices:* This is related to interaction with the community, linkages with industry, educational extension and innovations, and other welfare activities. Its weight is 10 points.

As soon as the NAAC receives a self-study report from the institution, it appoints a committee (Peer Team) of the professionals from other states, which will visit the institution along with one or two experts from NAAC. After careful study and deliberations, the Peer Team will award a simple score (out of 100) for each of the parameters. These simple scores will be converted into weighted scores by multiplying each of them by corresponding weights, the sum of which is finally divided by 100 to obtain the institutional average. This institutional average is evaluated against the following classification scheme to award the given institution an appropriate Grade:

A***** 75 and above (Five Star)
A**** 70 to 75 (Four Star)
A*** 65 to70 (Three Star)
A** 60 to 65 (Two Star)
A* 55 to 60 (One Star)

In more than 50 countries where some form of accreditation is in practice, the accrediting agencies base their evaluation on a set of predetermined criteria or standards. The existing procedures for accreditation in the member countries of the International Network of Quality Assurance Agencies in Higher Education (INQAAHE) is based on two things—self-study report of the institution and peer judgement on the predetermined criteria or standards. The peer judgement with reference to the predetermined standards becomes the indicator of quality. If we want to evaluate an institution as a system in totality, we can have performance indicators with reference to input, process and output. Input indicators are concerned with the resources and factors employed in order to produce an institution's output. Process indicators relate to the way in which resources and factors are combined and used in order to produce the institution's output. Output indicators describe the outputs produced by the institution. These indicators are certainly useful to see whether the inputs have been transformed to the outputs of expected standards through appropriate processes.

The UGC had asked all the universities of India to undergo the process of assessment and accreditation by December 31, 2000, and all the colleges by December 31, 2003, but unfortunately, the eight-year old scheme could not achieve much success. Consequently, the UGC had to revise its deadline for accreditation of the universities to December 2002. However, by October 2002 (TOI, September 25, 2002) only 61 universities had got themselves accredited. Similarly, the compulsory accreditation deadline announced by the government for 12,000 odd colleges in the country is also drawing near and may be revised because only 200 colleges had got themselves accredited by October 2002. This means that the process is very slow. The NAAC has been functioning for the last 8 years but output is not satisfactory. This raises the basic question why universities and colleges are trying to shy away from undergoing evaluation of performance. The university community, including teachers and students, should realize that the common people who do not reap its benefits are financing higher education system. The universities have to be answerable to them.

The UGC and the NAAC have time and again warned the universities that if they did not come forward for assessment and accreditation, their annual grants would be frozen, but due to such a poor response, the drastic punitive step seems difficult to be exercised. The Expenditure reform Commission (ERC) of the Ministry of Human Resource Development, deploring the response of the universities and indifference of the UGC, has warned the NAAK to give a presentation. It has recommended that UGC should actively promote accreditation system by confining its assistance to only those universities and colleges, which acquire a grade above a specified minimum level during accreditation and also by offering assistance at a higher level to those who acquire a high grade. But, there is nothing new in it. The UGC has issues such warnings several times on several other matters, but has never withheld the grant of any university on the grounds of non-fulfilment of the requisite conditions.

PROBLEMS AND ISSUES

Despite visibly impressive achievements, there is a widespread dissatisfaction among the public in general and youth in particular. Some of the obvious problems are: poor quality of education, large scale unemployment, limited coverage, and in-built mal-practices coupled with heavy demand for higher education at low cost. This shows that there is something fundamentally wrong, and the entire system of higher education needs to be re-engineered. In this context, certain burning issues have to be examined and resolved. The discussion to follow concentrates on these issues (Chauhan, 2000).

Quantity Vs. Quality

Other things being equal, the quantity of a product is negatively correlated with its quality. When quantity of production is increased without corresponding increase or improvement in the input, the quality of the product is bound to deteriorate. This is exactly what has happened with our higher education system. The huge quantitative expansion has taken place at the cost of quality, especially, during the post-independence period. As stated by J.P. Naik (1982), the post-independence period might be described literally as the "Era of Higher Education" in the history of independent India.

During the period of five decades since 1947, there has been a phenomenal quantitative growth of higher education system. The number of universities and university level institutions has gone up from only 20 in 1947 to over 256 at present (1999-2000). The number of affiliated colleges has gone up from 500 to 12,000 during the same period. The total enrollment of students has also witnessed corresponding increase from less than 2 lakhs to over 77 lakhs (Gautam, 1999). Quantitatively, this has been a remarkable development characterized by 12-fold increase in the number of universities, twentyone-fold in the number of affiliated colleges, and over forty-fold in student enrollment. This disproportionate increase in the number of institutions and the enrollment has caused serious problems in maintaining classroom discipline. An unplanned expansion and establishment of substandard institutions has led to deterioration in the quality of teaching and research. About 45% of the affiliated colleges are listed in the category of non-viable colleges and are not eligible for UGC grant, because, these colleges do not fulfil the minimum requirements for this purpose. Consequently, there are full registers but empty classrooms.

There is large-scale unemployment among the university graduates. Of all the job-seekers registered with the employment exchanges about 67% are educated including over 5 million graduates and postgraduates. These figures also include doctors and engineers whose education and training costs the nation very heavily. Most of them are not only unemployed but also unemployable. About 88% of the total students enrolled at first degree level and 56.5% at postgraduate level attend the affiliated colleges most of which do not have adequate facilities (UGC Report, 1996-97). Moreover, the majority of those enrolled, about 82% are concentrated in the faculties of Arts, Science, and Commerce receiving general education in these areas without any vocational training. This means that professional education accounts for only 18% of the total enrollment. It is only this last group that can expect an early availability of jobs. Within this group also, only about 10% enrolled in engineering, technology, medicine, agriculture and veterinary science may expect smaller waiting period.

Despite such an unplanned and rapid expansion of higher education, only about 6% of the relevant age-group 18-23 years participate in it, whereas in USA, the corresponding figure is 50%.

Even in some of the developing countries, the participation in higher education is as high as 30% of the relevant age group. This shows that even in terms of quantity, our progress is not satisfactory. Now we should shift emphasis from linear expansion to qualitative development of higher education. It is good news that UGC plans to do so in the 9th plan period.

Equity Vs. Excellence

In Indian conditions, it appears that equity and excellence cannot go together. Although, linear expansion referred to earlier has taken care of equity in the sense that colleges are now available to common people, even in remote villages, within a radius of 100 kms. and universities and colleges have been set up in the culturally disadvantaged and geographically isolated areas, yet there is unending outcry regarding equity in higher education, especially in political circles. As guaranteed in the Constitution, reservation of seats has been made to the extent of 15% for Scheduled Castes and 7.5% for Scheduled Tribes, not only in general education but also in professional and technical courses. In some states, reservation is also available for "Other Backward Classes". For these groups even relaxation in minimum qualifications and age is provided under the law. Sometimes, reservation acquires such a high proportion that highly meritorious students are ignored in order to accommodate those belonging to reserved categories. Even teaching posts have not been spared. Our political system is responsible for this state of affairs. Perhaps, India is the only country in the world where talent is least honoured. The categorization of people on caste lines for the purpose of reservation is purely a political strategy to divide people to garner votes. The phenomenon of reservation based on caste is generating social conflicts on the one hand and encouraging brain drain on the other. It will backfire if not checked at the earliest.

In India, 75% of the people live in villages, most of them being under poverty line. The children of rural people remain at disadvantage, as they are obliged to study in schools and colleges having poor facilities. Therefore, they are unable to compete with their urban counterparts. Reservation policy would have been a little justified had it been based on socio-economic considerations. It is doubtful whether the existing approaches to achieve equity would promote excellence. Equity and excellence seem to be enemies of each other. There has to be some compromise between the twin objectives of achieving 'equity' and promoting 'excellence'. Higher education has to be reconstructed to take care of these issues. Can we sacrifice excellence over equity, which is a distant dream in Indian conditions? The concepts of equity and social justice need to be redefined so as to avoid wastage of talent and save higher education from the fatal attack of mediocrity.

Autonomy Vs. Accountability

The term 'autonomy' has proved to be a misnomer in Indian conditions. It has been both misinterpreted and misused. Everybody is asking for autonomy, be it an institution or an individual teacher. To them autonomy means "freedom for not accepting inconvenient or stringent norms". The UGC, which is a funding and monitoring body, is autonomous, and every university is also autonomous, the only relationship being that of funding. Under section 12 of the UGC Act, 1956 it can issue guidelines to the universities for improvement and maintenance of standards in teaching and research, but universities are not obliged to accept these guidelines. The governing bodies of the universities tend to accept these guidelines on selective basis picking up favourable elements and following them promptly, and ignoring the stringent norms. Therefore, in the name of autonomy, UGC guidelines are either not accepted or are implemented partially. The UGC has been issuing guideline regarding teaching, research, and examination from time to time, but many of these have not been implemented. Under the umbrella of autonomy, the universities frequently dilute the UGC norms so as to make them suitable to their local and often non-academic requirements. Sometimes, various pressure groups inside the university force the university bodies to dilute these standards. These situations arise because the UGC does not have mandatory powers, and hence, cannot force the universities to follow its guidelines.

Sometimes, there is slackness on the part of the UGC also. For example, UGC issued guidelines regarding qualifications and selection of teachers in the universities and colleges. As a part of these guidelines, the clearance of the National Eligibility Test (NET) was made an essential requirement for recruitment of lecturers in the universities and colleges. But, UGC has revised these guidelines several times leading to a lot of confusion. At present, different universities are following different patterns, some treating NET as an essential requirement while others using Ph.D. as a substitute for it. This is giving rise to malpractice in the teacher recruitment process. Autonomy should be taken to mean "freedom to grow in academic quality". It is freedom "to choose right ways and means" to achieve the objective of academic excellence, not to dilute the objective itself. The universities should be made to understand this point. Moreover, the UGC must exercise its powers to withhold grants to defaulter institutions in the case of delay in following its guidelines or diluting them. Accountability should be ensured at all costs.

Some kind of performance-based funding system should be evolved. The establishment of National Assessment and Accreditation Council (NAAC), an autonomous organization, by the UGC is an excellent step. The main function of this organization is to evaluate the performance of universities to encourage self-evaluation and accountability in higher education. Unfortunately, the idea is not being digested by the vested interests. There is some opposition to this process from some quarters. As assessment and accreditation is on voluntary basis, only a fraction of higher education system has come forward (Gautam, 1999) to be assessed and accredited. Consequently, the UGC is seriously considering making it compulsory for aided institutions to undergo the assessment and accreditation process conducted by the NAAC. Such an assessment will be linked with additional grants and awards. All the universities in the country will have to get assessed and ranked by December 31, 2000 and all colleges by December 31, 2003. The NAAC will grade the universities and colleges on a five-point scale on the basis of teaching, research, and infrastructure in addition to other parameters. The grading will range from 'outstanding' to 'disqualified'.

Public Vs. Private Funding

As the system of higher grew in size, its maintenance required more and more funds. At the same time, the proportion of non-governmental financial resources successively reduced. Consequently, the contribution of the government to educational finance increased from 57% in 1950-51 to about 92% at present, and that student fees decreased from over 20% to mere 7.5% during the same period. The expenditure on education as a proportion of GNP has marginally increased from 1.2% in 1950-51 to about 4% at present. In terms of plan expenditure, the share of education as a percentage of total plan outlay also decreased from 7.86 % in the First Plan to 2.97% in Sixth Plan, then marginally increased to 3.55% in Seventh Plan. In Eighth Plan, it was 3.7%, again a marginal improvement (Chauhan, 1999). We are still far behind the target of spending 6% of the GNP on education as recommended by the Education Commission (1964-66). The government had planned to achieve this goal by the end of Eighth Plan but failed.

It appears that the government is feeling shy of making any sizeable investment in higher education. In the First Plan, 22% of the plan outlay was earmarked for higher education (including technical education). The percentage rose to 38 during Fourth Plan, but came down to 33 in Sixth Plan (Azad, 2000). In Eighth Plan, the corresponding figure was 22 per cent, and in Ninth Plan it is 24%. This shows that most of the money to maintain the universities at present is provided by the government from public funds. In the case of central universities, dependence on government funds varies from 89% (Delhi University) to 98% (Vishva Bharti), and contribution of fees varies from less than 1% (JNU) to 10% (Delhi University). Punayya Committee (1993) has reported this. The situation in state universities is still worse. The overall scenario is that higher education is being subsidized by the government to the extent of 90-95%. It has been estimated that beneficiaries of higher education received about Rs. 10,000 crores as subsidy while paying only 1.3% of the total cost of their education. A survey conducted by the NCERT during 1960s showed that 80% of university and high school completers came from the top 20% of the income groups. A similar study conducted by the UGC during 1970s revealed that 70% of the university students came from top 20% of the income groups. On the other hand, 70% of the government revenue came from indirect taxes paid by all citizens of which 60% were living in poverty (Mitra, 1993). This shows that through education scarce financial resources are being passed on from poor to the rich. Therefore, one important issue is the extent to which we can subsidize higher education.

Those who are benefited by the subsidy in higher education do not bother about its quality because they are getting it free. When beneficiary of education has to pay (as in the case of public schools), he expresses concern about its quality. But, in the case of higher education, the amount of fees has been kept frozen for decades and there has been no upward revision. As higher education has been monopolized by the well to do, the major part of the subsidy is going to those who do not need it. Another paradox is that the more expensive the course (such as medicine, engineering and management), the larger the subsidy (Balachander, 1993). A graduate in general education pays about 14% of the cost of his education while a graduate in more expensive professional courses pays only 9 per cent. Is it not contrary to all norms of equity and social justice? Here is a case for increasing fees so as to cover at least 50% of the cost in general education. In professional education, the fee may be even higher because these courses lead to higher personal economic returns. But, how to accommodate those who cannot pay, is a million-dollar question. This is an important issue requiring an intensive national debate till a workable solution is found.

English Vs. Regional Languages

One of the important recommendations of the Education Commission (1964-66) was that regional languages be used as media of instruction in universities and colleges instead of English. But, this recommendation could not be implemented so far because of certain controversies involved in it. Although everybody agrees that English has not been very effective as a medium of instruction, yet no consensus has so far been evolved on this issue. It has been observed and proved through researches that poor linguistic ability is a serious handicap in learning and causes downfall in the quality of education. In our universities and colleges, undergraduate students, in general, have poor linguistic ability, which tells upon their academic achievement. English is used as a medium of instruction in most of the courses taught in our universities. This is truer for scientific and technological courses.

It is now believed that English is not working well as a medium of instruction for an average student. Students read books in English but do not comprehend the substance given in them. This is evident from the large-scale failures (about 50%) in examinations at undergraduate stage. With phenomenal growth in the number of

English medium schools after independence, the literacy in English might have increased, but quality of knowledge of English as a language has been decaying. The situation is so bad that a graduate, sometimes, cannot write an application in English. Whatever may be the arguments, it is true that we cannot pull on with English as a medium of instruction indefinitely as standard of English language is deteriorating very fast in India. Not to talk of students, even teachers fail to speak/write correct English. It is, sometimes, argued that good literature, in all subjects and fields, is available only in English. Hence, English should continue as a medium till good books are produced in Hindi or in other regional languages. Some universities, especially in Hindi speaking areas, have already started using Hindi as a medium of instruction in Arts, Commerce, and Social Sciences. This shows that there has been some progress in the direction of 'Indianization' of medium of instruction, but still it continues to be a burning issue.

Open-door Vs. Restricted Entry

Article 45 of the Indian Constitution guarantees free and compulsory education for all children in the age-group 6-14 years. Hence, elementary education may be considered as a right granted by the Constitution, and a responsibility of the government towards every citizen. But, education beyond elementary stage is supposed to be provided on selective basis, the selection being made on the basis of well-defined criteria. In view of this, all the commissions and committees on education appointed by the government during the post-independence period have suggested some kind of selective approach of admission to institutions of higher learning. Hence, secondary and higher education cannot be claimed by anybody as a matter of right, and may not be provided free of cost or at a highly subsidized price. However, due to certain socio-political reasons, the government of India has been following an open-door policy in college admissions, thus providing admission to all those who desire higher education even if many of them do not deserve. Consequently, three kinds of students are enrolled in colleges and universities (Chauhan, 1997):

(i) Those who, both desire and deserve *i.e.* those who are genuine learners interested in and capable of receiving higher education;

(ii) Those who desire but do not deserve *i.e.* those who attach a social status to a university degree and higher education but lack basic capabilities to benefit from it;

(iii) Those who neither desire nor deserve *i.e.* those who are not genuine learners but seek admission to colleges/ universities for passing their leisure time.

The first of these categories constitutes a small minority of students enrolled in colleges and universities. It is this group that keeps the system going and passes out as a quality product followed by second group of second graders who fill up ministerial positions in the government and private sector. The third group consists of trouble-makers coming from middle class families busy in status making and sending their children to schools and colleges to keep themselves free. It is this group that creates and organizes campus problems, mostly at the instance of outsiders, anti-social elements, and political parties. The college/university authorities are, most of the times, busy in managing the conflicts created by them. Dr. Amrik Singh called this phenomenon 'babysitting'. The main business of this group is to organize strikes, dharnas, lock-ups, and gheraos, mostly on non-academic issues. A handful of these trouble-makers emerge as student leaders, teacher politicians, and then as national leaders. This explains the rampant corruption, not only in public life, but also in the government. Therefore, open-door policy of admissions at higher education stage has proved to be counter-productive. Can we risk the future of higher education by continuing with this approach indefinitely? The following statement of the Education Commission (1964-66) should have acted as warning for our policy makers:

> A system of university education, which produces a high proportion of competent manpower, is of great assistance in increasing productivity and promoting economic growth. Another system of higher education with the same total output but producing a large proportion of indifferently educated graduates of arts, many of whom remain unemployed or are even unemployable, could create social tensions and retard economic growth. It is only the right type of education, provided on an adequate scale that can lead to national development; when these conditions are not satisfied, the opposite effect may result.

Competitive Vs. Time-Bound Promotions

Prior to 1983, there was only one avenue of promotion for university and college teachers to higher grades/ranks, that is, open competition on all India basis through general advertisement of vacancies. Those who showed distinctively superior performance in teaching and research filled up the few seniors and sanctioned positions available. But, this method denied opportunities of promotions to many erudite and deserving teachers for want of adequate number of senior positions. Due to this problem, many scholarly persons stagnated for a long time on the same positions of Lecturers or Readers. This created frustration among them and had adverse impact on their job-satisfaction and efficiency. In order to solve this problem, the UGC launched what was called the Merit Promotion Scheme (MPS) to be implemented by the universities and colleges under certain norms and guidelines formulated and circulated by the UGC. The main objectives of the scheme were: *(i)* to recognize "outstanding work" done by the university and college teachers in areas of teaching and research; *(ii)* subject such work to 'objective' evaluation by 'experts' in the subjects/areas concerned; and *(iii)* to provide for reasonable opportunities for professional advancement to such teachers who merit academic recognition on a 'competitive' basis.

Although, the procedure of implementation of the scheme was clearly spelled out by the UGC, yet sufficient room was left for manipulation and misuse. As stated in the objectives, the scheme was meant for those who were deserving and qualified to be appointed against open posts, but could not be appointed/promoted because sufficient sanctioned posts were not available. Unfortunately, contrary to the spirit of the scheme, the major advantage was cornered by under-qualified and undeserving persons. In fact, many of those who were not found qualified, and hence were not called even for interview for open posts, were interviewed and promoted under merit promotion scheme. Not only this, in some universities, the condition of objective evaluation of academic work by external experts in the concerned subjects was also strategically done away with in order to serve vested interests. Consequently, some persons having consistently poor academic record and without any academic/published work at their credit, got promoted to the higher academic positions of

Readers and Professors, mostly on extra-academic considerations. Instead of recognizing and rewarding outstanding work, some of those without doing any work were also promoted, thus rewarding not only under-performance but also non-performance.

This, however, is not to say that only undeserving persons were benefited by this scheme. There were some beneficiaries who really deserved promotion on the basis of their excellent work, but many of them were considered under merit promotion scheme even though open posts were available. This was a kind of punishment to them for doing work. There have been instances when the same selection committee promoted a deserving teacher under MPS and a not so deserving one on open post. Thus, the scheme proved to be a via media of punishment for some (erudite) teachers and reward for many (mediocre). There were two important conditions attached to the scheme; one, that nobody would be promoted under this scheme more than once in life; two, that not more than 33.3% teachers would be promoted under this scheme to the next higher ranks. The universities set both of these conditions aside and the scheme reduced practically to a "Mass Promotion Scheme". The scheme has been misused to such an extent that in some departments/institutions, where even a single sanctioned post does not exist, dozens of persons have been designated as professors under MPS.

When pay scales were revised in 1986 after the implementation of the recommendations of the Fourth Pay Commission, the UGC formulated another parallel scheme known as Career Advancement Scheme (CAS), with the same intentions. But, this time separate pay scales were recommended for those promoted under open selection and MPS/CAS schemes. This created further confusion and universities availed of the opportunity to utilize both, MPS and CAS schemes, to the advantage of favourites, and to satisfy pressure groups. It is no wonder as the universities, in order to dilute standards and violate norms, generally use the concept of autonomy. At present, the majority of Readers and Professors in the universities consists of those who have been promoted under MPS or CAS schemes. Every body is a winner, the only losers being the "academic standards" and the "public exchequer". Recently, on revision of pay scales after Fifth Pay Commission Report, the pay scales of Readers/Professors promoted under open and MPS/CAS schemes have been equated, again to satisfy the pressure groups. This is another reward for non-performance.

The entire episode has raised several contentious issues about seniority, workload, and administrative responsibilities. Who will be senior—the one who has been selected on an open post or the one who has been promoted under MPS/CAS? Who should be appointed as Dean of the Faculty or Head of the Department? These are the common disputes. Various Courts of Law, including the Supreme Court of India, have given conflicting judgements in these matters by interpreting the Acts and Statutes of different universities. In fact academic contentions cannot and should not be settled on the basis of technicalities, and hence should not be settled by courts. The legal experts interpret the 'language' of the acts and statutes and deliver judgements, without comprehending the "academic spirit" of the original scheme of the UGC. In some decisions, the courts have ordered preparation of separate seniority lists for the two categories of teachers—those promoted against open posts and those promoted under MPS/CAS. In certain other cases the courts have equated the two categories.

Recently, Dr. Sarup Singh, a former Vice Chancellor of Delhi University, through a petition in Delhi High Court has challenged the promotion policy for university and college teachers, followed by the UGC and has alleged that the academic standards are getting diluted through it (The Hindustan Times, Nov. 3, 2000). The petition seeks to quash the circular relating to the promotion of readers to professors and give directions to review the entire scheme propounded by the Malhotra Committee (1986) and Rastogi Committee (1997). The petition states that the MHRD and the UGC have, under the sustained pressure of teachers' organizations, been appointing teachers to the post of professor through promotion, and consequently, lowering the standards of academic performance. According to Dr. Sarup Singh "India is the only country in the world where a teacher can become professor through promotion". Out of a total strength of 3.5 lakh college/university teachers in India, 22.7% are professors. The petition further states that the MHRD, in implementing the scheme in college education also, virtually rewrote every report of the committees appointed by the UGC.

Another controversy has been about 'workload'. The UGC had given clear guidelines saying that a person promoted under MPS/CAS will carry the workload of his substantive position as every sanctioned post is justified by the workload attached to it. No teacher promoted under MPS/CAS can be given reduced workload.

But unfortunately, many universities are not following these guidelines in their letter and spirit. When a teacher promoted under the CAS/MPS scheme is given reduced workload, a part of his workload goes to the younger staff, thus, overburdening the young teachers with teaching load and hampering their research efforts.

According to the UGC Act, 1956 the main function of the UGC is to coordinate the development of higher education along with determination and maintenance of standards of teaching, research and examination. But, unfortunately, the UGC has been a silent witness to all that has been going on. The seriousness of the UGC and the Ministry of Human Resource Development about standards in higher education appears to be doubtful. If at all the situation is to be brought under control and the system of higher education is to be saved from blackmailing, the UGC must act. The implementation of the UGC schemes is not properly monitored. That is why minimum programme of examination reform, the teachers' workload suggested by the UGC, and measures to improve quality of research have met lukewarm response.

8

Teacher Education

It has been rightly remarked by an educationist (Saraf, 1996) that "there can be muddy teaching in marble halls and marvellous teaching in muddy walls". What he means is that a school does not mean simply a magnificent building with beautiful gardens and lawns, rich laboratories and libraries and large playgrounds. The school also does not mean simply a good curriculum with modern equipment such as computers, teaching machines and other technological devices. School, in fact, means a "learning environment", in which teacher has an important role to play. The technology cannot replace a teacher; it can only help him teach better. A bad teaching can undo the effect of a good curriculum and precious equipment.

The role of a teacher is not just limited to classroom teaching; he has to perform a very significant role in the community, of which he is a member. As an academic and intellectual member of the community, he cannot remain indifferent to what goes on in the social environment around him (Chauhan, 1998). Education is a social system which goes on changing along with changes taking place in the society. The role of the teacher also changes in order to cope with the changes in the society and education. This justifies the need, not only of pre-service training, but also of in-service training of teachers. When the 10+2+3 pattern of school and college education was being implemented during early 1970s, new demands were thrown on teachers and consequently, on teacher education institutions. The new structure of education brought about drastic changes in the existing system by introducing the concepts of vocationalization, work-experience, diversification and general education up to class X. These, and similar other changes, threw new challenges before teachers and teacher education institutions. Consequently, there was a strong move to revise teacher education programmes and to launch large-scale in-service teacher education courses to help teachers adjust to the new situation effectively. Similarly the NPE-1986 brought new ideas and fresh proposals to improve the quality of education at all levels with the introduction of concepts like Operation Blackboard, Minimum Levels of Learning, Micro-planning, Decentralized Management and modernization of teaching learning process. The implementation of these ideas required a large-scale orientation of teachers and a drastic change in pre-service teacher education programmes. This shows that every bit of change in school education has its implication for teacher education. The kind of teacher training imparted earlier, say 20 years ago, is no more relevant to the current educational scenario. Teacher training, therefore, is not a one-time affair; it is continuous process in a teacher's life. The following statement of Rabindra Nath Tagore is worth quoting here:

> A teacher can never truly teach unless he is still learning himself. A lamp can never light another lamp unless it continues to burn its own flame. The teacher who has come to the end of his subject, who has no living traffic with his knowledge, but merely repeats his lesson to his students, can only load their minds. He cannot quicken them. Truth not only must inform, but also must inspire. If the inspiration dies out and the information only accumulates then truth loses its infinity. The greater part of our learning in the schools has been a waste because for most of our teachers, their subjects are like dead specimens of once living things, with which they have a learned acquaintance, but no communication of life and love.

The theory and practice of teacher education is closely associated with how we define teaching. One controversial issue in this regard has been whether 'teaching' is an art or a science. Different schools of thought have taken different positions over this issue. One group argues that many great teachers like Socrates, John Dewey, Dr. Radhakrishnan and Dr. Zakir Husain did not receive any formal training, but they were regarded as great teachers. Therefore, teaching is an art, and proficiency in it depends on certain innate capacities and talents. The other group, on the other hand, emphasizing the role of certain acquired skills and capabilities in teaching, asserts that it is essentially a science. In order to take an objective view of the matter, we have to make a clear distinction between a social reformer who preaches certain moral and religious values, and a classroom teacher who teaches in a school setting and is responsible for modifying or changing the behaviour of a group of learners with varying capabilities and levels of motivation. Certainly, a classroom teacher in the latter sense of the term requires both innate capabilities and a set of acquired skills to deal with amazingly heterogeneous groups of learners. This ground reality makes us believe that teaching is both an art and a science. Any kind of formal training can hardly make an impact on those aspects of teaching behaviour which are related to teaching as an art, but as a science, teaching behaviour may be modified through education or training (Chauhan, 1999). This forms a basis for formulating and launching teacher education programmes for various levels of education.

HISTORICAL PERSPECTIVE

The idea of teacher education is perhaps as old as teaching itself. In the ancient times, teaching was considered neither a vocation nor a profession. It was a natural duty of a certain class of people called Brahmins who performed it, not for earning money, but for discharging their social obligation (Singh, 1996). Brahmins and priestly classes/castes had dominance on teaching profession because of their cultural superiority and other factors. Teachers enjoyed a respectable position in the society. The teacher-pupil relationships were extremely cordial. The teacher treated his students like his own sons and they lived with him like other members of his family. Sir Philip Hartog (1938) has made the following remarks about this phenomenon:

> I must say a word on that relation of guru and chela, of teacher to disciple, inseparable from the tradition of Hindu education. It is a relation of unselfish learning and devotion on the one side, of profound respect on the other. To the Brahmin guru teaching is no lucrative profession, but its own reward; the institutes of Manu forbade the payment of fees; the guru lived on a minimum and sometimes fed his own scholars; and we shall perhaps find the reflection of that ideal in what seem to us the absurdly low stipends of Indian teachers in primary schools.

About the dedication and simplicity of teachers during the pre-British period, Adam (1835) made the following remarks:

> The Pundits are of all ages from twenty-five to eighty-two; some just entering upon life, proud of their learning and panting for distinction; others of middle age, either enjoying a well-earned reputation or.....The humbleness and simplicity of their characters, their dwellings and their apparel, forcibly contrast with the extent of their acquirements and the refinements of their feelings. I saw men not only unpretending, but plain and simple in their manners.....living constantly half-naked, and realizing in this respect the descriptions of savage life;.... and yet several of these men are adepts in the subtleties of the profoundest grammar of what is probably the most philosophical language in existence;....They are in general shrewd, discriminating, and mild in their demeanor. The modesty of their character does not consist in abjectness to a supposed or official superior, but is equally known to each other.

Although, during that period no formal qualification or training was prescribed for becoming a teacher, yet very strict and stringent conditions were laid down, which were both academic and moral. However, no formal training programme for teachers was organized. Teachers followed the teaching methods of their own teachers. Thus, the teaching techniques were handed down from one generation of teachers to another. A teacher was expected to possess several qualities such as patience and impartiality. He was to be well grounded in his own branch of knowledge and was expected to continue to read throughout life. He must have a fluent delivery, readiness of wit, presence of mind, a great stock of interesting anecdotes, and must be able to expound the most difficult texts without any difficulty or delay (Altekar, 1951, p. 53).

The formal training programme for teachers was transplanted in India along with the British system of education, which though broad based, was alien to Indian traditions. The teaching profession broke the caste barriers and became available to the people of non-Brahmin castes also. The British Raj prescribed formal qualifications for becoming a teacher, which were gradually raised. In the course of time the formal training was also introduced as one of the qualifications of school teachers. The Danish missionaries made the formal beginning of teacher education, by setting up a Normal School at Serampore (Bengal) in 1793. In the beginning, the missionaries were interested in elementary education, but later on became enthusiastic about secondary education also. The first institution to train the secondary school teachers was opened at Madras (now Chennai) in 1856 (Singh, 1997). The second was set up at Lahore in 1880. In 1881-82, the total number of training schools was 113 enrolling about 4100 trainees. Their number increased to 152 in 1891-92, 179 in 1901-02, 575 in 1911-12, 1,072 in 1921-22, and then decreased to 612 in 1941-42. In 1946-47, the total number of training schools was 650 with an enrolment of 38,770 trainees (Table 8.1). In 1944, the Sargent Committee suggested that duration of training in normal schools, to award diplomas, should be of two years. We are still following the same pattern.

The development of secondary teacher education also took place slowly. Even by 1902, the total number of secondary teacher training institutions was not more than 6, in addition to a few secondary training schools. In 1904, the Government of India Resolution on Educational Policy desired that "teachers be trained in the art of teaching" and made the duration of training to be one year for graduates and two years for non-graduates. The Calcutta University Commission (1917-19) pointed out that poor quality of training is imparted in existing training colleges, and recommended the establishment of a Department of Education at the University to be manned by a Professor, Readers and Lecturers with a demonstration school attached to it, for experimentation with new methods of teaching, curriculum planning, and school organization. The Mysore University was the first to have a Faculty of Education (1925). In 1932, 13 universities had departments of education, and Bombay University was the first to launch M. Ed. programme in

1936. However, the number of secondary teacher training colleges increased to 31 by 1941-42 and 42 by 1946-47. The total enrollment of secondary teacher-trainees in these institutions was 3,100 in 1946-47 (Misra, 1962).

During that period, there was acute shortage of teachers. In the best primary schools, as reported by Philip Hartog (1939), there were four or five classes with three or more teachers. In the worst a single untrained teacher attempted to teach two, three, or four classes at the same time. The provinces differed greatly in this matter. Over 70% of the total 24,700 primary schools for boys in Bihar and Orissa, and 80% of the 45,600 in Bengal, were single-teacher schools in the year 1934-35. Of the 4,280 schools in the Central Provinces, the most advanced province in this respect, only 23.2% were single-teacher schools, and of 5,600 odd schools in Punjab, only 27.3% were single-teacher schools. The Government, therefore, inspired by Adam's suggestion, gave first priority to providing trained teachers. In 1932, half of the teachers in boys' primary schools were designated as trained, but of those more than one-third (61,895 out of 1,59,820) had themselves only received a primary education before receiving a year's training in a normal school. The Punjab had a higher proportion of trained teachers than any other province, 86.8% in 1936. The normal schools were sometimes separate institutions, as in England, and sometimes they consisted of a special class under the head teacher of a selected primary school.

Table 8.1
Teacher Education During the British Period

Year	*Training Schools*		*Training Colleges*	
	Number	*Enrollment*	*Number*	*Enrollment*
1881-82	113	4,080	*	*
1891-92	152	5,150	*	*
1901-02	179	5,700	*	*
1911-12	575	12,880	*	*
1921-22	1,072	26,930	*	*
1931-32	*	*	*	*
1941-42	612	32,120	31	2,500
1946-47	650	38,770	42	3,100

* Not available.

By 1947, the year of Independence, the system of teacher education in England had undergone considerable change. All educational changes in England had their impact in India also for obvious reasons. However, after independence a fresh thinking started. The University Education Commission (1948-49) was the first national body to give some serious thought to teacher education and a well-organized system of teacher education got established. In the beginning, teacher education programmes were available only to primary school teachers. But, later on, such facilities were made available to upper primary and secondary school teachers also. At present some kind of training is considered necessary even for teachers working in the colleges and universities. Thus, teacher education not only has developed into a full-fledged professional programme, but also widened its scope to cover the entire spectrum of education.

From the organizational point of view, there are mainly three types of agencies in India that carry out programmes of teacher education:

(i) Universities, which impart pre-service and in-service training through their departments of teacher education and affiliated teacher training colleges;

(ii) State governments, which have created state level training facilities in the form of State Institutes of Education (SIEs) and State Councils of Educational Research and Training (SCERTs); and

(iii) Autonomous bodies like the National Council of Educational Research and Training (NCERT) and National Institute of Educational Planning and Administration (NIEPA), which conduct in-service and pre-service training programmes at national level.

There are mainly three types of teacher training institutions for imparting training to teachers of elementary, secondary, and tertiary levels of education respectively. For elementary stage, a comprehensive training, generally of two years' duration, is organized, which leads to the award of a Diploma or a Certificate in teacher education. The candidates holding these diplomas/ certificates are eligible for appointment as teachers in primary as well as in upper primary schools. The minimum qualification for admission to these courses is High School or Matriculation. For the secondary school stage, training programmes are offered by the university departments of education or by colleges of education, which lead to the award of B.Ed. degree. These courses are of two years' duration. The B.Ed. degree holders are considered eligible for appointment as teachers in secondary schools. The minimum qualification for admission to these programmes is graduation (B. A., B. Sc., or B. Com.) from a recognized Indian or foreign university.

Training for teachers in higher education is relatively a new phenomenon. In pursuance of the proposals of the NPE-1986, the government of India has established 48 academic staff colleges (ASCs), which impart in-service training to teachers in higher education. Later on, a few more academic staff colleges were set up. At present, 51 of such ASCs are functioning. These institutions are fully financed by the UGC and are supposed to conduct orientation courses for newly recruited teachers and refresher courses for existing ones. The details of this scheme have been given in an earlier chapter. It is, therefore, evident that in India teacher education programmes are being organized at all level of educational ladder.

POLICIES AND PROGRAMMES

Education Commission (1964-66) had rightly said, "A sound programme of professional education of teachers is essential for the qualitative improvement of education. Investment in teacher education can yield very rich dividends because the financial resources required are small when measured against the resulting improvements in the education of the millions." The Commission made several useful recommendations for removing the isolation of teacher education from other sectors of education, improving the quality, and raising the status of teachers. Some of these recommendations are listed below:

(i) In order to remove the isolation of teacher education institutions from the academic life of the university, education should be recognized as an independent academic discipline, and should be introduced as an elective subject at first and second-degree levels. In pursuance of this recommendation 'education' has been

introduced at B.A. level, and in some universities an M.A. (Education) course is also being offered.

(ii) Selected universities should have "schools of education" to develop new programmes in teacher education and undertake quality research involving interdisciplinary approach.

(iii) Extension work should be regarded as an essential component of teacher education programmes and every teacher education institution should have an Extension Services Department as an integral part.

(iv) Recognized schools should be attached to teacher education institutions for practice teaching work, and periodic exchange of staff between the teacher education institutions and practicing schools should be arranged. Alumni associations should be established and strengthened for periodic dialogue and discussion.

(v) Attempts be made to upgrade the level of all the teacher education institutions so as to bring them under universities. Each state should have some Comprehensive Colleges of Education and a State Board of Teacher Education to coordinate their activities.

(vi) The quality of teacher education be improved by organizing subject oriented/upgradation programmes, introducing integrated teacher education courses, using improved methods of teaching and evaluation, improving practice teaching by introducing internship approach and revising curricula at all levels of teacher education.

(vii) The duration of teacher education courses should be two years for primary teachers who have completed the secondary school qualification, and one-year for secondary school teachers with graduate qualifications. The number of working days in a year should be 230.

(viii) The quality of staff in teacher education institutions should be improved. The secondary teacher training institutions should have staff members having double masters' degree, one in an academic discipline and another in education.

(ix) Staff in subjects like, psychology, sociology, science and mathematics may be appointed without any training if

otherwise qualified and competent. In primary teacher training institutions one masters' degree with B.Ed. should be an essential qualification for staff. The knowledge and skills of the staff should be improved through Summer Institutes.

(x) For untrained teachers working in the schools adequate arrangement of training through correspondence courses be made with liberal concessions. The universities and other bodies, at all levels, should organize a large-scale and coordinated programme of in-service teacher education. Every working teacher should be required to participate in some kind of in-service training programme after every five years.

(xi) For teachers in higher education also some kind of training programme be introduced so as to orient them to the profession. Regular orientation courses for new staff should be organized in every university and/or college. In bigger universities such programmes may be placed on a permanent basis by establishing a Staff College.

(xii) In addition to State Boards of Technical Education, the UGC should take the responsibility of maintaining standard in teacher education at national level by setting up a joint standing committee in collaboration with the NCERT. The government of India should make provision for adequate funds for teacher education sector both in state and central budget.

These recommendations of the commission were reflected in the statements of the National Policy on Education, 1968, which was the first policy resolution on education after independence. Regarding status, emoluments, and education of teachers, the Policy said:

(a) Of all the factors that determine the quality of education and its contribution to national development, the teacher is undoubtedly the most important. It is on his personal qualities and character, his educational qualifications and competence that the success of all educational endeavors must ultimately depend. Teachers must, therefore, be accorded honoured place in the society. Their emoluments

and other service conditions should be adequate and satisfactory having regard to their qualifications and responsibilities.

(*b*) The academic freedom of teachers to pursue and publish independent studies and researches and to speak and write about significant national and international issues should be protected.

(*c*) Teacher education, particularly in-service education, should receive due emphasis.

These proposals of the policy, though very comprehensive, and attractive, ended in smoke. The only recommendation that caught the attention of the decision-makers was that of enhancement of salaries to ensure that teachers get adequate remuneration so that the best talent is attracted to teaching profession. These recommendations made Mr. M.C. Chagla, then Minister of Education describe the report of the Commission as "Magna Charta of Teachers" (Naik, 19982). For various socio-political reasons, these recommendations of the Commission were implemented more effectively than others were. At the time of 1973 pay-revision exercise, teachers' salaries, at all levels, were improved. However, there was hardly any significant change by way of improvement in the programmes of teacher education.

Emphasizing the role that teachers can play in qualitative development of education, the Draft National Policy on Education (1979) also stated that professional competence of teachers be improved, their academic freedom be assured, and their awareness about their own role be strengthened. The Policy Document stated:

> The curriculum of teacher education at the elementary and secondary stages will be suitably changed in order to enable teachers to play their proper role in reforming education. Pedagogical and professional preparation of teachers in higher education should also be provided. Facilities for in-service education of teachers will also be expanded. Centers for developing curriculum material and teaching aids will be established, especially, for the benefit of teachers in rural areas and for both formal and non-formal systems of education.

During the period of about two decades from the publication of the Education Commission Report in 1966 and launching of the

NPE-1986, the progress of teacher education was rather slow. Hardly any new programmes were launched during this period except when 10+2+3 pattern of school and college education was implemented during seventies. During that period some reorientation/refresher programmes were arranged to acquaint teachers with new curricula and methodologies of instruction. Teacher education, therefore, has remained a neglected field.

When the NPE-1986 was launched, the matter attracted the attention of the policy makers again and the role of teachers in social transformation was emphasized. The Policy Document states:

> The status of the teacher reflects the socio-cultural ethos of a society; it is said that no people can rise above the level of its teachers....Teachers should have the freedom to innovate, devise appropriate methods of communication and activities relevant to the needs and capabilities of the pupils and the concerns of the community.

This statement clearly indicates the significance attached to teachers and their education. The policy statement proposed to reorganize the methods of recruitment of teachers "to ensure merit, objectivity, and conformity with spatial and functional requirements" and to improve pay and service conditions of teachers to make them "commensurate with their social and professional responsibilities." Clear guidelines would be formulated to ensure objectivity in postings and transfers. An open, participative, and databased system of teacher-evaluation would be evolved, for promotion of teachers to higher grades. Norms for accountability would be laid down with "incentives for good performance and disincentives for non-performance."

The policy also emphasized the need for continuing education of teachers, saying that pre-service and in-service components of teacher education are inseparable. Separate proposals were made for elementary and secondary teacher education. For elementary teacher education, the creation of District Institutes Education and Training (DIET) was proposed for each district with the capability to organize pre-service and in-service training courses. The DIET would also take care of personnel working in the non-formal and adult education systems. For secondary teacher education, the proposal was to upgrade selected teacher training colleges to complement the work of State Councils of Educational Research and Training. Another important policy proposal was to provide the statutory status to the National Council for Teacher Education (NCTE) with enhanced resources and capability to accredit teacher education institutions. The policy made several other proposals to improve the living and working conditions of teachers as well as to improve the quality of teacher education in the country as a whole. However, the results would depend on how the programmes were implemented.

SOME NEW DEVELOPMENTS

As mentioned in the previous section, the NPE-1986 made several proposals to create new bodies/institutions to act as monitoring and coordinating mechanisms at national as well as state levels. In this section, further details about these bodies/institutions are discussed in terms of their functions, roles and powers. The NPE-1986 has been under the process of implementation for the last one decade. During this period several new developments have taken place, the most notable being the creation of DIET, CTE, IASE and the NCTE.

District Institute of Education and Training (DIET)

The establishment of DIET in all the districts was an important proposal of the NPE-1986 for the development of teacher education at district level. Prior to 1986, the primary function of state level elementary teacher education institutions had been to provide pre-service training with limited resources and outdated curricula. The massive expansion of facilities for elementary and adult education generated a need for a decentralized approach of management to ensure better administration and increased efficiency. Consequently, a district level body was envisaged in the NPE-1986, and the idea of DIET originated. Pursuant to the provisions of the NPE-1986, a centrally sponsored scheme of restructuring and organization of teacher education was approved in October 1987 (GOI, 1989). The establishment of DIET was one of the five components of the said scheme. The main functions of a DIET are:

(*i*) Training and orientation (both pre-service and in-service) of elementary school teachers, head masters, block level officers, instructors and supervisors of non-formal and adult education, the members of District Board of Education and Village Education Committees, local volunteers and resource persons;

(ii) Academic and resource support to elementary and adult education systems in the district by way of organizing extension activities, providing resource support to teachers/instructors, developing locally relevant teaching/instructional material, and serving as an evaluation center of elementary and adult education; and

(iii) Action Research and experimentation to deal with specific problems of the district in achieving the objectives in the areas of elementary and adult education.

Each DIET would have qualified staff in all the important branches of pedagogy, foundation courses and teaching subjects. The size of the staff will depend on the number of schools, NFE centers and adult education centers in the district. However, each DIET will have adequate facilities in terms of man and material. It was proposed that each state would have a DIET in the course of time. By the end of 1998-99, 451 DIET had been set up in the whole country (GOI, 2000).

Institutes of Advanced Study in Education (IASE) and Colleges of Teacher Education (CTE):

> Another important proposal of NPE-1986 was to upgrade selected teacher education institutions to complement the work of SCERT. The government of India has expressed the view that secondary teacher education in this country presents a mixed picture—some spectacular achievements, innovations of far-reaching significance and rigorous observance of norms along with alarming distortions and structural shortcomings. On the one hand, there are good quality institutions, which have given evidence of enormous capacity to meet the challenges of growing new demands on them having kept pace with latest developments in teacher education and engaged themselves in experimentation and innovation of highest order. On the other hand, there are training colleges/institutions, which have been providing teacher training of substandard quality indulging in grave mal-practices, not only in

admissions and appointments, but also in utilization of funds available to the institution. There is large number of teacher education institutions, which suffer from inadequacy of physical facilities including teaching staff, laboratories, libraries, and other support services. Even the minimum essential physical facilities are not available in some of the colleges of teacher education.

In addition to this, some of the teacher education institutions and university departments are offering B.Ed. programme through correspondence, the credibility of which is being questioned not only by technical experts but also by general public. The university departments are providing limited support to teacher education colleges for want of effective interaction among them. In the light of all this, the NPE-1986 proposed to revitalize secondary teacher education by devising functional strategies, which would consist of the following (Ed. CIL, 1987):

(i) Reorganization of content and methods of secondary teacher education to enable it to play its proper role and discharge the functions envisaged under this scheme;

(ii) Improvement of standards of selected teacher education institutions which are already well established, by providing additional inputs by way of qualified staff and physical facilities;

(iii) Promotion of research, interdisciplinary studies, and setting of norms of excellence by up-gradation of a small number of institutions as institutions of advanced study; and

(iv) Phasing out institutions, which are substandard and surplus or have been indulging in mal-practices.

Under a Centrally Sponsored Scheme (CSS) of strengthening selected secondary teacher education institutions, it was proposed that about 250 selected teacher education institutions be identified during the Eighth Plan period and be provided financial assistance, on a project basis, for staff and physical facilities. Only those institutions would be selected under this scheme, which have given evidence of a good quality and reputation. Out of these 250 selected institutions, 50 would be provided enhanced grant so that they may develop into centers of excellence in research. These 50 institutions would be referred to as "Institutes of Advanced Study in Education (IASE)", while the remaining 200 would be known as "Colleges of Teacher Education (CTE)". The functions of CTE will include organization of pre-service teacher education for preparation of secondary school teachers, organization of short-term and subject-centred in-service teacher education programmes, provision of extension and research support-services to secondary schools, promotion of research and experimentation in secondary education, conducting research and training in new and emerging areas of education, encouragement of community participation in teacher education and providing support to professional bodies.

The functions of IASE would be more broad-based and, in addition to the above, would include preparation of elementary teacher educators, organization of post-graduate and research programmes leading to M.Ed, M.Phil and Ph.D. degrees, to prepare secondary teacher educators and educational researchers, to start 4-year integrated secondary teacher education programmes, to conduct in-service courses for teachers, teacher educators, supervisors and educational administrators, to provide guidance to DIET and CTE and to prepare quality instructional material.

The scheme of identifying and upgrading selected teacher education institutions has been in operation since 1987-88. Till 1996-97, 108 secondary teacher education institutions had been upgraded to the status of IASE/CTE against the target of 135 during the Eighth Plan. Among these, 25 had been upgraded as IASE against the total target of 50. According to the new reports of the government, 76 CTE and 34 IASE have been established under the scheme till the end of 1998-99.

Some Other Programmes

The NPE-1986 followed by POA-1986 called for a substantial improvement in the conditions of work and the quality of teachers' education and spelt out the main aspects of strategies to implement its proposals. In pursuance of this, efforts have been made to evolve an appropriate mechanism for periodic in-service teacher education. In this connection a Centrally Sponsored Scheme of restructuring and reorganization of teacher education was launched (1987-88) and implemented during the Seventh Plan period with the following objectives (NIEPA, 1990):

(*i*) to impart pre-service and in-service training to school teachers in order to equip them with teaching competencies; and

(*ii*) to provide meaningful academic support to formal and non-formal school systems as also to adult education, through professionally organized teacher education institutions.

Under this scheme, a Programme of Mass Orientation of School Teachers (PMOST) was launched for improvement of professional competence of teachers. During the year 1988, 9,113 camps were organized through the NCERT and State governments, for primary and secondary school teachers aimed at increasing their motivation and professional expertise, and equipping them to play a key role in the process of reorientation of content and process of school education. These camps trained 4,39,261 primary, upper primary, and secondary school teachers. In addition, Special Orientation for Primary School Teachers (SOPT) has also been taken up since 1993-94, to provide orientation to primary school teachers in the use of teaching learning material supplied under Operation Blackboard, and in the Minimum Levels of Learning (MLL) strategy with focus on the teaching of language, mathematics and environmental studies. By 1995-96, about 17.62 lack teachers had been oriented under SOPT. These programmes have given encouraging results. The government of India has, so far, approved 18 projects to strengthen the SCERT. Several university departments have been selected by the UGC, for strengthening under Special Assistance Programme (SAP), for encouraging research and innovation in teacher education.

NATIONAL COUNCIL OF EDUCATIONAL RESEARCH AND TRAINING (NCERT)

The NCERT is an autonomous organization, which was established on 1st September 1961, and registered under the Societies Registration Act, 1860. It is an apex resource organization with its headquarters at New Delhi. The main function of this body is to act as an academic advisor to the Ministry of Human Resource Development, Government of India, in the implementation of policies and programmes in school education and teacher training by providing necessary expertise. The NCERT is fully financed by the Government of India through the Ministry of Human Resource Development.

Structure of the NCERT

The Union Minister of Human Resource Development is the ex-officio president of the General Body of the NCERT. The members of the General Body include the Education Ministers of all the States and Union Territories, Chairman of the UGC, the Secretary to the Department of Education HRD Ministry, four vice chancellors of the universities—one from each region, the Chairman of the Central Board of Secondary Education, the Commissioner of Kendriya Vidyalaya Sangathan, all members of its Executive Committee (not included among the above), and some other members (not exceeding twelve) nominated by the Minister of Human Resource Development as President of the NCERT. At least four of these nominated members have to be the school teachers. The NCERT has a full-time Director, a Joint Director and the Secretary appointed by government. The government also appoints the Joint Directors of the Central Institute of Educational Technology (CIET) and the Central Institute of Vocational Education (CIVE). These two institutes are subsidiaries of the NCERT. The main governing body of the NCERT is the Executive Committee. The Union Minster of Human Resource Development is its President and the Union Minister of State in the Ministry of HRD is the ex-officio Vice-President. Standing Committees, related to different activities assist the Executive Committee in its work.

The NCERT has five major constituents, namely, the National Institute of Education (NIE) at New Delhi, five Regional Institutes of Education (RIE) located at Ajmer, Bhopal, Bhubaneshwar, Mysore, and Shillong, the Central Institute of Educational Technology (CIET) at New Delhi, Pandit Sundar Lal Sharma Central Institute of Vocational Education (CIVE) at Bhopal, and seventeen Field Offices in different States (NCERT, 1988). The NIE has several academic departments actively engaged in research, development, training and extension activities in their respective fields of specialization. For example, the Department of Education in Science and Mathematics (DESM) undertakes research and developmental activities including production of instructional material in Science and Mathematics Education. The Regional Institutes of Education (RIE) cater to the research and training needs of the five regions—Northern, Western, Eastern, Southern and North-Eastern. Each region covers several States under its jurisdiction. The CIET and CIVE undertake research and developmental activities in their respective areas. The Field Offices function as important links between the States and the NCERT through Regional Institutes of Education.

Major Functions

The major concern of the NCERT is the improvement of quality of school education and teachers' training in India. In order to discharge these responsibilities, the NCERT undertakes the following activities:

- *(i)* Promotion and coordination of research in all branches of school education, including teacher education, by conducting and financing research projects in identified fields;
- *(ii)* Organization of pre-service (mainly through RIE) and in-service teacher education programmes in emerging areas according to the changing requirements;
- *(iii)* Organization of extension services for institutions, voluntary organizations and other agencies engaged in educational activities;
- *(iv)* Development of, and experimentation with new and improved techniques of teaching, training and research;
- *(v)* Collection, compilation, processing and dissemination of educational information to be used by the government and educational institutions;
- *(vi)* Collaboration with States and State-level institutions, agencies and organizations in development and implementation of educational policies and programmes for improvement of quality of education;
- *(vii)* Collaboration with international organizations like UNESCO, UNICEF etc. and the equivalent educational organizations/institutes of other countries;
- *(viii)* Provision of training and research facilities to scholars and educational personnel from other countries;

(ix) Publication of journals, research reports, books, teacher-guides and other useful material for the benefit of teachers, research workers, students and educational administrators; and

(x) Organization of a National Talent Search Scheme to identify and nurture talent in various academic fields by holding a national level test and providing scholarships.

In addition to the above functions, the NCERT conducts All India Education Surveys after every five years to evaluate the status/progress of educational development. Six such surveys have already been published. The sixth survey was conducted by using information technology in communication for compilation and processing of data. The NCERT also has an Educational Research and Innovations Committee (ERIC), which provides financial assistance to outside institutions/organizations for research in priority areas of education. The government for its better re-organization and prioritization of its areas of work reviews the functions of the NCERT so that it may function as an effective national body.

NATIONAL COUNCIL FOR TEACHER EDUCATION (NCTE)

The National Council for Teacher Education (NCTE) is a statutory body established by an Act of Parliament. In fact, a non-statutory NCTE was in existence since 1973. During the last more than two decades, the NCTE has been working for improvement in the quality of teacher education. Its headquarters being at New Delhi, the NCERT used to serve as academic secretariat of the non-statutory NCTE. Even as a non-statutory body, the NCTE made continuous efforts to upgrade the quality of teacher education in India. In 1978, the NCTE brought out a document "Teacher Education Curriculum—A Framework" which took a comprehensive review of the existing realities and perceived futuristic scenario. The current teacher education programmes in India are, more or less, based on 1978-Framework, even though it was revised in 1988. During the period from 1973 to 1993, a long period of 20 years, the NCTE could not make any significant impact on the quality of teacher education in India. The main reason for this was that it had no statutory status.

The government realized that a body like the NCTE needs to be given statutory status before it can make some impact. Consequently, the NPE-1986 proposed to give the NCTE a statutory status and provide it with necessary resources and capability to accredit institutions of teacher education and provide guidance (NPE modified-1992) regarding curricula and methods. In pursuance of this, a bill of the proposed statutory NCTE was drafted by MHRD, which was passed in 1993 by the Parliament. With the passage of the NCTE Act (No. 73 of 1993), a statutory body came into existence on 17 August 1995 with the objective "to achieve planned and coordinated development of teacher education system throughout the country and to ensure the maintenance of norms and standards in teacher education system". The mandate given to the NCTE is very broad and covers the whole gamut of teacher education programmes, including research and training of persons.

Structure and Organization

The NCTE has a full-time Chairman, a full-time Vice-Chairman, a full-time Member-Secretary, and some supporting staff. With its headquarters at New Delhi, the NCTE has four Regional Committees situated at Jaipur, Bhopal, Bhubaneshwar and Bangalore for Northern, Western, Eastern and Southern regions respectively. Each Regional Committee is headed by a Regional Director and is constituted by including prominent educationists/ teacher educators of the region. The NCTE also has a General Body, which includes its Chairman, Vice-Chairman, Member-Secretary, Union Education Secretary, Director NCERT, Director NIEPA, Member-Secretary AITCE, Chairman CBSE, Chairman UGC or his nominee, Advisor Planning Commission and 13 educationists nominated by the government, three MPs and others. The NCTE headquarters at New Delhi as well as the Regional Committees have administrative and academic wings, both having different types of functions.

Functions of the NCTE

As detailed in NPE-1986 and POA-1992, the objectives of the NCTE are as follows (NCTE, 1996):

(i) To create mechanism for determination and maintenance of standards in teacher education;
(ii) To regulate institutions of teacher education with a view to phasing out substandard and mal-practicing institutions;
(iii) To lay emphasis on continuing education of teachers; and
(iv) To reduce the gap between the demand and supply of trained teachers.

In the light of these objectives, the main functions of the NCTE have been spelt out as follows:

(i) To undertake surveys and studies relating to various aspects of teacher education and publish the results thereof;
(ii) To make recommendations to central and state governments, universities, UGC and other recognized institutions in the matters of preparation of suitable plans and programs in the field of teacher education;
(iii) To coordinate and monitor teacher education and its development in the country;
(iv) To lay down guidelines in respect of minimum qualifications for a person to be employed as teacher in schools or other recognized institutions;
(v) To lay down norms for any specified category of courses and training in teacher education including the minimum eligibility criteria for admission thereof, and the method of selection of candidates, duration of the course, course content and mode of curriculum;
(vi) To lay down guidelines for compliance by recognized institutions, for starting new courses or training, and for providing physical and instructional facilities, staff pattern and staff qualifications;
(vii) To lay down standards in respect of examinations leading to teacher education qualifications, criteria for admission to such examinations, and develop schemes of courses and training programmes;
(viii) To lay down guidelines regarding tuition fees and other fees chargeable by recognized institutions;
(ix) To promote and conduct innovations and research in various areas of teacher education and disseminate the results thereof;

(x) To examine and review periodically the implementation of the norms, guidelines and standards laid down by it and to suitably advise the recognized institutions;

(xi) To evolve suitable performance appraisal systems, norms and mechanisms for enforcing accountability on recognized institutions;

(xii) To formulate schemes for various levels of teacher education and identify recognized institutions and set up new institutions for teacher development programmes;

(xiii) To take all necessary steps to prevent commercialization of teacher education; and

(xiv) To perform such other functions as may be entrusted to it by the Central Government.

Performance of the NCTE

Although, the NCTE Act was passed by the Parliament in 1993, yet it was brought into force with effect from July 1, 1995. However, some preparatory work had been done in 1994. By a formal notification in the Gazette of India, the NCTE was established with effect from August 17, 1995 in terms of the provisions of the Act (NCTE, 1996). In addition to the publication of several documents on teachers, their status and profession, the NCTE has conducted many seminars/meetings to discuss the issues involved in teacher education. In pursuance of its main functions, the NCTE has taken five major steps during the last few years:

(i) It has developed norms and standards for quality control in teacher education at pre-primary, elementary, and secondary levels. These norms are to be followed by existing institutions as well as by new institutions, to be established in future.

(ii) It has issued guidelines for improvement of quality of teacher education programs being carried out through correspondence /distance education mode.

(iii) It has undertaken a major task of conducting inspections of teacher education institutions in the whole country for the purpose of recognizing their programmes. Each institution of teacher education (old or new) must seek recognition of the NCTE.

(iv) After proper consultation with the experts and educationists on several issues, the NCTE brought out the "Curriculum Framework for Teacher Education: A Discussion Document" in 1996, which was circulated widely throughout the country. It was expected that the issues identified and presented in the discussion document would provide the basis for a nationwide debate (NCTE, 1997) leading to a meaningful curriculum framework.

(v) On the basis of discussions and debates, the NCTE published another document entitled "Curriculum Framework for Quality Teacher Education" in 1998. This document is supposed to provide broad-based guidelines for development and improvement of quality of teacher education in India. It provides several new ideas regarding content and process of teacher education, duration of various teacher education courses, and development of required skills in teacher-trainees through various means of curriculum transaction.

A careful analysis of the contents of the 'Quality' curriculum framework shows that when compared with the traditional programmes, there is hardly any major shift in the philosophical orientation and structural approach of training strategies proposed in it, excepting the proposals regarding enhancement of the duration of B.Ed. course. It has suggested at least six different teacher education courses each related to a different stage of education. For each suggested teacher education programme, at least 9 or 10 compulsory components/courses have been proposed. In addition, a four-year integrated teacher-training course has also been proposed for aspirants to become secondary school teachers. It is worth noting here that such courses started earlier in some universities/ institutions had to be closed down for some reason or the other. It would have been prudent had our educationists taken some lessons from these experiments.

We, the Indians, have a peculiar way of thinking. We generally believe in repeating the experiments, which repeatedly fail or are bound to fail. A live example is that of the Integrated Courses in teacher education, which were introduced in some universities/ institutions only to be discontinued later on. Our proposals/efforts to re-introduce such courses, as recently suggested in the latest

"Curriculum Framework" brought out by the NCTE, should not surprise anybody. A four-year integrated course was first introduced by the Kurukshetra University in 1960, Sardar Patel University in Gujarat, and thereafter by the NCERT, in the four Regional Colleges of Education under its control. But, all these courses were closed down at some point of time due to one reason or the other. It was found that bright students did not prefer to join teaching profession at an early age of 16 or 17 years, that the share of enrollment in these courses was only about 5-10% of the total enrollment in teacher education, and that the integrated programmes seemed to have "marginal impact" on the quality of teacher education, and thus, had no "promising future" (NCTE, 1998). In view of these issues/problems Education Commission (1964-66) had cautioned against such experiments. The Commission stated:

> We feel that it would be wrong to place an undue emphasis on such marginal experiments and that, from the point of view of raising standards in teacher education, it would be better to concentrate on improving the professional one-year course following the first or the second degree.

Regarding increasing the duration of one-year courses in teacher education to two years, the Commission had said:

> At the secondary stage, where the duration of the course is only one year, it has been suggested that it should be increased to two years, to do justice to the existing heavy courses and to incorporate the proposed subject matter courses. From a financial and practical point of view this does not seem feasible. However, it is possible to make better use of the existing duration by extending the working days in the academic year from the existing level of 180-190 days to 230 days.

In view of these arguments of the Commission, extension of the duration of the B.Ed. programme from one year to two years does not seem to be reasonable. Perhaps, we are proposing to do so because we are unable to regulate the existing one-year course.

PROGRESS AND ACHIEVEMENT

Teachers constitute a major chunk of manpower in India. In absolute terms, a substantial increase in the number of teachers has been registered from 1950-51 to 1998-99 in different types of schools. During this period, the total number of teachers increased from 7.51 lakhs to 52.9 lakhs (Govt. of India, 2000). It is over seven-fold growth. The number of women teachers increased from 1.15 lakhs to over 18 lakhs during the same period. At present, the percentage of women teachers to all teachers is 32 in primary schools, 35 in upper primary schools, and 34 in secondary and senior secondary schools. On the basis of school enrollment and number of teachers, the Teacher-Pupil Ratio (TPR) has also undergone considerable change. The TPR at primary school stage was 1:24 in 1950-51, which had changed to 1:47 till 1995-96. The corresponding TPRs for upper primary and higher secondary stages are 1:38 and 1:33 respectively. A steady increase in TPR during the last 50 years explains the increased rush in the classrooms. The increase in the number of teachers has not kept pace with the increase in enrollment. If this phenomenon continues as it is, there will be acute shortage of teachers in future. Moreover, the increase in TPR without corresponding improvement in techniques of teaching will have adverse impact on the quality of education. During the post-independence period there has been a spurt in the teacher education institutions as well as in the number of trained teachers in India.

Table 8.2
Percentage of Trained Teachers in Indian Schools at Different Stages (1948-1996)

Year	*Pre-primary*	*Primary*	*Upper primary*	*Secondary*
1948-50	45.64	58.32	52.61	53.59
1950-55	69.88	62.31	58.33	54.66
1955-60	72.56	65.85	62.48	67.34
1960-65	73.34	66.69	66.33	72.46
1965-70	73.96	69.76	66.86	74.84
1970-75	74.77	74.32	76.38	76.56
1975-80	76.39	78.94	82.86	83.56
1980-85	76.88	86.36	89.08	89.03
1985-89	78.24	88.31	92.06	91.08
1991-92	82.98	85.31	88.25	88.07
1995-96	NA	88.00	88.00	89.00

Sources: 1. Malhotra S. P., Indian Teacher Education and Challenges of Change, Education and Society, James Nicholas Publishers, Volume 8, No. 1, 1990, page 37.
2. Govt. of India, HRD Ministry, Education in India 1991-92, Vol-I(s).
3. Selected Educational Statistics, Govt. of India MHRD, 1995-96.

As indicated in the figures given in Table 8.1, the percentage of trained teachers has progressively increased at every level of education. Every year, a large number of teachers is trained and added to the existing pool of trained teachers. According to the latest available data (2000), the percentage of trained teachers is 88 at primary school stage, 88 at upper primary stage, and 91 at secondary and senior secondary stage. This shows that still there are 10-12 per cent untrained teachers working in the schools at all India level. Also, there are regional disparities in this regard. While there are 100 per cent trained teachers in certain states like Kerala, Orissa, Panjab and Haryana, the percentage of trained teachers in Arunachal Pradesh, Nagaland, Tripura and other North Eastern States, ranges between 30 and 45. This shows that there is acute shortage of trained teachers and training facilities in some states.

In 1995-96, there were as many as 5.9 lakh primary schools, 1.7 lakh upper primary schools, and 95 thousand high/higher secondary schools in India (NCTE, 1996). As against this there were 1221 teacher-training institutions for preparing elementary school teachers and 633 colleges of education and university departments, preparing teachers for secondary and senior secondary schools. Out of about 44 lakh teachers in the country, about 29 lakh were teaching in elementary schools. A sizeable number of them were untrained or poorly trained teachers, such as in the case of north-eastern regions. In certain states, there are even unqualified and under-qualified teachers. Such a situation points to a pressing need for developing teacher education programmes both in quality and quantity. In certain regions, there is an overflow of trained teachers, which has created a serious problem of unemployment among them. So, the problem of regional imbalances in teacher education facilities has to be dealt with carefully.

The Regional Committees the NCTE received 2426 applications by the end of 1998-99, from existing teacher education institutions for recognition and conducting of teacher-training courses. Recognition was subsequently granted to 408 institutions. In addition, 1294 institutions were granted provisional recognition. Similarly, 1349 applications were received for starting new institutions/courses. Out of these, recognition has been granted to 77 new institutions/courses (GOI, 2000), provisional recognition to 1035 institutions and recognition refused to 131 cases.

PROBLEMS AND ISSUES

While looking at the overall current status of teacher education in India, one finds a mixed picture. On the one hand, there exist teacher education institutions, which have made a mark in the field of teacher education by promoting excellence, and on the other hand, there are teacher-training colleges which do not have even the minimum physical facilities and may be rated as substandard. This, however, is not the whole story. There are some bright spots in the overall picture of darkness. Practically, in all parts of the country, teacher education institutions have given evidence of enormous capacity to meet the challenges of new demands thrown on them by the growing system of school education. Some of them have been engaged in experimentation and innovation to keep pace with the new developments in pedagogy and allied sciences. But, still there is much to be done. A large number of teacher education institutions need overhauling. The entire system is faced with certain grave problems and issues, which need to be resolved. There is much scope for improvement, especially, in the qualitative aspects of teacher education.

State of Isolation

About three decades ago, Education Commission (1964-1966) had talked about the isolation of teacher education system from other educational institutions. A teacher training college is not only isolated from schools in the surrounding area but also from other teacher education institutions. Similarly, the department of education in a university remains isolated from other academic departments in the university. There is very little interaction between an academic department and education department in the university.

Similarly, colleges of education receive inadequate and insufficient support from university departments of education and SCERTs, and the linkages between them are very weak and ineffective. Therefore, there has to be a planned and sustained effort to establish linkages between teacher education institutions and apex bodies on the one hand, and between teacher education and school education on the other.

Regional Imbalances

Due to unplanned and ill-planned expansion of teacher education, there has been a wide gap between demand and supply of teachers in certain areas. In some regions of the country, there are surplus trained-teachers resulting in the serious problem of their employment, while in some other parts there is acute shortage, like in the North-East, of teachers and untrained teachers have to be employed. Therefore, planned efforts have to be made not only to establish new institutions in some areas, but also to check the mushrooming growth of substandard institutions in certain other areas. Moreover, the imbalance in the quality of teacher education from one region to another has to be removed through judicious planning and implementation of strategies. There has been an enormous growth in the number of substandard institutions in teacher education and corresponding downfall in the quality of training imparted in them. At the same time, there are reports of grave mal-practices in the admission of students, appointment of teachers and utilization of funds.

Inadequate Physical Facilities

A sound professional training requires sufficient physical facilities in terms of both men and material. It is the group of the qualified and competent teacher educators and good classrooms, library and laboratories that make a good teacher education institution. A large number of teacher education institutions suffer from inadequacy of physical facilities, laboratories and related equipment are not available, libraries, if available, do not have good books and journals, classrooms are also not adequately furnished, and the overall learning environment is not conducive. In certain cases, teacher educators are neither sufficient in number nor satisfactory in quality.

A large number of teacher-training colleges do not have experimental schools attached to them. These institutions find it difficult to carry out the practice teaching programmes of trainees effectively. Whatever practice teaching is being done is on the traditional lines. This situation has to be carefully studied and improved.

Commercialization

During the last five decades, there has been an enormous growth in the number of substandard teacher training institutions many of them being indulged in grave mal-practices. Several of them are now offering B. Ed. and M. Ed. courses through correspondence/ distance education mode the suitability of which is being questioned and doubted in the professional circles as well as in the general public. These institutions are charging very high fees from the poor students, most of which come of lower-middle stratum of the society. This practice is highly undemocratic and unjust. Reports have been received that in certain correspondence/distance education programs the enrollment of students has been as high as 30,000 in one academic session. These practices, not only lead to the downfall in the quality of training, but also encourage commercialization of teacher education. Although, universities have laid down norms for such institutions/colleges including those for staff requirement, admission process, examination process, practice teaching and physical facilities, yet these norms are not strictly followed. Moreover, these norms, as prescribed by the universities, are not very rigorous.

Therefore, there is an urgent need to stop commercialization of teacher education programmes resulting in dilution of standards, by developing strict and national level norms. The NCTE has taken welcome steps in this direction by developing separate norms for pre-primary, elementary, and secondary school teacher education courses, and conducting nationwide inspections of teacher education institutions. This process has developed a strong, reliable, and useful database for future planning and development of teacher education.

Duration of Courses

In general, the teacher education programs for elementary school teachers are of two years' duration, and those for secondary school teachers these are of one-year duration. There is a general feeling these days that one-year B.Ed. programme is inadequate to meet the demands of the profession in view of the multi-dimensional development in various related aspects such as school curricula, information technology, knowledge of the subject matter, and pedagogical sciences. It is argued that in actual practice, the one-year B.Ed. programme reduces to 7 or 8 months' exercise because of many reasons, which are beyond the control of the teacher training institutions. However, the argument does not sound very reasonable. "Because the teacher education institutions, and hence the teacher educators, are unable to regulate the existing one-year teacher education programme, the duration of courses should be increased" is not a convincing argument in favour of increasing the duration of teacher education courses. The NCTE has also been very cautious in recommending enhancement in the duration of courses. It has stated (1998):

> There has been a strong demand from a large section of teacher educators and educationists to increase the duration of B.Ed. course from one year to two years. However, changeover from one year to two years' duration may require two-three years' preparatory time. It is, therefore, recommended that the two-year B.Ed. courses may be instituted after careful planning, development of detailed curriculum, and suitable augmentation of infrastructure and necessary orientation of teacher educators during the next two/three years. During the intervening period, the suggested general teacher education programmes may be offered. However, if some institutions have the necessary infrastructure, staff and other resources and are willing to start these two-year programmes early, they need to be encouraged and assisted.

Out-dated Curricula

The teacher training programmes in India are being run on traditional lines without any noticeable change or modification to keep pace with the changing realities. The skill development aspect of the programme is the most neglected. The practice teaching aspect is heavily loaded with activities like writing lesson plans, memorizing them, and presenting them in the classroom in order to fulfil the requirement of completing 40 or 45 lessons as prescribed in the ordinances. On the other hand, the teaching of theory courses consumes most of the time and energy of the staff and students. The time being given to the teaching of theory in most of the teacher training colleges is about 70% of the total time available and only

30% is left for practice teaching and other activities. This trend needs to be reversed.

The supervision of practice teaching has become a routine and drab exercise. There is hardly any seriousness or rigour in it. The teaching practice aspect needs to be completely revamped. Several committees and commissions have recommended the "Internship Model" of training, but it has never been implemented, probably because of inertia. Also, the theoretical courses such as Philosophy of Education, Psychology of Education etc. should be thoroughly revised so as to incorporate new developments in these fields. Certain new components need to be included in the curriculum so as to make it more relevant to the socio-economic needs of the area. The NCTE (1996) has rightly stated that, "any attempt to impose a rigid, uniform and common curriculum on a plural and heterogeneous society is not desirable". Therefore, a requisite degree of flexibility is essential to provide for social and cultural diversity. The NCTE has already brought out a National Curriculum Framework for Teacher Education, which is to be implemented during the years to come.

Dr. R.P.Singh, former Dean (Research), National Council of Educational Research and Training (NCERT), has rightly stated, "around one lakh people take 'teaching' every year but few are adequately trained to face the classrooms. Nor is the curriculum designed to help them provide quality teaching in schools. No evaluation of the teacher training courses and how best the curriculum relates to the quality of effective teaching in schools has been done in the last 130 years of the formalized teacher education system in India. What is being offered in the name of teacher education today is not only irrelevant but also unhelpful and B.Ed. courses are being commercialized and there is hardly any in-service training programmes or a separate curriculum for senior secondary teachers." He further stated, "according to the data available with the Ministry of Human Resource Development, the quality of pre-service teacher education has fallen over the years and only about 40% of the teachers get in-service training. Teaching which is a skill area is taught theoretically and no one seems to take the curriculum seriously. The authorities need to undertake the evaluation exercise before a curriculum is framed or text book is written."

Limited Scope

The function of teacher education institutions is limited. By and large it is confined to pre-service teacher education only with practically no provision of in-service training and continuing education of teachers. Wherever such facilities are available, these are confined to limited number of teachers serving inside a limited area. The NPE (1986) had envisaged a regular in-service education of all teachers, and systematic programs of continuing education to update their knowledge and skills were launched.

The teacher education institutions cannot function in isolation from the other components of the education system. Their programmes must be influenced by changes in school education, because the main target of training institution is a 'school'. Any change in the nature, purpose, quality or character of school education throws new demands on teacher education and reinforces the process of programme evaluation and re-adjustment, especially in the area of curriculum reconstruction. Not only that the curricula should be modified, rather, the entire teacher education programme at all stages should undergo drastic changes. It would be possible only when academicians of forward-looking and modern vision are involved in the process of change.

9

Early Childhood Care and Education

Education for All (EFA), in the Indian context, implies not only the universalization of elementary education and adult literacy, but also the expansion of early childhood education and development activities, especially for the poor, disadvantaged and disabled children. In fact, the goal of EFA cannot be effectively achieved without giving proper impetus to the development and expansion of pre-school education. The development of pre-primary education in India has been of comparatively recent origin. During the past a few decades, tremendous significance has been attached to Early Childhood Care and Education (ECCE), that would not only complement the role of the family in care and stimulation of the young child, but also function as a support service to the primary education system. The research studies carried out in this area have established that as far as learning and growth are concerned, the period from birth to about six years is of exceptional significance, and if it is not utilized for the development of the child, it would be too late in the life of the child to make up for the loss. The circumstances created by rapid socioeconomic change have also boosted the growing interest in this field.

Due to the phenomenon of migration caused by increased urbanization, the traditional pattern of joint family system has broken, and the members of the family, other than the parents, are no more readily available for childcare. There is now greater pressure on women to work for wages than ever before, and men have migrated to cities in search of work. These situations have affected the traditional childcare practices and created the need for alternative strategies for this purpose.

EARLIER ATTEMPTS

In the pre-colonial days, formal education was meant only for the older children and was a privilege of the ruling classes. No education was considered necessary for the young child. The young children drew information from their interaction with the parents, grandparents and other members of the family. During the British period, the little attempt made by individuals and private agencies took the shape of the prevalent formal public school system of education and resulted in the establishment of a few KG and Nursery schools. One of the first such schools was set up by Gopaldas and Moti Amin (1915) at Baroda. Such attempts generated awareness about the significance of preschool education, especially through the efforts of urban-based national NGOs, and the Montessorian ideology took concrete shape when it was experimented in Sevagram (1946) in terms of the idea of pre-basic education proposed by Gandhiji. Gandhiji emphasized the need for an inexpensive and 'Indianized' system of pre-school education to meet the needs of the masses (Khalakdina, 1998).

The early sporadic efforts by voluntary organizations came to be gradually accepted and recognized especially after the recommendations of the Central Advisory Board of Education (CABE) in 1944. This led to the expansion of pre-primary education as a necessary adjunct to elementary education. The government of India played its active role in early childhood education only after 1953, when the Central Social Welfare Board (CSWB), through its various schemes, sponsored Balwadis for children of less privileged groups in rural and urban areas. However, the ECCE received the real impetus in 1974 when the government launched the Integrated Child Development Services (ICDS) scheme to make some form of ECCE accessible to children aged 3-6 years. Today, the ICDS has been universalized to all the blocks in the country with a network of 5614 sanctioned projects intended to reach out to 35 million young children below the age of six years from the disadvantaged groups (NIPCCD, 1998). However, only 12% of the target children of this age group are being covered by the ICDS. In addition to this, there are several other schemes such as Early Childhood Education, Creches, Day Care Centres, Statutory Creches etc.

By far, as mentioned by NIEPA (1990), the most widespread model is that of the Integrated Child Development Services (ICDS) with the single largest outreach program, having a comprehensive package of services for meeting the total development needs of children in the 0-6 age group. The coverage under ICDS when combined with various other Early Childhood Care and Education (ECCE) facilities, such as Balwadis (creche/day care centers) run by voluntary agencies and pre-primary schools run by the state governments, municipal corporations and other agencies, adds up to 6,224,000 children (NIEPA, 1990). The coverage, though impressive in terms of total numbers, is minimal and constitutes less than 10% of the corresponding age group who require these services.

The importance of Early Childhood Care and Education (ECCE) has been recognized as a preparatory aspect of a child's development, especially as learning begins at birth and the early formative years are crucial to all future learning. The National Policy on Education, 1986 defined the objective of ECCE as being the total development of the young child in the age group 0-6, and added that stress must be laid on children of underprivileged (GOI, 1994 p. 47) groups and those who were first generation learners. The NPE-1986 (as revised in 1992) stated:

> Recognizing the holistic nature of child development, viz., nutrition, health, and social mental, physical, moral and emotional development, early childhood care and education will receive high priority and be suitably integrated with the Integrated Child Development Services (ICDS) programme wherever possible. Day-care centers will be provide as a support service for universalization of primary education, to enable girls engaged in taking care of siblings to attend school and as a support service for working women belonging to poor sections.

The NPE also proposed that the ECCE would be child centered, based on play-way methods, community participation, and without formal introduction of 3Rs. The ECCE, as a concept, has emerged as an integration of child-care and pre-primary education. It would function as a feeder and a strengthening factor for primary education. The period between birth and attainment of the age of six years is a vital period in the process of human development during which the foundations for intellectual, cognitive, socio-emotional, linguistic and physical/motor competence are laid. During this period, not only the physical development takes place, but also social and mental, and emotional aspects of behaviour acquire necessary directions and momentum. Therefore, the assistance, direction and guidance provided during this period play a decisive role for child's al-round development in future.

THE CONCEPT AND MECHANISM

It is a well-recognized fact that development of a child begins at the time of conception, but the child goes to school at the age of 6 years. Therefore, some program has to be devised to guide his development and learning between the age-span 0-6 years. Being a support service to the UEE, the ECCE aims at ensuring that every child is prepared to join class I of a primary school as soon as he acquires the age of six years. Psychologically, the ECCE is proposed to be activity-based and play-based, involving joyful activities with less or no emphasis on formal teaching of reading, writing, and arithmetic. It is an integrated programme consisting of the following components (Gopalan, 1996):

(i) The Integrated Child Development Services (ICDS);
(ii) The scheme of assistance to voluntary organizations for conducting Early Child Education (ECE) centers;
(iii) Ballades and day care centers run by voluntary organizations with government assistance;
(iv) Pre-primary schools run by the state governments, municipal corporations and other agencies; and
(v) Maternal and child health services through primary health centers, sub-centers and other agencies.

The ECCE services are to be provided in two phases: (a) healthy home-based stimulation practices for the 0-3 age-group such as play activities, children's games and health programs, and (b) early childhood education (ECE) for the children of 3-6 age-group to prepare them for primary schooling, especially, by relieving girls from child/sibling care responsibilities. The first phase of early childhood care (ECC) would help girls attend school regularly, and the second phase of early childhood education (ECE) would help both girls and working women from the lowest socio-economic groups.

The ECCE programmes would be introduced in urban slums, ecologically deprived areas, skilled and unskilled workers' clusters, and unorganized work places on a priority basis so as to cater to the needs of those who most need it.

The early childhood education or pre-school education has been, more or less, a neglected area of educational system in India. Traditionally, the education has been divided into three major stages namely, pre-primary, elementary, and secondary corresponding roughly to the three stages of in the development of a child-infancy, childhood and adolescence. But, greater emphasis has been placed on primary, and secondary stages, than on pre-primary stage. Education Commission (1964-66) had made the following remarks (Para 7.06):

> While we recognize the need to develop pre-primary education as extensively as possible, our advance in this sector will necessarily be restricted on account of the inadequacy of resources available, and especially because primary education must be accorded higher priority. It is also necessary to reconcile the competing claims of quality and quantity.

The objectives of pre-school education, according to the commission, are to develop in the child good health habits and build up basic skills for personal adjustment, to develop good social attitudes, to develop social maturity, to stimulate intellectual curiosity, to encourage creativity and ability of effective verbal expression. The Commission also stated that for the first time in our educational history Sargent Plan (1944) had emphasized the significance of pre-primary education as an essential component of National System of Education. However, the development of pre-school system has been very slow as compared to other sectors of education.

PROGRESS

In 1950-51, the number of pre-primary schools was only 303 with 866 teachers and an enrollment of about 28,000. In 1965-66, the number of pre-primary schools increased to 3500 with 6500 teachers and a total enrollment of about 250,000. In rural areas, there were 20,000 Balwadis having an enrollment of 600,000. The Education Commission (1964-66) was the first to discuss the issue and support the idea that the state should accept the limited responsibility (Naik, 1982) for pre-school education, especially, among the underprivileged groups. But, these recommendations received least attention and the pre-school education, till the launching of the NPE-1986, developed in response to the demand from the urban upper and middle classes, because of the requirements of the working women among these groups. The development of pre-primary education from 1965-66 to 1992-93 is given in the following table.

Table 9.1
Development of Pre-primary Education
(From 1965-66 to 1992-93)

	1965-66	*1975-76*	*1977-78*	*1992-93*
No. of Schools	3,235	5,658	7,050	32,998
No. of Teachers	6,832	9,951	11,021	17,899
No. of Pupils	26,2073	56,9296	73,4757	1,31,8403
Expenditure (Rs. in millions)	11.4	33.00	41.00	NA

Sources: 1. Naik, J.P. Education Commission and After, Allied Publishers, New Delhi (1982).
2. NCERT New Delhi, Sixth All India Educational Survey, Selected Statistics (1998).

These data do not include the figures about the unorganized pre-primary schools and Balwadis/Anganwadis, which are run by the Department of Social Welfare of the Ministry of Human Resource Development. In 1971, pre-school education was available to only about 2% of the population in the age group 3-6 years.

NPE-1986 AND AFTER

As mentioned earlier in this chapter, the NPE-1986 laid special emphasis on pre-school education under the banner of ECCE. The NPE-POA-1986 suggested that "70% of the target group (aged 0-6) should be covered by the ECCE services by 2000 A.D. A minimum of 2.50 lakhs centers should be established by 1990, most of them being in the tribal development blocks and blocks having substantial scheduled caste population and slums in large cities. Expanding ICDS services and opening more pre-primary education centers of various kinds such as day-care centers would mainly achieve these targets. A component of training will also be introduced for ECCE functionaries at various levels such as a two-year vocational course in ECCE at +2 level, and a higher course in ECCE for senior level functionaries."

The ICDS programme, which was launched on October 2, 1976, is today the largest outreach programme in the world with most comprehensive package of services for meeting the developmental needs of children in the age group 0-6 years. By 1987-88, the ICDS outreach had already expanded to cover approximately 4.65 million children (NIEPA, 1990) through 88,400 centers spread out in the rural and tribal areas and urban slums. This coverage, when combined with other ECCE services such as Balwadis, creches/ day-care centers and other types of ECE centers, added up to a total coverage of about 6.22 million children, which constituted a little less than 12% of the corresponding age-group who required these services. The development up to 1991-92 is given in the Table 9.2. It can be seen from the table that the number of pre-primary schools has increased from 303 in 1950-51 to 3500 in 1965-66, 4500 in 1986-87. The corresponding increase in the enrollment has been from 28,000 through 250,000 to 1.3 million children (GOI, 1993). In 1991-92, the estimated number of institutions rose to 13,515 while enrollment figures registered a rise to 3.9 million. However, in addition to pre-primary schools, there are ICDS service centers, which covered by 1993, about 15 million children through 339,000 centers. The latest figures regarding the outreach of ICDS (1995-96) is over 21 million children. It is expected that ICDS, the main vehicle of ECCE, will cover 80% of the vulnerable population, by the end of the Eighth Plan. Its impact will be enhanced by strengthening its pre-school component, adapting its location and duration to the needs of the target groups (especially girls), and adapting its location and duration to the requirements of working mothers. In order to give a further boost to UEE and improve enrollment, retention, and attendance in primary schools and also the nutritional status of children, a nationwide mid-day meal programme was launched on Aug. 15, 1995. The whole programme was built around community participation, teachers' empowerment, decentralization and flexibility.

The recent report (The Hindustan Times, Jan. 20, 2001) of the Comptroller and Auditor General (CAG) on ICDS, 25% of the target group lies uncovered even after 25 years of implementation of the Scheme. In an appraisal of the performance of the scheme between 1992-99 the CAG lamented that the ICDS has done little to improving the health status of children or making any appreciable dent in the prevailing conditions of child development, child health and maternal care. When the HRD Ministry's Department of Women and Child Development launched the scheme, it envisaged delivery of an integrated package of services that included supplementary nutrition, immunization, health check-up and referral services to the targeted children adolescent girls, and pregnant and lactating mothers. The specific goals were to reduce Infant and Child Mortality Rates. But, CAG found glaring shortcomings and shortfalls. These were related to poor quality of expenditure, execution or monitoring of the scheme and the government's failure to provide adequate resources for expansion of the programme. The report further states that in eight states the Adolescent Girls Scheme, which was woven into the ICDS in 1991-92, covered not a single beneficiary. In the majority of States, there was no supply of vitamin A solution during this period. In seven states, including U.P., Himachal Pradesh and Bihar, the ICDS funds were diversified. There was little or no supply of therapeutic food in nine states because of non-identification of severely malnourished children. In 15 states, neither the beneficiaries for immunization were identified nor achievements monitored. In 13 states, the records of monthly progress were not maintained or were incomplete or inaccurate. Only 4200 of the required 5618 projects were made operational after the scheme was universalized in 1997. There was a discrepancy in the number of projects sanctioned and operated in the records of the Ministry.

Table 9.2
Pre-primary Schools/Institutions and Enrollment

Year	*No. of Schools*	*Enrollment*
1950-51	303	28,000
1965-66	3,500	250,000
1986-87	4,500	1,272,000
1991-92	13,515	3,900,000

Appropriate linkages are being worked out between ECCE programmes, primary schools, non-formal education centers and UEE-related schemes to enhance the efficiency and output of ECCE schemes. The following steps are being taken to achieve this end (GOI, 1993):

(i) Coordination of timings between primary schools and Anganwadi/Balwadi centers,
(ii) Using primary school buildings for the activities of Anganwadis/Balwadis wherever possible,
(iii) Planning the visits of primary school teachers to Anganwadi/Balwadi centers to ensure better enrollment at primary school level,
(iv) The organizations such as SCERTs to be identified to draw-up pre-school material and curriculum in local languages and locally available techniques which could be used in ECCE activities,
(v) The personnel imparting early childhood education to be trained specifically in ECCE component, by SCERTs and other organizations,
(vi) Identification of institutions which could run ECCE training courses and to provide recognition to these courses, and
(vii) To impress upon all employers to open ECCE centers at work sites wherever women are employed.

With increased awareness among the people of India about the importance of education as a vehicle of social mobility, the trend of admitting young children of the age-group 3-4 years in schools is increasing day by day, not only in the large cities and urban clusters, but also in the remote rural habitations. The facilities for pre-primary education are available in three different kinds of institutions; *viz.* Anganwadis/Balwadis, independent pre-primary schools and pre-primary classes attached to the recognized schools. According to the Sixth All India Educational Survey (NCERT, 1998), there are 1,74,540 villages where pre-primary education facility is available. Of these 1,58,779 have Balwadi/Anganwadi, 7,386 have independent pre-primary schools, and in 17,489 villages, the pre-primary classes are attached to other schools. These villages constitute 29.76% of the total villages in the country. There are many villages where more than one type of pre-primary education facility is available. In the states of Assam, Bihar, Himachal Pradesh, Jammu & Kashmir, Madhya Pradesh, Rajasthan, Uttar Pradesh and West Bengal the facility is available in less than 30% villages. On the contrary, Manipur, Sikkim, Tripura, Dadra & Nagar Haveli and Pondicherry have pre-primary schools in more than 80% villages.

There are 2,34,422 Balwadis/Anganwadis located in 1,58,779 villages showing that there are big villages having more than one Balwadi or similar institution functioning in them. These institutions have 2,57,143 teachers in which 97.17% are female teachers. There are about 112 million children in these Balwadis of which 47.83% are girls. In urban areas, 23,490 Balwadis/ Anganwadis are functioning, which have 27,789 teachers and over 12 million children. Girls constitute 47.92% of the total enrollment. Like rural centers, urban centers have 96.95% female teachers. Besides the Balwadis and Anganwadis, there are 10,376 independent pre-primary schools in the villages having 15,028 teachers and 4,72,835 children. Also 22,622 schools in villages have pre-primary classes attached to them, with 2871 teachers and 8,45,568 children.

These developments clearly indicate that the concept of ECCE is increasingly receiving public recognition and support. With the globalization of economy accompanied by faster rise of consumerism, the Indian society is likely to face greater challenges in future than ever before. The childcare practices are likely to be adversely affected by these situations with greater involvement of women in the workforce. The working mothers will find it very difficult to take due care of their children due to pressure of work on the one hand and psychological strain on the other. In such circumstances, the pre-schools will be required in large numbers to serve as support services for the working mothers and centers of care and socialization for children. Therefore, it is high time for the Government of India to boost the process of establishment of ECCE centers by providing liberal financial and academic support.

10

Educating the Weaker Sections

One peculiar characteristic of Indian Society is that it is highly stratified, not only on the basis of socio-economic status, but also according to caste, community, language and religious affiliation. In addition, there are geographical, cultural, political, and ethnic divisions, which constitute a unique diversity nowhere seen in the world. Although, after independence, there has been an all-round development of the society in all fields, yet there are many gaps to be filled up. There are sections of Indian people who, have lagged behind in the race of socio-economic development. These sections are popularly termed as "weaker sections". The term "weaker sections" has not been properly defined in the Constitution. Therefore, sometimes it becomes very difficult to decide as to which segments of the society should be included in the list of weaker sections. However, the socio-economic scenario of the society indicates that women, scheduled castes, scheduled tribes and some minority communities are backward socially, economically, and educationally. In the ultimate analysis, it may be stated that their educational backwardness is the major cause of backwardness in other fields.

This has led the society to another weakness *i.e.* elitist character in which all power-political, economic, and knowledge, is concentrated in the hands of a small elite, which despite its internal jealousies and quarrels, always keeps a united front vis-a-vis the masses of the people who are marginalized and unable to assert themselves or to plan their destiny (Naik, 1982). The advent of Islam did not change this picture materially because the Muslim society itself got divided into similar elite groups and the masses of the people and the overall society continued to present the same elitist model. Thus, the society is divided into two visibly distinct groups with different ways of living—one influenced by the western world, and the other struggling for bread and butter.

It has been recognized that education is a powerful tool of socio-economic transformation and upward social mobility. That is why the framers of the Indian Constitution, having realized the need of social support to the weaker sections, made special constitutional provisions for the education of these groups. Since the enforcement of the Constitution in 1950, efforts have been made by the government of India to reduce the educational disparities based on sex, caste and religion. As mentioned and discussed in Chapter II, the directive principles of state policy throw on the government a special responsibility of educating the weaker sections. The purpose of this chapter is to discuss, in detail, the progress made on this front during the period of last five decades since independence. In the following sections the major policies and programmes, progress and problems of the education of women, scheduled castes and scheduled tribes, and minorities have been discussed in that order.

EDUCATION OF WOMEN

Historical Perspective

The history of India, especially the portion related to the glorious ancient period, records that women enjoyed a high status in the society. They were provided educational opportunities comparable to men. The social evils like purdah, sati, enforced widowhood and child-marriage crept into the Indian society much later and resulted in the degradation of their status. The upanayan ceremony, which marked the introduction of a child to the study of Vedas was performed for boys as well as for girls. During Vedic and Upanishadic times, girls used to wear the sacred thread, live a life of celibacy and study Vedas, Vedangas and other subjects studied in those times along with their brother pupils. A girl student was not allowed to marry until she had completed her Brahmacharya (student life). Some women advanced so much in studies that they are said to have challenged educated men of their times in public debates on religious philosophical and metaphysical subjects. The learned women were known as Brahmavadini (women having attained the knowledge of the Supreme Being) or Mantravid (having the knowledge of mantras), or Pandita (learned women). For instance, Kaushalya, the mother of Lord Rama, and Tara, wife of Bali, were known as mantravid and Draupadi, in the Mahabharata, was known as Pandita. Women, therefore, also studied the sacred religious scriptures and acquired knowledge of the highest order.

As mentioned in Chapter 1, there were no institutions for education of girls during the Muslim period, but girls did receive religious education in the recitation of the Quran in their homes. However, the women or royal and aristocratic families received education of high quality and practical character. Notable among them are: Razia Begum, Gul Begham (Babar's daughter), Noor Jahan, Mumtaz Mahal, Jahanara Begham (daughter of Shah Jahan), and Zebunnissa Beghum (Aurangzeb's daughter).

Under the British rule, the East India Company was reluctant to take up the responsibility of girls' education for a long time, due to the doctrine of religious neutrality, which was adopted by the government so as not to offend the natives even on social customs that had nothing to do with religion. However, missionaries did some pioneering work in this direction. The American Missionary Society opened its first girls' school in Bombay (1824). Similarly, the Church Missionary Society opened 5 schools for girls belonging to the upper classes of Hindus in 1826 somewhere near Poona. Missionaries in Madras and Bengal also took some other similar initiatives. The year 1850 is characterized by the historical event of recognition of the claim of girl's education, officially, by the then government. The government informed the Bengal Council of Education that it was to consider superintendence of girl's education as one of its functions. The standing instructions were issued to the Council to encourage and consider the plans of Indians to set up schools for girls, as their duty. In the meantime some Indians, such as some followers of Raja Ram Mohan Roy in Bengal, also came forward to spread female education. The efforts made by Mahatma Jyotiba Phule need special mention. He set up a school for girls in Poona as early as 1851.

The 19th century Industrial Revolution in Europe had its impact on Indian society also. Because of economic reasons, women had to work in factories along with men, which in turn generated and strengthened the need of educating women. When Wood's Education Despatch (1854) was received, there were 288 girls' schools with 6869 pupils in Bengal, 65 girls' schools with 3500 pupils in Bombay, and 256 girls' schools with about 8000 pupils in Madras (Nurullah and Naik, 1943).

The Indian Education Commission (1882) took a serious note of the status and education of women and rated it to be extremely backward, and recommended measures for improvement. But, because of certain socio-political reasons, no noticeable progress could be observed. During the Freedom Struggle, the All India Conference on Women's Education (1927) proposed to encourage women to participate actively in educational, political and social activities and help bring about reforms in these fields. In 1944, three years before independence, the Central Advisory Board of Education submitted its report (commonly known as Sargent Report) on post-war Plan of Educational Development. This visualized, among other things, free and compulsory education for all boys and girls between the ages of 6 to 14 years.

After independence, the University Education Commission (1948-49), set up by the government of free India, laid special emphasis on the education of women and recommended that in view of the similar fields of activity for men and women, and some specific requirements of women, maximum facilities should be given for education in Home Economics, and Home Management. On the significance of women's education, the Commission quoted Arthur Mayhew (1926):

> If the government, by the initial exclusion of the masses accentuated segregation of the masses from the privileged few by their initial restriction of their educational efforts to the male population, they brought a line of division where it had never existed before, within the household.

The Commission further stated:

> The educated, conscientious mother who lives and works with her children in the home is the best teacher in the world of both character and intelligence. There cannot be an educated people without educated women. If general education had not to be limited to men then opportunity should be given to women, for then it would most surely be passed to the next generation.

However, rejecting the idea of separate curriculum for girls at school stage, the Secondary Education Commission (1952-53) recommended diversification of courses at secondary and higher secondary stages with special facilities for teaching Home Science to girls. On the recommendation of the Educational Panel of the Planning Commission (1957), and a subsequent approval of the State Education Ministers' Conference, the National Committee on Women's education (1958-59) headed by Mrs. Durgabai Deshmukh, was appointed to examine the problems of education of girls in depth. The Committee studied the whole issue in detail and made the following recommendations:

(i) The education of girls should be regarded as a major and special problem of education for a good many years to come, and that a bold and determined effort should be made to bridge the wide gap existing between educational levels of male and female populations.

(ii) This committee surveyed the historical development of women's education till 1959 and expressed grave dissatisfaction over the dismal situation as it was. The Committee also suggested that a National Council for the Education of Girls and Women should be set up, and a separate unit for women's education under an Educational Advisor should be set up at the Center.

(iii) In each state, a woman should be appointed as Joint Director and be placed in-charge of girl's education, and lady teachers should be appointed in all schools where there are no women.

(iv) There should be identical curricula for boys and girls at the primary stage, and differentiation may be made at the

secondary stage. Arrangement should be made for vocational training of girls by adjusting the timings to suit their convenience.

(*v*) Educational facilities of shorter duration should be created for adult women so as to prepare them for different formal examinations such as Middle School Examination and High School Examination.

(*vi*) Part-time employment of women teachers should be encouraged as largely as possible in order to enable women to manage their responsibilities at home as well as do some teaching work and cooperation of voluntary organizations and local bodies should be sought in this connection.

Regarding the deterioration in the status women over the years the Committee observed:

> Unfortunately, this high level of culture as well as the status, which our women enjoyed at this dawn of Indian history, was brought low by the social, economic, and political changes of the later years. Women gradually lost their right to education; while the age of marriage was lowered until even the practice of marrying infants became fairly common. In course of time, a social code in which women had hardly any rights in property, marriage and divorce came into existence. Customs like enforced widowhood, and sati were also evolved through the religious concepts then prevailing. Purdah and seclusion of women came a little later and became generalized during the Muslim period. By the end of the eighteenth century, therefore, the sphere of life of the average woman was restricted to her home and her social status was one of the subjection with a few exceptions.

These days, a large majority of Indian women is confined inside the narrow walls of their home. The National Family Health Survey (NFHS), in its second round of investigation which interviewed 90,000 women in the age-group of 15 to 49, reported that up to 58 to 65 per cent women had been beaten by their husbands, fathers, brothers or sons for reasons ranging from neglecting the home, being 'disrespectful' to their in-laws and going out without informing their husbands. A survey of 10000 Muslim and Hindu women, conducted by Zoya Hasan and Ritu Menon, reported (The Hindustan Times, Jan. 5, 2001) that 85-90 per cent women accepted to have experienced physical abuse at the hands of their husbands. Even more shocking, women over 55, probably widowed, simply move from one male destination to the next. In the absence of husbands, sons step in to continue the mistreatment. The NFHS reports that wife beating cuts across the religious barriers. These data indicate the current status of Indian women. However, there are bright spots in this dark picture. There are highly educated and respected women holding high position in public life and the government.

Major Policies and Programmes

During the post-independence period, the main strategy of achieving equalization of educational opportunities has been the expansion of educational facilities on a massive scale so as to make school accessible to every child. It was thought that expansion of educational facilities, as a part of providing universal elementary education for all would make education available to the weaker sections of the society including women. It was found that there had been a phenomenal development in the education of women. Emphasizing the significance of women's education, the Education Commission (1964-66) observed:

> The significance of the education of girls cannot be overemphasized. For full development of our human resources, the improvement of homes, and for molding the character of children during the most impressionable years of infancy, the education of women is of even greater importance than that of men. As stated earlier, the education of women can assist greatly in reducing the fertility rate. In the modern world, the role of the women goes much beyond the home and the bringing up of children. She is now adopting a career of her own and sharing equally with man the responsibility of the development of the society in all its aspects. This is the direction in which we shall have to move. In the struggle for freedom, Indian women fought side by side with men. This equal partnership will have to continue in the fight against hunger, poverty, ignorance and ill health.

As per the data presented by the Commission, in 1901, the percentage of literacy among women was only 0.8. The number of girls enrolled for every 100 boys was only 12 at the primary stage and 4 at the secondary. The total enrollment in higher education was only 264 including 76 girls studying in medical colleges and 11 in colleges of education. Much faster progress was made during the next 50 years, both in raising their social status and in developing their education; and the progress after independence had been phenomenal. However, the recommendations of the Commission regarding education of girls seemed to have made no significant impact on the then ruling party, and the National Policy on Education (1968), which was subsequently formulated did not contain any significant proposals excepting the statement, "The education of girls should receive emphasis, not only on the grounds of social justice, but also because it accelerates social transformation." Due to the existing programmes, and some initiatives on the part of the government, the girls' education had developed faster than that of boys during the post-independence period. Consequently, the gap between the educational levels of boys and girls had decreased at all stages from 1947 to 1965; and further narrowed down between 1965 and 1985.

The progress of education was reviewed in 1985, and it was found that the gap between the education of male and female populations was still very large. The government took note of the situation and made specific proposals for development of women's education in the National Policy on Education, 1986. The NPE-1986, which was launched the same year, stated:

> Education will be used as an agent of basic change in the status of women. In order to neutralize the accumulated distortions of the past, there will be well-conceived edge in favour of women. The National System of Education will play a positive, interventionist role in the empowerment of women. It will foster the development of new values through redesigned curricula, textbooks, the training and orientation of teachers, decision-makers and administrators, and the active involvement of educational institutions. This will be an act of faith and social engineering. Women's studies will be promoted as a part of various courses and educational institutions encouraged to take up active programmes to further women's

> development....The removal of women's illiteracy and obstacles inhibiting their access to, and retention in, elementary education will receive overriding priority, through provision of special support services, setting of time targets, and effective monitoring. Major emphasis will be laid on women's participation in vocational, technical and professional education at different levels. The policy of non-discrimination will be pursued vigorously to eliminate sex stereotyping in vocational and professional courses and to promote women's participation in non-traditional occupations, as well as in existing and emergent technologies.

In order to implement these proposals of the NPE-1986, Government of India launched several programmes. One such programme was the Mahila Samakhya, whose main emphasis was on women empowerment. The programme endeavours to create a learning environment where women can collectively affirm their potential, gain the strength to demand information and knowledge and move forward to change and take charge of their lives. The Sangria (village level women's collective) is the nodal point around which the programme revolves. The process of mobilizing and organizing women is facilitated by a 'sahayogini' who is a cluster coordinator in-charge of 10 villages. Sahyogini serves as a link between the district implementation unit, which provides resource support to the programme to meet the needs of women. State Office supports the district unit, and at the national level, a Project Director coordinates the programme.

Mahila Samakhya has expanded its coverage to 51 districts and over 7335 villages (GOI, 2000) in the states of Uttar Pradesh, Karnataka, Gujarat, Andhra Pradesh, Bihar, Madhya Pradesh, Assam and Kerala. The sangha, the nodal point of the programme, has emerged as an effective umbrella for women to come together, at the village level. The sanghas address a wide range of issues, which relate to the livelihood, education and health of women, as well as accessing resources among others. Kishori sanghas and kendras/centers have been started in all States. There are about 900 kendras with over 20000 adolescent girls studying in them, in the whole country.

There are several other programs, which have been launched by the government of India in order to implement the proposals of

NPE-1986 (as revised in 1992). In fact the effectiveness of the programme, however good at the face of it, largely depends on its implementation. During the last 53 years since independence, the government has been striving hard to achieve its targets in different aspects of education including that of women. Let us examine the progress of women's education in terms of literacy rate, enrollment of girls at school stage and their participation in the educative process.

Progress and Achievements

As per the figures based on 1991 census, women constitute about 48.27% of the total population of India. In fact this percentage should have been 50. But, in the field of education these disparities are still larger. The gap between the literacy rates of males and females has been persisting since 1901 when the female literacy rate was 0.60% as against 9.83% among males. The disparity index (ratio of male literacy rate to female literacy rate) in 1901 was 16.38. The literacy rate of women rose to 7.97% in 1951 and to 39.29% in 1991. As shown in Table 10.1, the literacy rate among women has increased at a faster rate than among men. This is evident from the successively decreasing trend of disparity indices, which from 16.4 in 1901 fell down to 3.1 in 1951, and to 1.6 in 1991. It is estimated that by 1997, it might have further declined to 1.5. Although, a little more than 60% of the country's adult population (62% in 1997) is now literate, about 50% of the female population still remain illiterate (Krishnan, HT, Dec. 26, 1998). The wide gap (70-50) between the male and female literacy persists at national level despite a spectacular improvement in a few states, led by Kerala. At the same time women responded far more enthusiastically than men to the Total Literacy Campaigns launched by the government in 1990s with the help of non-governmental organizations and the cooperation of volunteers. Turning to statistics, it appears that the material realities of the lives of the majority of Indian women have not improved significantly. Indeed, in some ways, their situation seems to have become worse. Take for example the sex ratio, which has come to be accepted as a revealing indicator of women's status. Only a few countries in the world—among them India—have fewer women than men. The Indian sex ratio has been abnormal since the turn of the century, with only 972 women for 1000 men in 1901.

It is currently at an all-time low 927 in 1991 down from 946 in 1951. Something is clearly rotten in the state of the nation (Manorama Yearbook, 2000).

Table 10.1
Sex Differences in Literacy Rates (1901-1997)*

Year	*Male Literacy Rates*	*Female Literacy Rates*	*Disparity Index*
1901	9.83	0.60	16.4
1911	10.56	1.05	10.1
1921	12.21	1.81	7.6
1931	15.59	2.93	5.3
1941	24.90	7.30	3.4
1951	24.95	7.93	3.1
1961	34.44	12.95	2.6
1971	39.45	18.69	2.1
1981	56.50	29.85	1.9
1991	64.13	39.29	1.6
2001	75.85	54.16	1.4

*Compiled from Selected Educational Statistics, HRD Ministry, Govt. of India, 1996-97 and Manorama Yearbooks, 2000, 2001, and 2002.

At school stage, the progress of girl's education has also not been satisfactory. In 1947, the enrollment of girls in school was 25% of the total enrollment. The situation did not change much by 1948-49. In 1950-51, the enrollment of girls was 28% (5.4 million out of 19.2 million) at primary school stage, and about 26.5% (5.9 million out of 22.3 million) at the total elementary school stage (class I-VIII). By 1998-99 (table 10.2), the situation had considerably improved (also see table 4.2) with girls' enrollment being 43.5% (48.3 million out of 111.0 million) at primary level and 42.7% (64.6 million out of 151.4 million) at elementary stage. The female teachers constitute about 35.3% of the total number of teachers working in elementary schools now, as against 16.8% in 1951

As mentioned earlier, the enrollment of girls has increased at a faster rate than that of boys, at primary, upper primary and the entire elementary levels. During the period 1951-1966, the Annual Compound Growth Rate (ACGR) of enrollment of girls was 8.8% as against 6.1% of boys. During 1966-1986, the corresponding figures were 3.8 and 2.8 respectively. During the period 1986-1996, the ACGRs in the case of both girls and boys, further decreased, perhaps because of higher base, the corresponding figures being 4.2 and 2.7. The foregoing analysis shows that during the whole period of 50 years since independence, the enrollment growth rate of girls has been higher than that of boys.

Table 10.2
Girls' Enrollment as percentage of Total Enrollment

Year	*Primary Upper Stage (I-V)*	*Primary Stage (VI-VIII)*	*Secondary Stage (IX-XII)*	*University*
1950-51	28.1	16.1	13.3	10.0
1955-56	30.5	20.8	15.4	14.6
1960-61	32.6	23.9	20.5	16.0
1965-66	36.2	26.7	22.0	20.4
1970-71	37.4	29.3	25.0	20.0
1975-76	38.1	31.3	26.9	23.2
1980-81	38.6	32.9	29.6	26.7
1985-86	40.3	35.6	30.3	33.0
1990-91	41.5	36.7	32.9	33.3
1995-96	43.2	39.0	35.3	37.2
1998-99	43.5	40.5	37.8	38.8

1. Selected Educational Statistics, HRD Ministry, Govt. of India, 1997.
2. HRD Ministry, Govt. of India (Department of Education), Annual Report, 2000.

At the secondary and senior secondary stages also the percentage of girls' enrollment has been consistently increasing. In 1950-51, the girls constituted 13.3% of the total enrollment in classes IX-XII, while this figure has increased to 37.8% by 1998-99. Similarly, at the university stage also, the enrollment of girls has increased from only 10% in 1950-51 to 38.8% in 1998-99 (GOI, 2000). These data indicate that the participation of women has been increasing.

These figures, which paint a very dismal picture, are further disappointing when actual participation of girls in elementary and secondary education is examined. As mentioned in Chapter IV, all the children who are enrolled in primary or elementary school do not complete elementary education. The dropout rate of girls has been consistently higher than that of boys. In 1960-61, the dropout rate of girls up to class V and class VIII were 71 and 85 respectively. This showed that out of every 100 girls enrolled in class I only 15 completed elementary education. Though, the situation has considerably improved now, yet the progress is still unsatisfactory. At present (1998-99), out of every 100 girls enrolled in class I, about 40 complete class VIII. At the secondary stage also the situation is similar. It is reported by the government agencies that 70% of girls enrolled in schools dropout before completing education up to class X.

As in the case of school stage, the enrollment of girls has increased at a faster rate than that of boys in higher education also. Like separate schools, there are also separate colleges and universities for women in India. Today, we have 5 universities and 1359 colleges exclusively meant for women. The first women was admitted to the University of Calcutta in 1877, the second to the University of Chennai in 1881 and the third to the University of Mumbai in 1883 (Desai, 1999), though these universities had been established in 1857. The period of 123 years since the first women entered the university for higher education, has witnessed a steady progress in women's higher education. While the percentage of women students in higher education institutions was only 9.3 in 1947, it has risen to 38.8 by the session 1999-2000, though there is state-wise variation with Kerala having enrolled the highest percentage of women and Bihar the lowest. From 14 women per 100 men enrolled in 1950-51, the increase is over fourfold now—53 women for every 100 men.

Another important thing about the enrollment of women in higher education is that their concentration is more in the faculties of Arts and Social Sciences than in other faculties. While 54.4 % of women are enrolled in these faculties, as against 40.4% of all students, their percentage is only 2.1 in the faculty of Engineering and Technology. Traditionally, a large majority of women continues to enroll in the faculties of Arts and Social Sciences. However, in recent years there has been a systematic shift in their preference towards science subjects, and consequently, the enrollment of women (19.2%) in the faculty of science is approximately equal to the overall enrollment (19.6%) in these subjects. But in professional subjects including commerce, except education where the enrollment of girls is 3.4% compared to the overall figure of 2.3%, their enrollment continues to be lower than the national average.

Problems

Though, the government of India has made earnest efforts, since independence, to improve the educational status of women, and met with considerable success, yet there is much to be done to bring them at par with men. There are certain factors, which hamper the progress of girls, both at school and college levels. First, a large number of girls of school going age are not enrolled because they have to assist their mothers in domestic work. They have either to participate directly in the cooking work or assist their mothers indirectly by bringing food and fodder for domestic animals, keeping younger siblings and bringing water and fuel. It has been reported that of all the non-enrolled children 70% are girls. While the enrollment ratio of boys is around 100%, it is only about 83% for girls at the primary stage. The attitude of parents, especially in rural areas, is also not favourable to girls' education. It is believed that girls are Paraya Dhan (the property of others), and hence need not be educated. As they are to be married off and sent to their in-laws' place. This points to the need of educating parents, especially, in rural areas.

Second, these beliefs have given rise to another related problem of "child marriage", which is still prevalent in some regions/states. Even as child marriage remains a legal offence, it continues to be prevalent in Madhya Pradesh where 15.4% of the girls, most of them from rural areas, are married off between the age of 10 and 14. According to the human Development Report 1998, 16.6% of the rural girls and 11% of the urban girls in the 10-14 age group in the country's biggest State married in 1997. The Child Marriage Restraint Act was enacted in 1929. This Act fixed the minimum age of marriage for boys and girls at 18 and 14 years respectively. Since then, this Act has undergone several amendments. The latest amendment made in 1978 raised the minimum age of marriage to 21 years for boys and 18 years for girls. But in violation of these laws, the evil of child marriage still persists. This is a great problem affecting the education of girls adversely. When a girl marries at the age of 11 year, how can she attend school?

Third, girls have been taught to believe that domestic work is the only occupation for them. They do not think of any thing other than getting married, going away to in-laws' house, and bearing and rearing children. Marriage and Motherhood are, practically speaking, the only career options for majority of Indian women, and for which they are groomed from girlhood. Marriage is near universal in India as 95% of all women are or have been married, the overwhelming majority by the age of 18. Most often within a year they are mothers (Menon, 2001), and the average number of children per women is 3.7, as per 1991 census. So, generally speaking, most Indian women do a good job of motherhood, whether they like it or not.

Fourth, illiteracy among mothers is another serious problem. Jawaharlal Nehru had once said that when we educate a boy we educate a single individual, but when we educate a girl we educate a family. There is a strong linkage between socio-economic factors and family size. This has been proved through numerous research studies conducted in India and abroad. Mothers who are illiterate or are educated only up to primary school level tend to have more than six children, while number comes down to five in the case of mothers with middle level education, four in the case of matriculates and only two in the case of those educated up to the university stage (HT, July 11, 1988). Thus, in order to have educated mothers, education of girls is important and necessary.

Fifth, the economic dependence of women on men (husbands or fathers) is a great barrier threatening their self-respect. The dominance of male members of the family over female members can also be explained in terms of economic dependence. The incidences of wife beating, wife abuse, physical exploitation by men, killings for dowry, and similar other acts of violence against women occur because of this reason only. Attempts have to be made to educate girls in such a way that they become economically independent. On the one hand, this will develop confidence in them, and on the other, they will be able to assist their families economically. This will lead to an overall improvement of the quality of life. For this purpose, women should be encouraged to join job oriented and professional courses such as engineering and technology, medicine, education, law and agriculture. The government should start separate institutions of these courses for girls.

EDUCATION OF SCHEDULED CASTES AND SCHEDULED TRIBES

Historical Perspective

In the traditional Varna Vyavastha (the caste system), the Indian society was divided into groups, known as castes, on the basis of traditional occupations. Among the four major Varnas, the Brahmins were considered superior and constituted a respectable class. The Kshatriyas were considered as warriors and Vaishyas as those who would take care of economy and supply of food. The Shudras had the responsibility of serving the upper castes. It is said that Brahmins came from mouth, Kshatriyas from arms, Vaishyas from stomach and Shudras from the feet of the creator (Ghurye, 1969). Gradually this categorization of people, which was purely based on occupation, generated certain social evils such has untouchability, social isolation and denial of opportunities to Shudra. The caste-based stratification of society adversely affected the equality of educational opportunities to the disadvantage of these groups as they were engaged in traditional family occupations, which did not require any kind of education or special training. This situation persisted throughout the ages and the depressed classes continued to be deprived of educational opportunities, which were cornered by the upper castes.

The Constitution identified another class of people living in remote areas and cut off from the society at large. These people known as Scheduled Tribes are mostly concentrated in states of Orissa, Bihar, Madhya Pradesh, Andhra Pradesh, Maharashtra, Gujarat and Rajasthan, where they are about 80% of the total tribal population of India. In some North Eastern States they are more than 80% of the total population, and mostly live on the hillsides and in forests. They are isolated from the rest of the society due to poor transportation and communication facilities and have remained educationally, culturally, economically and socially disadvantaged (Chauhan, 1990). Scheduled Castes (SCs) and Scheduled Tribes (STs) have been considered to be the lowest in the social hierarchy. They were labelled as untouchables, and hence, denied all educational opportunities in the past. Being mostly illiterate, they have been subjected to all kinds of exploitation—social, economic and political. They feel that they have also been subjected to social segregation, rejection, atrocities, and harassment. It has been only after independence that the government of India thought of improving their lot by providing some guarantees in order to facilitate their socio-economic uplift.

Policies and Programmes

During the British Period, the policies of the then rulers also perpetuated and strengthened the caste-based division of Indian society and used it to their advantage. The expression "Scheduled Castes" was coined by the British Simon Commission and was embodied in the Government of India Act of 1935 to refer to the groups, which were then known as depressed classes. Later on, Mahatma Gandhi, the Father of the Nation, called them Harijans meaning the "People of God". One of the main features of the British policy of education in India was its adherence to what was called the "downward filtration theory", which consisted in providing education to the few elite classes who in turn were expected to educate the masses. As mentioned in Chapter 1, the British policies forced Indian people to study English, which was also the medium of instruction for the education of the elite. The policy, in effect, resulted in the neglect of the education of the masses including Scheduled Castes and Scheduled Tribes who were the worst sufferers. However, some sporadic attempts were made to educate the Scheduled Castes, largely by Christian missionaries and some prominent social reformers. In fact, the British policy of education in India was egalitarian, at least in theory, and the educational institutions set up and supported by the government were open to all irrespective of caste or community affiliation. Among the social reformers, the attempts made by Jytiba Phule who opened schools for the lower castes were commendable. Other individuals and reform movements such as Prarthana Samaj and Arya Samaj further carried on the initiative taken by Jyotiba Phule in a big way. But these efforts were inadequate in view of the prolonged disadvantage suffered by the Scheduled Castes. For instance, in 1921-22, the enrollment of the Scheduled Caste at different stages of education in India was 6.1 per cent (Aikara, 1996). The vast majority of Scheduled Caste students were enrolled at the primary school stage. Their enrollment at every stage above this was less than two per cent. Thus, at the time of independence in

1947, India inherited an educational system in which depressed classes had a very low level of participation.

When the Constitution of India was drafted, special attention was paid to these classes by making special provision for their welfare. The founding fathers of the Indian Constitutions made special provisions for educational development of the Scheduled Castes and the Scheduled Tribes. There are some clauses in the Constitution (also see Chapter 2 for details), which provide for equality to all classes of citizens. For instance, Article 15 prohibits "discrimination against any citizen on the ground only of religion, race, caste, class, place of birth or any of them." The equality of opportunity to all citizens in the matters related to employment or appointment to any office under the state is guaranteed under Article 16, which states, "No citizen will be considered ineligible or discriminated against in respect of any employment or office under the State." Article 46 of the Constitution has placed on the government a responsibility of promoting with special care the educational and economic interests of the weaker sections of the people, and in particular, of Scheduled Castes and Scheduled Tribes, and protecting them from social injustice and all forms of exploitation.

In addition to this, the Constitution has also safeguarded the interests of Scheduled Castes and Scheduled Tribes against any kind of discrimination in the matters related to establishment of separate educational institutions or admission in the existing institutions. The state would also not discriminate against the institutions established and managed by these classes in the matters of providing grant from the State funds. The government has also issued notification and instructions to various State governments, universities and the administrations of Union Territories to reserve 20% of the seats in different educational and technical institutions for students belonging to Scheduled Castes and Scheduled Tribes sharing 15% and 5% of the seats respectively. Moreover, this reservation would be interchangeable (Prasad, 1986), that is, if sufficient number of candidates is not available to fill up the seats reserved for Scheduled Tribes, these may be filled up by suitable Scheduled Caste candidates, and vice-versa. The government also suggested that a minimum qualifying standard should be prescribed for admission, and the Scheduled Caste and Scheduled Tribe candidates should be considered eligible for admission to the reserved seats if they attain that standard without any reference to the gap between their marks and the marks of the last person admitted to the open seats. In case a minimum percentage of marks is prescribed as a criterion for eligibility, a reduction of 5% be made for SC/ST candidates provided the reduced percentage is not less than the minimum pass percentage in the qualifying examination. No policy can be so liberal and biased in favour of a particular class of people as this. This reveals that the government of India has left no stone unturned in making protective discrimination in favour of the weaker sections of the society.

Education Commission (1964-66) further clarified the intentions of the government regarding the education of Scheduled Castes and Scheduled Tribes saying, "It is necessary to pay special attention to the education of children from the backward classes which include the Scheduled Castes, the Scheduled Tribes, denotified communities and a few nomadic and semi-nomadic groups." The Commission felt that so far as Scheduled Castes were concerned, the problem had become a little easier because of the diminution in the rigour of untouchability. However, for its early solution, the Commission recommended that the ongoing programmes for the education of Scheduled Castes should continue and be expanded.

On reviewing the situation the Commission found that, on the whole, the progress of education of Scheduled Castes during the period from 1947 to 1965 was satisfactory. At the secondary stage, the coefficient of equalization (the proportion of enrollment of SC/ST groups to their total population divided by the proportion of all enrollments to total population and multiplied by 100) also indicated satisfactory progress of these groups. What worried the Commission (Naik, 1982) was that the progress was not uniform because the dominant people/groups among these classes cornered the maximum benefit and those who actually needed it were again denied the opportunities. Secondly, the rate of wastage remained high with a large incidence of dropouts and failures among the students belonging to these classes. Their achievement was generally low and it was often difficult to find suitably qualified candidates among these classes to fill up the posts reserved for them in the government services. Thirdly, the students belonging to these categories could not find places in the quality institutions such as IITs and IIMs either because of low achievement or because of low merit in competitive tests. But, the National Policy on Education, 1968, which was formulated after the Commission and was to be based on its recommendations made no special proposals for the education of scheduled castes and scheduled tribes. It was, perhaps, because the then ruling party had some different way of thinking and approaches to deal with the problem. Pundit Nehru, while addressing all the Chief Ministers in June 1961 (Jain, 2000) had once said:

> I dislike any kind of reservation in service. I react strongly against any thing, which leads to inefficiency and second-rate standards.... The only real way to help a backward group is to give opportunities for a good education.... But, if we go in for reservations on communal and caste basis, we swamp the bright and able people and remain second-rate or third-rate... It has amazed me to learn that even promotions are based sometimes on communal and caste considerations. This way lies not only folly, but also disaster. Let us help the backward groups by all means, but never at the cost of efficiency. How are we going to build our public sector or indeed any sector with second-rate people?

The Draft National Policy on Education, 1979 expressed grave concern over the dismal educational condition of certain disadvantaged sections of the society including Scheduled Castes and Scheduled Tribes. It stated:

> While there has been considerable expansion in all sectors of education in our country, imbalances and inequalities still persist. Girls, Scheduled Castes and Tribes, land-less labourers, backward classes and urban slum poor generally continue to lag behind in education. Special effort must be made to identify the problems in these cases and to bring all such people into the fold of education.

The government if India reviewed the progress of education in 1985 and published a discussion document, and subsequently, formulated the National Policy on Education (NPE)-1986 followed by a Programme of Action (POA). In these documents, the detailed proposals (NPE-1986) and schemes (POA-1986) to be pursued for the improvement of educational status of Scheduled Castes and Scheduled Tribes were given. The relevant statements of the NPE-1986 are given below:

THE EDUCATION OF SCHEDULED CASTES

The central focus in SCs' educational development is their equalization with the non-SC population at all stages and levels of education, in all areas and in all the four dimensions—rural male, rural female, urban male and urban female. The measures contemplated for this purpose include:

(i) Incentives to indigent families to send their children to school regularly till they reach the age of 14;

(ii) Pre-matric scholarship scheme for children of families engaged in occupations such as scavenging, flaying and tanning to be made applicable from class I onwards. All children of such families, regardless of income, will be covered by this scheme and time-bound programmes targeted on them will be undertaken;

(iii) Constant micro-planning and verification to ensure that the enrollment, retention and successful completion of courses by SC students do not fall at any stage, and provision of remedial courses to improve their prospects for further education and employment;

(iv) Recruitment of teachers from Scheduled Castes;

(v) Provision of facilities for SC students in students' hostels at district headquarters, according to a phased programme;

(vi) Location of school buildings, Balwadis and Adult Education centers in such a way as to facilitate full participation of Scheduled Castes;

(vii) Utilization of NREP and RLEGP resources so as to make substantial educational facilities available to Scheduled Castes; and

(viii) Constant innovation in finding new methods to increase the participation of Scheduled Castes in the educational process.

THE EDUCATION OF SCHEDULED TRIBES

The following measures will be taken urgently to bring the Scheduled Tribes on par with others:

(i) Priority will be accorded to opening primary schools in tribal areas. The construction of school buildings will be undertaken in these areas on a priority basis under the normal funds for education, as well as under the NREP, RLEGP, Tribal Welfare schemes, etc.

(ii) The socio-cultural milieu of the STs has its distinctive characteristics including, in many cases, their own spoken language. This underlines the need to develop the curricula and devise the instructional materials in tribal languages at the initial stage, with arrangements for switching over to the regional language.

(iii) Educated and promising Scheduled Tribe youths will be encouraged and trained to take up teaching in tribal areas.

(iv) Residential schools, including Ashram schools, will be established on a large scale.

(v) Incentive schemes will be formulated for the Scheduled Tribes, keeping in view their special needs and lifestyles. Scholarships for higher education will emphasize technical, professional and para-technical courses. Special remedial courses and other programs to remove psychosocial impediments will be provided to improve their performance in various courses.

(vi) Anganwadis, Non-formal and Adult Education Centers will be opened on a priority basis in areas predominantly inhabited by Scheduled Tribes.

(vii) The curriculum at all stages of education will be designed to create an awareness of the rich cultural identity of the tribal people as also of their enormous creative talent.

Population and Literacy

Scheduled Castes and Scheduled Tribes are two important segments of the people of India. The census experience indicates that the population of these segments increases faster than the overall population of the country. The details of the population and literacy profile of these two sections in relation to the total population of the country are given in Table 10.3 below:

Table 10.3
Population and Literacy Profile of Scheduled Castes and Scheduled Tribes (1951-1991)

Year	*All*	*Scheduled Castes*			*Scheduled Tribes*		
	Persons	*Population*	*Percentage*	*Literacy*	*Population*	*Percentage*	*Literacy*
1951	361						
1961	439	64.5	14.7	10.27	29.9	6.8	8.53
1971	548	80.0	14.6	14.67	38.0	6.9	11.30
1981	683	104.8	15.3	21.38	51.6	7.6	16.35
1991	846	138.2	16.3	37.41	67.8	8.0	29.60

Source: Selected Educational Statistics, MHRD, the Government of India, New Delhi 1996-97.

As shown in the table, the population of scheduled castes in India has increased from only 64.5 million in 1961 to 80 million in 1971, 104.8 million in 1981 and 138.2 million in 1991. There has been over 2.14 times growth in 30 years, while the total population increased 1.93 times during the same period. The literacy rate of scheduled castes has increased from 10.27% to 37.41. In their case also there have been wide disparities based on sex and rural-urban location. The female literacy rate among scheduled castes was 23.76% against 49.91% among males. The disparity is clearly wider than in the case of general population including the scheduled castes (see Table 5.1). The literacy rate among rural scheduled caste population had a literacy rate of 33.25% while urban scheduled caste population had a literacy rate of 55.11%. This shows that, there is much to be done to bring the literacy rate of scheduled castes at par with the general population.

The Scheduled Tribe population has also increased 2.27 times from 1961 to 1991. The growth rate, in this case also, has been more than that of the general population. The literacy rate among scheduled tribes was 8.53% in 1961 which has increase to 29.60% by 1991. During the same period, the literacy rate of Scheduled Caste males has increased from 13.83% to 40.65%, and that of scheduled caste females increased from 3.16% to 18.19%. Similarly, the literacy rate among scheduled caste rural population increased from 8.16% to 29.60%, and that of urban population increased from 22.41% to 56.60%. The scheduled tribe rural females had the lowest literacy rate of 3.16%. The situation will become clearer if we examine the comparative figures related to these groups and the non-scheduled population as given in table 10.4.

Table 10.4
Comparative Literacy Rates of Scheduled and Non-scheduled Populations (1991)

Particulars	*Scheduled Castes*	*Scheduled Tribes*	*Non-Scheduled Population*
Total			
Male	49.91	40.65	69.53
Female	23.76	18.19	44.81
Total	37.41	29.60	57.69
Rural			
Male	45.95	38.45	63.42
Female	19.46	16.02	35.38
Total	33.25	27.38	49.86
Urban			
Male	66.50	66.56	83.40
Female	42.29	45.66	67.48
Total	55.11	56.60	75.93

The literacy rates of Scheduled Castes and Scheduled Tribes when compared with the literacy rates of non-scheduled communities indicate that the persons belonging to the scheduled groups are far behind the persons belonging to non-scheduled communities. It can be observed from table 10.4 that there are wide disparities between the literacy rates of scheduled and non-scheduled sections of the society in India. The total literacy rate of non-scheduled communities (57.69%) is 1.54 time the total literacy rate of SC, and 1.95 times the total literacy rate of ST communities. Almost similar differences are visible in the literacy rates of non-scheduled rural population and scheduled rural populations. The widest difference may be observed between the literacy rates of non-scheduled caste urban males (83.40%) and the scheduled tribe rural females (16.02%). This indicates that we have to do a lot to bridge these gaps in literacy rates, which are based on sex, caste and rural-urban location.

School Education Among SC/ST Communities

The government of India has been making continuous efforts to equalize educational opportunities between the privileged and disadvantaged sections of the society by way of implementing the provisions of Article 46 of the Constitution. After independence, a number of steps have been taken by the government to strengthen the educational base of the weaker sections including SC/ST communities and other backward classes. Ideally, the participation of these classes in educational process should be according to their proportion in the total population of India. Though, overall progress in this direction is satisfactory, yet much work has to be done to remove the educational disparities, which exist on various grounds. The progress of school education among scheduled castes in relation to total population is presented in Table 10.5 below.

Table 10.5*
Enrollment of Scheduled Caste Children by Sex and Level of School Education

(Fig. in 000s)

Year	Primary (Classes I-V)		Upper Primary (Classes VI-VIII)		Secondary/Senior Sec. (Classes IX-XII)	
	Total	Girls	Total	Girls	Total	Girls
1978-79	7926 (16.4)	— —	3108 (11.7)	— —	2170 (10.3)	— —
1980-81	10981 (15,1)	3768 (12.9)	2223 (11.2)	602 (8.8)	1152 (10.5)	246 (7.2)
1985-86	13921 (16.1)	5194 (14.8)	3619 (12.9)	1082 (11.3)	1810 (11.0)	432 (8.6)
1990-91	15794 (15.9)	6057 (15.0)	4160 (12.5)	1413 (11.3)	2338 (12.2)	635 (10.0)
1995-96	17906 (16.3)	7353 (15.5)	5956 (13.2)	2255 (12.1)	2940 (11.8)	935 (10.6)

*The figures within the parentheses indicate the SC enrollment as per cent of the total enrollment at the corresponding stages. The figures for enrollment of girls during the 1978-79 session were not available.

Sources: 1. Govt. of India, Education of Scheduled Castes and Scheduled Tribes 1988-89, MHRD, Department of Education, New Delhi, 1993.
2. Govt. of India, Selected Educational Statistics 1996-97, Department of Education, MHRD, New Delhi.

As shown in the table, the enrollment of the children belonging to Scheduled Castes, at the primary stage, is around 15-16% of the total enrollment at that stage, in the case of both boys and girls. This corresponds to the proportion of their number in the total population of India. But, at the upper primary stage, their enrollment is around 12-13% of the total enrollment at that stage. The situation at the Secondary and Senior Secondary stages is also not satisfactory with the enrollment of students belonging to SC communities being about 10-12%, the girls' enrollment being still lower. This points to the need of under taking some special measures to encourage the SC parents to send their daughters to school. There is a need to establish schools in the areas predominantly inhabited by these communities, on a priority basis. The government of India has taken measures like providing scholarships, free-ships, mid-day meals, free uniforms, books and stationery, reservation of seats in educational institutions for SC/ST children, relaxation in the standards for admission to the institutions of higher education, coaching classes for competitive examinations and hostels specifically meant for these children.

The Scheduled Tribes constitute another important section of our society needing special attention as for as educational opportunities are concerned. The educational problems of these communities are more serious than any other section of the society because of their special geographical and environmental constraints. The progress of enrollment of children belonging to Scheduled Tribes is presented in Table 10.6 below.

Table 10.6*
Enrollment of Scheduled Tribe Children by Sex and Level of School Education

(Fig. in 000s)

Year	*Primary (Classes I-V)*		*Upper Primary (Classes VI-VIII)*		*Secondary/Senior Sec. (Classes IX-XII)*	
	Total	*Girls*	*Total*	*Girls*	*Total*	*Girls*
1978-79	3398 (7.0)	1124 (4.3)	1279 (4.8)	401 (6.8)	460 (2.7)	154 (5.4)
1980-81	4660 (6.3)	1527 (5.4)	742 (3.6)	205 (3.0)	329 (3.0)	83 (2.4)
1985-86	6580 (7.5)	2406 (6.8)	1283 (4.7)	390 (4.1)	585 (3.6)	165 (3.3)
1990-91	7869 (8.1)	2911 (7.2)	1707 (5.0)	576 (4.6)	805 (4.2)	238 (3.8)
1995-96	8794 (8.0)	3608 (7.6)	2545 (6.2)	938 (5.9)	1207 (4.9)	396 (4.5)

*The figures within the parentheses indicate the ST enrollment as per cent of the total enrollment at the corresponding stages.

Sources: The same as for Table 10.5.

As in the case of SC communities, the enrollment of ST children at primary stage also corresponds to the proportion of their number in the total population. The table 10.6 shows that during 1990s, the enrollment of ST children, including girls, has been about 7-8%, which approximates the percentage of their population (8.08%) in the total population of India. But, at upper primary and secondary school level their enrollment has not been satisfactory. It may be seen in the table that the enrollment of ST children at the upper primary stage varies between 5% and 6%, and that at the secondary school stage the corresponding figures vary around 4-5%. These data indicate that the progress of education of ST children at upper primary and secondary stages is not satisfactory, and sustained efforts have to be made to raise their educational status during the years to come. The government should provide attractive financial incentives to enhance the enrollment of ST children, especially, at upper primary and secondary stages. In view of their specific problems emerging out of their geographical and environmental location.

Government should set up more schools in the vicinity of their habitations. Attempts may be made to utilize the services of voluntary agencies by way of helping them in opening non-formal education centers and pre-primary schools.

Higher Education Among SC/ST Communities

Despite the policy of protective discrimination in favour of SC and ST groups followed by the government of India during the last five decades, these groups still continue to be educationally backward. This is truer in the case of university education than in the case of school education. The situation has been so dismal that in 1921-22 the enrollment of these communities in higher education was only 0.5% of the total (Goyal, 1984) enrollment in colleges and universities. As a special provision, a scheme of Central Scholarships was launched by the government in 1944, which was initially meant for SC communities only, but later on was extended to cover ST communities (1948-49) and Other Backward Classes (1949-50) also. Since then, the scheme is continuing covering larger and larger number of castes/students and involving huge expenditure. The situation had not improved much by 1947, the year of independence. The University Education Commission

(1948-49) laid special emphasis on the education of weaker sections of the society including SC and ST communities. The Commission stated that "In the democratic society, the opportunity of learning must be open not only to the elite but also to all those who have to carry the privilege and responsibility of citizenship. Education is a universal right, not a class privilege." In order to provide adequate opportunities to the candidates belonging to the weaker sections of the society, the government of India provided reservation of seats to the extent of 20%–15% for Scheduled Castes and 5% for Scheduled Tribes.

In view of the slow progress, the Committee on the Welfare of Scheduled Castes and Scheduled Tribes (1973-75) recommended that statistics regarding reservation of seats for SC and ST students should be collected from all universities and should be published in the Annual Report of the UGC. The Committee also suggested that a separate cell with adequate staff should be created in regard to the effective implementation of reservation orders in favour of SC and ST candidates and a note on the activities of the cell included in the UGC Annual Report.

The UGC, in 1975, invited the attention of the universities to the guidelines issued by the Ministry of Education and Social Welfare regarding reservation of seats for SC/ST students in universities/colleges. It was mentioned that according to the existing arrangement, 20% seats were reserved for SC/ST candidates and they were also given a concession of 5% marks in the minimum percentage of marks required for admission to any course. Later on it was observed that even with these concessions, some of the seats in the reserved quota remained vacant due non-availability of suitably qualified SC/ST candidates. Accordingly, it was suggested that in such a situation, a further relaxation in the minimum qualifying marks, might be given to SC/ST candidates in orders of merit (among them) so that candidates belonging to these communities fill all the reserved seats. In the light of the recommendations of the Commission for Scheduled Castes and Scheduled Tribes (1973-74), the UGC asked the universities/colleges to provide reservation of 20% seats for ST and ST students in the hostels. In July 1975, the UGC agreed in principle that reservations may be provided for SC/ST candidates for recruitment to the post of Lecturers in the universities/colleges and mechanics for such reservations may be worked out. It was also decided that in order that a teaching post may not remain vacant for long periods, such reservations may not be operated on roster basis nor should the reserved posts be carried forward from year to year. These reservation percentages in enrollment, recruitment and hostels facilities were revised to 15% for SC and 7.5% for ST communities since August 1982.

Progress

No authentic and systematic data are available regarding the enrollment of SC and ST students in higher education. However, a survey conducted by the National Commission on Teachers-II (1985) provided some information about the enrollment of SC students in general and professional courses at the university stage. In 1964-65, the SC students enrolled in general education were 64,000, which constituted 5.5% of the total enrollment in these courses. In professional education, their number was 31,000 constituting 4.3% of the total enrollment in these courses. These figures had increased to 3.30 lakhs and 68,000 respectively by 1977-78, constituting 7.7% and 6.8% in general and professional courses.

In order to implement the provisions of reservation effectively, the UGC has created a special cell known as SCT Cell. The responsibility of the SCT Cell is to circulate the decisions of the government of India and the UGC to the universities and colleges and to collect regularly, on annual basis, the factual information/position regarding admissions of SC/ST candidates though reservation policy. Accordingly, the SCT Cell conducted a survey regarding admission of SC/ST students in different faculties during the academic sessions 1977-78 and 1978-79. The report of this survey was published by the UGC in 1985. On the basis of the finding of the survey, the following observations may be made:

(i) The total enrollment of Scheduled Caste students was 7.33% (1978-79) at undergraduate level and 7.62% at postgraduate level. The highest concentration of SC students was in the faculties of Arts and Medicine (about 10% each), showing that these candidates were more attracted towards professional courses. In other faculties, their enrollment ranged from 4.5% (Science) to 7.5% (Law). As compared to their proportion (15%) in the total population of India, this progress is highly unsatisfactory.

(ii) The total enrollment of ST candidates was 1.7% at undergraduate stage and 1.46% at postgraduate stage. These students also enrolled themselves mostly in the faculties of Arts (2.5%) and Medicine (1.8%). In other faculties their enrollment was also very small and ranged from 0.71% (Science) to 1.32% (Law). The overall progress is highly deplorable as compared to their share (7.5%) in the total population of the country.

Table 10.7
Growth of Enrollment of SC and ST Students in Higher Education

(Figures in 000s)

Year	*Total Enrollment*	*SC Enrollment*	*ST Enrollment*
1978-79	2,618	180 (6.88)	41 (1.57)
1993-94	5,817	392 (6.74)	—
1995-96	6,426	497 (7.73)	170 (2.65)
1998-99	7,418	633 (8.53)	220 (2.97)

The information given in table 10.7 shows that during a period of 20 years, from 1979 to 1999, the progress of enrollment of SC/ST candidates in higher education has been very slow. While the overall enrollment of SC candidates has increased from 6.88% to 8.53% of the total enrollment, the corresponding figures for ST candidates are 1.57% and 2.97%. However, the share of their enrollment in professional/special higher education courses is reported to be higher (Bhalla, 2001). In 1957, the enrollment of SC and ST students taken together was 13.76% in general education and 7.93% in professional education. The corresponding figure, in general education, is reported to have decreased to 10.59%, while in professional education; the figure has increased to 10.22%. In absolute terms, the number of SC/ST students was 6.7 lakhs (1997) and that in professional education was 66,300.

Recently, the UGC has taken a few additional measures to improve the educational status of SC/ST communities. Notable among them are: reservation of 50 Junior Research Fellowships (annually), 25 Scholarships and 20 Research Associate-ships exclusively for SC/ST students; provision of relaxation up to 10% cut off marks in the Junior Research Fellowship examination, and award of fellowships to all the SC/ST candidates who, subsequently, qualify; provision of 50 Junior Fellowships every year in Science and Humanities including Social Sciences, to SC/ST candidates who appear in National Eligibility Test (NET) and qualify it for Lecturership; provision of relaxation of 5% marks, from 55% to 50%, at the master's level for appointment as lecturer to SC/ST candidates and reduction of minimum percentage of marks required for appearing in the NET examination in respect of SC/ST candidates; and establishment of SC/ST cells in 98 universities including central universities to ensure proper implementation of reservation policy, and appointment of a standing committee to review the implementation of this policy.

Problems

In addition to the general problems faced by all, the SC/ST candidates face certain specific problems. First, there is the problem of adjustment of these students, not only at the school stage, but also in the institutions of higher learning. After mandalisation of Indian politics during the mid-1980s, there has been increased consciousness about caste affiliation in the people of all section of the society. The politicization of the institution of caste to create and patronize vote-banks has cast its shadow on the seats of learning also. The students belonging to the weaker sections are feeling isolated and disadvantaged due to lack of proper interaction with the students of other communities as well as with the teachers. This situation has an adverse and lasting impact on their personality. It has been shown through researches that SC/ST students admitted on the basis of caste-based reservation policy face serious adjustment problems in the educational institutions. These problems are caused not only by their low caste status and low parental income, but also by their more than ordinary academic deficiencies. The social distance, which the society and the academic setup impose upon them, enhances their social isolation and feeling of inferiority (Omprakash, 1993).

Second, the students for the institutions of higher education come from the schools in which there is a high rate of dropout, especially among the SC/ST students. According to the reports published by the Government of India, the dropout rate among the SC/ST children is higher than among the overall dropout rate.

In 1988-89, the general dropout rate up to class X was 75.36%, while among scheduled caste and scheduled tribe children the dropout rates were 79.88% and 86.72% respectively. The dropout rates among SC and ST girls were 85.62% and 89.91% respectively as against the dropout rate of 79.46% among all girls. The overall situation indicates that out of every 100 SC children enrolled in class I only 20 passed class X. The corresponding figure for ST children was only 13. Out of these 16% SC/ST children, who pass class X, a large majority does not complete education up to class XII. Thus, the number of SC/ST students seeking admission to the institutions of higher learning remains microscopically small. This is an important reason why the reserved seats are sometimes not filled up for want of suitable candidates belonging to weaker sections.

Third, education of children, to a great extent, depends on the parents' attitude towards education. Due to low level of literacy, the SC/ST parents do not appreciate the value of education for their children. They are sometimes opposed to the idea of sending their children, especially daughters, to school. The evils of child marriage and child labour are more prevalent in SC/ST communities than in the non-scheduled population. However, with the increase in the literacy rate among these groups over the years, the enrollment of children belonging to these communities has been increasing. It has been discovered through studies that academic performance of SC/ST students is lower than their non-scheduled counterparts. Due to this factor, their aspirations and motivational level fall much below expectations resulting in loss of interest, not only in studies, but also in other social activities. This isolates them further from the main community life of the institution. They have poor interaction with the teachers, with counsellors, with classmates, and with hostel-mates. Their interaction is limited to their caste fellows.

Fourth, while India as a whole is rated as a poor country, the weaker sections including SC/ST communities are living under acute poverty. The majority of the members of these sections consists of land-less labourers who earn their livelihood through their own labour, either on the land belonging to others, or in occupations like scavenging, flaying and tanning of leather. More than 75% of the SC workers are engaged in primary occupations and the proportion of those engaged in tertiary sector is nearly half the national average. Due to these reasons the children of these communities are compelled to start earning at an early age, and hence, are deprived of education of any kind. Though, the government of India has started many schemes to provide financial assistance to the SC/ST students at all levels of education, yet, the impact of these programmes has been marginal.

Fifth, the policy of reservation launched by the Government of India in government services and educational institutions has not given expected results. On the one hand, the benefits of reservation have been cornered by the small minority known as "creamy layer" among these classes, and on the other, a large majority has still remained deprived, and in the process, developed a feeling of inferiority. The policy of reservation has always remained a contentious issue on the social and political platforms. On the one hand it has not significantly benefited the beneficiaries, and on the other, is rated as the root cause of large-scale migration of talented youth to the developed countries of the west. Due to certain more recent constitutional amendments effected by the government, against the verdict of the Supreme Court, to provide reservation in super-speciality courses, and in the promotion of employees to higher positions in the government jobs, the incidence of "brain drain" has considerably increased. As if that was not enough, some vested interests have started talking of providing reservation in the jobs available in the private sector also where in some efficiency is left. India is the only country in the world where talent is sacrificed over political expediency.

EDUCATION OF MUSLIM MINORITY

The word 'minority' forms more a part of political vocabulary in India than of a social interaction or conversation. Also, the Constitution of India has not properly defined this term. In a narrow sense, it is usually used to denote those non-Hindu communities whose members tend to assert their distinctiveness in relation to the Hindu majority. Various sections of the society are loosely described as 'minorities' on the basis of language, religion and ethnicity. Thus, Muslims, Christians, Sikhs, Buddhists Jains, Parsis and Jews are commonly described as minorities in India. Generally, the questions related to educational backwardness are raised only in the case of Muslims, as it has been assumed that the educational development of other minorities has kept pace with the educational development of the society as a whole. In the case of Jews and Parsis, the educational status may be even higher than that of the society as a whole (Chauhan, 1990). Another significant point is that the 'elite' among these classes has seldom raised any questions about the educational backwardness of their communities. However, the Muslim community is becoming increasingly aware of this problem and making attempts to educate its members. It is a good development.

Demographic Profile

According to the 1991 census, the religious minorities constitute about 17.5% of the total population of India. Among the minorities, the population of Muslims is the largest and amounts to more than twice the population of all other minorities taken together. Alongwith the overall population of India, the population of minorities has also increased during over the decades.

Table 10.8
Indian Population by Religion

Groups	*1951*	*1961*		*1971*		*1981*		*1991*	
Hindu	85.0	366.5	83.5	453.4	82.7	549.7	82.6	672.6	82.4
Muslim	9.9	46.9	10.7	61.4	11.2	75.6	11.4	95.2	11.7
Christian	2.3	10.7	2.4	14.2	2.6	16.2	2.4	18.9	2.3
Sikhs	0.7	7.8	1.8	10.4	1.9	13.1	2.0	16.3	2.0
Buddhist	—	3.2	0.7	3.9	0.7	4.7	0.7	6.3	0.8
Jains	—	2.0	0.5	2.6	0.5	3.2	0.5	3.4	0.4
Others	1.1	1.6	0.4	2.2	0.4	2.8	0.4	3.5	0.4
Total	100.0	439.2	100.0	548.2	100.0	665.3	100.0	812.3	100.0

Sources: Manorama Yearbook 2000, Malayala Manorama, Kottayam, India.

As may be observed from the table, the population of Muslims has increased at a faster rate than all other major religions with the community registering a rise of 32.76% during the decade 1981-91. From 35.5 million in 1951, their number has increased to 95.2 million in 1991. In terms of percentage, this increase is from 9.9% in 1951 to 11.7% in 1991. The report published by the Census Commissioner of India (The Hindustan Times, Nov. 8, 1995) showed that Muslims had recorded a rise of 10% more than that of the Hindu population. The population growth of the majority community (22.70%) had been one per cent below the national average. The population of Sikhs has also increased from 0.7% in 1951 to 2.0% in 1991. But, they are educationally advanced and economically sound. However, population growth has nothing to do with religion or caste, it can be attributed to their low level of education and high level of poverty. The faster growth of population among Scheduled Castes and Scheduled Tribes may also be similarly interpreted.

Historical Perspective

After independence, information about education of religious minorities was never collected either at National level or at State level. In fact government agencies were not authorized to collect information based on caste and religion except in the case of SC and ST sections. Even if they were asked to do so, it was to be only in terms of number of persons in these categories. It was never categories further in terms of literacy or other demographic variables. However, information available from different sources may lead us to understand certain trends.

The history of education of Muslims may be traced in the Mughal period (see Chapter 1) that opened a new chapter in the history of Muslim education. During this period a large network of educational institutions was set up throughout the country, which included centers of higher education at various places. Education had become a matter of right during those days, as all citizens were to receive education. Hindus freely joined Muslim institutions and Muslims learnt Sanskrit.

Historically, Muslims adopted the western system of education at a later stage than Hindus. During the British period, educational degeneration of Muslim community started, as in the beginning, they were not ready to accept the British system of education, which compelled to learn English language and western science. On the other hand, Hindus accepted the British System of education more readily and from an earlier stage than Muslims, and consequently, advanced in the socioeconomic field at a faster pace. Sir Syed

Ahmad Khan (1817-96) was the first to recognize this contrast between the two communities. He made earnest efforts to change the mode of thinking of Muslims and founded, in 1875, the first modernist educational institution in Islam. He was inspired by the idea that England and other western countries owed their wealth and power to their enlightenment and their learning in arts and sciences. But by this time, the Muslims were almost left behind a complete generation in education (Saini, 1980). In 1875, Sir Syed Ahmad Khan founded the Mohameddan Anglo Oriental (MAO) College at Aligarh. The founding of this college was a real turning point in the educational history of Muslims. It was this college that later on (1920) emerged as a prominent university of India known as "Aligarh Muslim University". The Government of India, through an Act of Parliament, created this university for educational and cultural advancement of Muslims of India.

It took another 30 years for Sir Syed to convince his Muslim brethren to accept English education. Therefore, till 1904, the rate of increase of Muslim enrollment was lower than that of other communities. Another milestone in the history of Modern education among the Muslims of India was the establishment of a school for girls at Aligarh by Sheikh Abdullah, which later on was raised to the status of a college for women. Aligarh Muslim University recognized this College and the related school in 1930, and affiliated it to itself. Thus, after the last quarter of Nineteenth Century, Muslim students from all parts of the country started being attracted to this institution. In this institution, a large number of Muslim girls, from different parts of the country, also come to receive education. Over a period of time, Aligarh Muslim University has emerged a premier institution of international fame for the education of Muslim youth.

In addition to this, some nationalist Muslims established the Jamia Millia Islamia at New Delhi in 1920. The main objective of this institution was to preserve the culture heritage of India, and at the same time, provide secular education to Muslims. In 1987-88, this institution had 237 faculty members including 48 women. For a long time, Jamia Millia Islamia was an institution deemed to be university established under Section 3 of the UGC Act. In view of its good performance, the Government of India has raised this to the level of Central University. Unlike Aligarh Muslim University, Jamia Millia Islamia does not enjoy the Status of a minority institution under article 30 of the Constitution.

Post-Independence Policies

In addition to the constitutional provisions, the government of India has been showing concern about the education of minorities at different times and at different levels. After independence, the Government of India announced its first National Policy on Education in 1968 in which it stated:

> Every effort should be made not only to protect the rights of minorities but also to promote their educational interests as suggested in the statement issued by the Conference of the Chief Ministers of States and Central Ministers held in August 1961.

In the same way, in the National Policy on Education announced in 1986, the Government referred to general principles related to the education of minorities and suggested some specific programmes. It observed:

> Some minority groups are educationally deprived or backward. Greater attention will be paid to the education of these groups in the interest of equality and social justice. This will naturally include the Constitutional guarantees given to them to establish and administer their own educational institution, and protection to their languages and culture. Simultaneously, objectivity will be reflected in the preparation of textbooks and in all school activities, and all possible measures will be taken to promote an integration based on appreciation of common national goals and ideals, in conformity with the core curriculum.

As a part of the strategies for implementing the NPE-1986 proposals, the government launched the following programmes (Choudhary, 1996):

(i) Setting up community polytechnics in the areas of predominantly minority concentration for imparting technical skills;

(ii) Evaluation of text books through the NCERT from the standpoint of national integration;

(iii) Organization of training programmes through the NCERT and SCERTs for Principals and Teachers of minority managed institutions;

(iv) Providing financial assistance to the universities and colleges conducting coaching classes for students belonging to educationally backward minorities;

(v) Setting up of early childhood education centers in the traditional schools and in areas predominantly inhabited by educationally backward minorities;

(vi) Promotion of teaching of English, science, and mathematics in traditional madarsas and other Muslim minority schools, on voluntary basis; and

(vii) Asking the State governments to compile statistical information, make textbooks available in minority languages, and provide for teacher-training facilities to teachers in the minority languages.

Progress

During the period of over 40 years between 1905-1947, the enrollment of Muslim scholars continuously increased in other educational institutions also, at all stages. The details of this trend are shown in the table 10.9 given below, which indicates that in 1906-07 the total enrollment of Muslims at school stage was 8.93 lakhs and at higher education level it was only 2040. By 1931-32, the total number of Muslim students at school level had increased to 30.17 lakhs and that at the college stage to 2362. However, as a percentage of total enrollments it was less than 1%.

Table 10.9
Muslim Scholars in Educational Institutions (1906-1932)

Year	*Higher Education (General)*	*Higher Education (Professional)*	*School Education (up to secondary)*
1906-07	1,569	471	8,93,162
1911-12	3,095	664	11,94,049
1916-17	4,921	1,152	15,22,142
1921-22	5,424	1,544	17,10,910
1926-27	8,456	2,331	24,37,373
1931-32	10,040	2,362	30,16,805

Source: Saini, S.K. Development of Education in India, Cosmos Publishers, 1980, page 225.

After the partition of India in 1947, the Muslim population remaining here faced certain unforeseen circumstances. However, Indian Constitution guaranteed certain privileges through Articles 29 and 30 (see Chapter 2), assuring the protection of educational and cultural rights of all minorities including Muslims. According to Article 29, all minorities are free to conserve their distinct language, script or culture and shall not be denied admission to any educational institution maintained by the State on the grounds of religion, race, caste or language. Similarly, under Article 30, minorities have a right to establish and administer educational institutions of their own choice. Further, the State shall not discriminate against such institutions in granting aid from the state funds on the ground that the minority community, whether based on religion or language, maintains them.

Unfortunately, the census reports do not publish data on community-wise educational status of Indian society, due to which systematic data regarding educational development of minorities during the post-independence period are not available. Although, the Constitution of India provides for equal educational opportunities to all citizens under the law, yet the educational advancement among Muslim community does not seem to have kept pace with that of the rest of the society. Some authentic reports published during the British period indicated that there was imbalance in the educational status of Muslims both at regional and national levels. For instance, in the western United Provinces, which was relatively more urbanized, women's literacy was higher than in the less developed and largely rural eastern part of the state. In the western Himalayan region, the literacy rate among Muslim women was higher because of less prevalence of the pardah system. In 1947, the proportion of college going Muslim women was 0.16 while that of Hindu women was only 0.10, but at the national level the enrolment of Muslim women was less than that of non-Muslim women. For example, out of 2966 college going women only 105 (3.5%) were Muslims, while 53.8% were Hindus, 6.6% Parsis and 24.5% Christians (Chanana, 1993).

Shah (1983) has stated that there has been a continuous degeneration of Muslims during the post-independence period, which has manifested itself in various forms, such as, poor performance of Muslim candidates in Civil Services Examinations, lack of adequate appearance in the merit lists of High School, Higher

Secondary and College Examinations, and sometimes, in the form of inferiority complex as exhibited in the state of indifference towards pressing for their rights and privileges. He has further stated:

> The poor, economically backward and least educated Indian Muslims cannot join the national mainstream unless they advance educationally in all fields, especially, in science and technology. A nation whose 12% population is seemingly ignorant and unconcerned with national plans, programmes and progress, will logically lose 12% of its efficiency and potential strength required for the country's development and progress. Therefore, it is in the wider national interest that the Muslim community is not neglected, but is educated and made economically prosperous. No country can afford to neglect its population of 90 to 100 millions to exist as parasite or become a drag on the nation as a whole. This will be too heavy a burden for a developing country to bear.

Despite a rapid educational development having taken place in India during the last 50 years, Muslim community has remained educationally backward, being unable to take advantage of increased educational facilities in the country. Two main explanations are advanced for this kind of deprivation. One, as Ahmed (1987) has stated, "They have been slow to take advantage of the vast educational development the country has witnessed since independence due to the particular ethos of their religion or a minority psychology." Two, "an invidious discrimination to which they have been subjected as a minority community" is another cause of their educational backwardness. These issues are very delicate and should be cautiously discussed in a secular country like India. In fact, the reasons for educational deprivation of Muslims are deeply rooted in their socio-economic structure. But, Muslims including their elite are prone to seeing it as a reflection of discriminatory treatment meted out to them. Secondly, Muslims carry the belief, for which there are potent historical reasons, that an average member of the majority community harbours a strong hostility towards them. It appears almost natural to them that an average Hindu should discriminate against them in the matters of admissions, evaluation etc. However, no reliable data are available, which allow us to assess whether Muslims are really discriminated against or they share educational deprivation with other disadvantaged sections of the society due to socio-economic or cultural reasons. The First Annual Report of the Minority Commission stated that lack of employment opportunities is posing serious problems for the minority communities. The same thing is true for educational opportunities. However, the members of the minority communities feel that they are denied admission in colleges, especially professional colleges, on the ground of lack of merit.

For want of adequate data, though it is difficult to study the real picture of educational progress of Muslims, yet some sporadic information available on the subject may be of some help in this regard. A high power committee for the minorities collected information about performance of Muslim students appearing in the examinations of 22 universities located in selected states (Table 10.10).

Table 10.10
Muslim Students' Performance in University Examinations (1981)*

Examination	*Total Number of Students*		*Muslim Students*	
	Appeared	*Successful*	*Appeared*	*Successful*
B.A., B.Sc., B.Com.	2,18,515	1,13,783 (52.07)	13,571 (6.21)	7,012 (51.67)
M.A., M.Sc., M.Com.	23,723	18,406 (77.59)	2,162 (9.11)	1,640 (75.93)
Engineering (B.E., B.Tech.)	2,698	1,768 (65.53)	92 (3.41)	42 (45.65)
Medicine (M.B.B.S.)	2,845	1,784 (62.71)	98 (3.44)	51 (52.04)

Source: Chanana, K. NIEPA, New Delhi, 1997, Saxena, (1983).
* Figures within brackets indicate percentages.

In 1981, out of the total 2,18,515 students appearing in the undergraduate examinations of the selected universities, 13,571 (6.21%) were Muslims. Out of the Muslim students 7,012 (51.67%) were successful in the said examinations while the 52.07% was the overall success rate. In the postgraduate examinations, out of the total 23,723 examinees 2,162 (9.11%) were Muslims, of which 1,640 passed the examination successfully. In terms of percentage, their success ratio was 75.93% as against 77.59% of the total examinees appeared. In the examinations of the Engineering Faculty of 9 universities, out of the total 2,698 students appeared 92 (3.41%) were Muslims, of which 42 (45.65%) were successful in the examination. The overall pass percentage of the candidates was 65.53. Similarly, in the Faculty of Medicine of 12 medical colleges, out of all the 2,845 students appeared in the examination, 1,784 (62.71%) were successful. But, out of 98 (3.44%) Muslim students having appeared, only 51 (52.04%) were successful. Second important point was that in professional education, the proportion of Muslim candidates appearing in the examination was very small, and far less than their proportion in the total population in the selected states. In fact, representation of Muslim students was small even in the general education courses.

The Hamdard Education Society (1983) conducted an All India Survey of Muslim-managed schools and colleges in India. It was found that in the 44 colleges sampled the number of Muslim students (40.4%) was less than that of non-Muslims. It was also found that dropout rate was higher among Muslim students than among the non-Muslims. In 430 Muslim-managed schools, it was found that as the level of education increases, the number of non-Muslim students in these schools also increases from 3.70% at the primary stage through 15.10% at the middle school stage to 36.70% at the higher secondary stage. The performance level of Muslim students was also lower than that of the non-Muslim students. Of the 430 schools surveyed, 202 were co-educational, 85 were exclusively for girls and 143 were exclusively for boys. Out of the total number of students enrolled only 6.10% were girls at the senior secondary stage. The dropout rate was also found to be higher among girls than among boys. At the senior secondary stage the dropout rate among girls was of the order of 75%. Most of the girls are married off at this stage.

However, this is not to say that all the Muslim women are educationally backward. Some of them are holding very high positions in the administration and the academic institutions. It has been found in a survey of two premier institutions, Aligarh Muslim University and Jamia Millia Islamia at New Delhi, conducted by Ahmad-1987 and Haider-1988, as quoted by Chanana (1993), that Aligarh Muslim University has an important place in the history of Muslim education in India. Established in 1920 as a Central University, this institution has grown into one of the largest residential higher education institutions of the country. At present, the University has 102 Departments of Studies under 12 Faculties. It has 4 hospitals, 8 constituent colleges, 2 polytechnics and 8 schools. The total enrollment in the University in the year 1999-2000 was about 25,100. The total number of employees is about 7,150. This includes 1,450 teachers and about 5,700 non-teaching employees (GOI, 2000). The Maulana Azad Library of the University has about 9,46,000 books. The Jamia Millia Islamia, which had been functioning as an institution deemed to be a university since 1962, was given the status of a Central University in December 1998. This institution also provides education from Pre-school classed to Doctorate. It has 29 departments under 6 Faculties, and several centers and schools. It enrolled 8,055 students during the session 1999-2000, and had 1,245 employees including 414 teachers. It also has a big library with about 2,46,000 books. But, the general conclusion is that Muslims, especially women, have largely remained educationally backward.

The most recent data have been reported by Rao (1995) as quoted by Choudhary (1996), which are based on the 43rd round of the National Sample Survey (NSS). It has been revealed that in rural India 51% of the Hindu males were illiterate. But the figure for Muslim males was 58%. The percentage of illiteracy in urban areas was 25.3% for Hindu males and 42% for Muslim males. Moreover, the illiteracy in urban areas was 42% for Hindu females and 60% for Muslim females. In another recent study conducted by Ahmad (1994) as quoted by Choudhary (1996), it was found that Muslims are more backward than Hindus regarding literacy. According to this study, the literacy rate was 32.20% and 53.65% among Muslims and Hindus respectively in Didwana town of Rajasthan, and 31.46% and 55.17% among Muslims and Hindus respectively in Kishanganj town of Bihar. The study also reflected that females lagged far behind males. The literacy rate of Muslim males was 50.94% and 39.73% in Didwana and Kishanganj respectively. But, the literacy rate of Muslim females was 12.18% and 22.20% respectively in the two towns. Although, no authentic data are available regarding literacy rate among Muslims at the national level, yet, the high power panel on minorities appointed by the Ministry of Home Affairs has identified Muslims, besides Neo-Buddhists, as educationally backward at the national level.

Problems

Regarding the quality of education imparted in Urdu medium schools, the excerpts from a write up by Ahmad (1993) is very relevant here. It was reported that about half a million students of Urdu medium schools all over India appeared in the 1993 board examinations for classes X and XII. It was the largest number of Muslim students appeared in these examinations after independence. The results, as analyzed and compiled by Friends for Education, a forum for the uplift of education and civic sense, projected a sorry plight of educational status of Muslims all over the country. The combined pass percentage was 30. In Bihar alone the failure percentage was as high as 73. West Bengal was a bit better with a pass percentage of 47. Madhya Pradesh had areas where pass percentage of Urdu medium students was as low as zero. In Gujarat the pass percentage was only 38 whereas in Rajasthan it was 40. Maharashtra had put up a poor show with only 30% students having passed and schools in Uttar Pradesh performed the worst with only 26 as a pass percentage. In Urdu schools of Delhi the failure rate was 73%. The pass percentage in Kerala, Karnataka, Andhra and Tamil Nadu fluctuated between 40 and 60. There were more than 50 schools whose pass percentage was zero a few of them being in Delhi. The more shocking thing that was reported was that the performance of schools in the year 1993 was better than that of the previous year, which was only 25% at all India level.

In order to know the causes of such a poor and deplorable performance, many people from the concerned cross-sections of the Muslim society and administration, were contacted. Some 80% of the parents contacted held the teachers teaching in the schools responsible for the poor results of their children. About 10% blamed the State for the social and educational backwardness of the community. The students blamed their schools for their failure. According to them the principals and teachers were not bothered at all about what was going on in the schools.

Some eminent Muslim educationists felt that the main cause of educational backwardness among their community was their lackadaisical attitude and complete lack of spirit for making advance in educational fields. A few of them blamed the parents for low level of performance of their children, and consequently, the appalling state of low level of education among Muslims. Some others were of the view that the ones who were responsible for the contemporary situation were the Muslim leaders who treated the community as a commodity, used them as a springboard for furthering their vested interests. A parliamentarian blamed the Muslim intelligentsia for not being responsible towards the community and the nation due to which most of the Muslim community could not be educated. According to him the rot started right in the primary sections of Urdu medium schools because the students passing out of them could not find the seats in the middle and secondary schools as they did not have the provision of Urdu. Some people blamed the entire community for remaining indifferent to education. The teachers and principals of the schools had their own stories to tell, both the groups blaming the parents for not taking adequate interest in the education of their children. Some of the parents contacted did not know even the name of the school where their children studied. Moreover, they hardly took any serious view of their wards' absence from the school till a letter was sent to them informing that the child's name had been struck off from the school records due to truancy.

It was also found that Urdu medium schools, in various parts of the country, existed almost in subhuman conditions. The buildings were inadequate and highly unhygienic. Some schools were without buildings. Most of these schools did not have Urdu textbooks even for important subjects like science and mathematics, and instead, Hindi medium books were being used by the teachers. The average number of vacant posts of teachers in senior secondary schools was 10 to 12 and the existing teachers were forced to teach the subjects which they had not mastered.

This survey has highlighted almost all the weaknesses of Muslim-managed educational institutions in India. The educational backwardness among Indian Muslims may be attributed to their overall social and economic condition, as their socio-economic status is comparable to the other socially and economically disadvantaged sections. In urban areas, the level of their education is generally higher than in rural areas, but this is true for all other sections of the society also. In fact, the Constitution of India has special provisions to ensure facilities for educational and cultural advancement of weaker sections of the society including Muslims. While Article 46 ensures reservation of seats for SC/ST candidates in educational institutions, Muslims are allowed to establish and administer their own educational institutions under Article 29 and 30. Of course, the Constitution does not ensure benefit to any section of the society under both the provisions.

It is believed that educational backwardness starts at school stage. A large majority of non-enrolled Muslim children is located in those areas where adequate schooling facilities are not available in or near their habitations. Therefore, the National Policy on Education, 1986 has stated that "some minority groups are deprived of education, and greater attention would be paid to ensure that the minorities properly avail of the existing provisions in the Constitution. The policy stated that lowest enrollment of girls is among the educationally most backward minorities. The future strategies of the Government emphasize the creation of schooling facilities in the areas, which are densely populated by minorities and other educationally deprived sections."

There are certain social traditions and preoccupations that stand in the way of girls' education such as reluctance of the parents to send their grown up daughters to schools and colleges. These problems were equally faced by both Muslim and Hindu women. For example, Arya Samaj wanted that the distance between the schools for boys and girls should be at least five kilometers. Under these circumstances no fundamental change could take place. Similarly, Pardah system was prevalent in both Hindu and Muslim well to do and urban families, which hampered the education of girls. But, it was practiced more in the Muslim families than in Hindu families.

11

Part-Time Open and Distance Learning

During the last five decades since independence, India has made tremendous progress in the field of education, though mostly quantitative in nature. Earlier, education was available only to elite classes of the society, and the large majority of the poor and marginalized people remained deprived of it. The democratic and socialistic values enshrined in the Constitution of free India brought a ray of hope for the common masses, especially, to the underprivileged and disadvantaged sections of the society including women, scheduled castes, scheduled tribes, and religious and linguistic minorities. Equalization of educational and employment opportunities has been the cherished goal behind all efforts of the government aimed at bringing about social and economic reforms. The major emphasis of the educational proposals during the last nine five-year plans, has been on the fulfilment of the constitutional obligation of providing free and compulsory elementary education to all children of the age group 6-14 years, as mentioned in the Article 45 of the Constitution. In order to achieve this goal, existing system of education was adopted without much required structural transformation and was subjected to a large-scale expansion. Due to rising social demand for education after independence, the expansion of elementary and secondary education has been phenomenal resulting in a tremendous pressure of students seeking admission to institutions of higher education. The main emphasis has been on establishment of new schools and enrollment of students at all stages of education. The government of free India rightly considered education, as a powerful tool of socio-economic transformation and encouraged expansion at all levels through private as well as official attempts. As the school education expanded, the number of students going for higher education also increased. In an attempt to accommodate the growing number of aspirants the system of higher education had to be expanded. The current trends indicate that enrollment in higher education doubles in every two decades.

Political considerations have an important role in the expansion of higher education, especially at the state level. The state governments experience tremendous pressure from the public to establish more and more colleges and universities. In a democratic society, even the strong governments find it very difficult to resist such pressures and are compelled to succumb. These considerations have led to fast expansion of higher education in our country, which in turn, has adverse impact upon its quality. The Education Commission (1964-66) had rightly stated that, "in a world based on science and technology, it was education that determined the level of prosperity, welfare and security of the people. On the quality and number of persons coming out of our schools and colleges would depend our success in the great enterprise of national reconstruction the principal objective of which was to raise the standard of living of our people." But quality education, imparted through the conventional system, is costly and beyond the reach of poor people who aspire for it. The facilities of quality education are confined to urban areas, and the great masses of the people living in the villages remain at a disadvantage. The children of the poor have to remain content with substandard education imparted in substandard institutions. Secondly, it is not possible to expand the formal system beyond a limit due to financial constraints. If we try to expand it without making adequate financial support available its quality will be poor. The annual public expenditure on education has been increasing since 1950-51, in absolute terms, but in real terms it has decreased. The problem has become more serious since the government has decided to reduce subsidy on higher education after the fourth five-year plan. Therefore, in order to ensure access and education of a reasonably good quality to all willing learners, we must think of some alternative system capable of supplementing the role of conventional system, and distance education is one of such alternatives. Through this, we can provide a larger number of learners an education of improved quality by introducing a variety of relevant courses. A statement by Prof. G. Ram Reddy (1988) is relevant here:

> There is a case of Ekalavya mythology who wanted to learn under the guru, Dronacharya, who as we all know, refused to take him as a student because he was neither a Brahmin nor a Kshatriya. However, Ekalavya was determined to learn and what happened subsequently is known to all of us. (The legend goes that Ekalavya built a figure in the image of Dronacharya and started practicing archery under its feet. Subsequently, his skills in archery surpassed those of the best pupil of Dronacharya. What happened subsequently is not relevant here. The point, however, that needs to be made is that today a motivated learner cannot be and must not be ignored for any reason whatsoever). In those days as Dronacharya could refuse to take Ekalavya as a student and the society would tolerate it. Today's democratic society cannot afford to overlook the interest of Ekalavyas nor can Dronacharyas say "no" to them. Distance education and the Open Universities facilitate him. Open Universities are the universities for the Modern Ekalavyas. Availability of communication technologies makes this possible today. It is said that there was a time when, if a student wanted to learn, he had to go the Aristotle. Today, we have the means to take the Aristotle to the student.

An open university has certain other distinctive features also. First, it can be compared with an "Industrial House", as it requires a massive organizational structure like an industry. It has the function of production and distribution of instructional material, of course, for a price. Second, it behaves like an organized concern providing for institutionalization of private learning independently learning facilities to the students without any restrictions imposed on them. In effect, it provides the learners a freedom from the rigidities of the conventional system like full-time attendance, rigid time-table, rigid curriculum, and compulsory listening to the face-to-face lectures delivered by the regular and full-time paid staff. Instead, it provides for a cost-effective, flexible, democratic and efficient system of learning.

LIMITATIONS OF THE FORMAL SYSTEM

During the last five decades, there have been two important developments, which have caused concern not only among the policy planners, decision-makers, and educationists, but also, other enlightened citizens.

First, there has been tremendous growth in the human population in the world. It took more than a million years for the human population, since its origin on the globe, to touch one billion mark by 1800. Second billion was added within a smaller period of 120 years upto 1920. The addition of third billion took only 40 years (1920-1960), and the next two billions were added within a still smaller period of 27 years from 1960 to 1987. It is estimated that sixth billion has been added by the end of 2000 AD. Proportionately, the population of India, which was only about 360 million in 1951, has crossed one billion mark by 2001. The number of persons eligible to receive formal education has also increased from only about 150 million to over 400 million during the same period. But, the formal system of education that we have created caters to the requirements of only 300 million. This figure also includes the contribution of the existing non-formal education system. Therefore, as a conservative estimate about 100 million eligible persons are still out of the ambit of the formal education system, which is second largest in the world. This shows that our formal institutionalized system of education is being increasingly rendered inadequate to cater to the requirements of the teeming millions. At the same time, due to our democratic system of polity and increasing socio-political awareness among the disadvantaged sections of the society, the demand for education has tremendously increased.

Second, during the later half of the 20th century, the rate of growth of knowledge, in all fields has been very high. This has been particularly so during the last two decades. It is said that knowledge doubles within every 3 or 4 years. Consequently, every citizen needs to update his knowledge and skills to cope with the changing social, vocational and professional circumstances. Now, we have more people to educate and more knowledge to be imparted than we had during 1950s. The situation became more paradoxical when the system of higher education, which was already inadequate, felt daunting pressure of enrollment due to expansion of school education and lack of employment opportunities after secondary education. In order to cope with the situation, the government of India resorted to the expansion of higher education during 1950s and 1960s mainly in terms of establishment of colleges of general education. During this period, expansion of higher education took place at an average rate of over 10% per annum. The graduates who passed out of these colleges found them unable to get gainful employment for want of practical knowledge. Moreover, unplanned expansion of higher education led to the problem of maintenance of standards, which required more funds to sustain it, thus exerting unbearable pressure on the public exchequer.

As a result of unplanned expansion and scarcity of funds, the quality of education imparted in the institutions of higher education successively deteriorated. The frustrated lot of students resorted to aggressive behaviour. The lopsided and unbalanced expansion of education diverted the efforts and resources of the government towards mass education through higher education to elite education at the cost of vocational training. This process produced an enormous number of unskilled and unemployable graduates with devalued degrees. This also led to the deterioration in the quality of education due to overcrowding of the educational institutions, curriculum constraints and lack of time. As a result there is a wide gap between what is needed by the society and what is produced by education system. This situation provided a golden opportunity to political parties to exploit the sentiments of the younger generation to their advantage, and campus unrest became the order of the day. Sometimes, the students' aggression took very ugly turn resulting in loss of public property, causing damage to educational institutions, railways, and other essential social services. This gave a glaring evidence of a complete failure of the conventional system to absorb, sustain and manage the growing numbers.

Although, the quantitative development of higher education, during the post-independence period, has been apparently very impressive, yet, it is inadequate to meet the growing demand of the people for higher education. Now, unlike the pre-independence period, the benefits of higher education are reaped by a sizeable number of youth even from underprivileged sections of the society. At present, we have one college for every 11,000 and one university for every 4.7 lakhs of persons in the relevant age group (18-23 years). Yet, in the real terms, only about 6-7% of the eligible age group are getting the benefit of higher education. This is insignificant compared to the corresponding figures of over 50% for the countries belonging the Organization of Economic Cooperation and Development (OECD), and about 30% for some other developed countries. Highlighting the significance of higher education in the modern times, the World Bank document (1994) states, "The development of higher education is correlated with the economic development: enrollment ratios in higher education average 51% in the countries that belong to OECD, compared with 21% in middle-income countries and 6% in low-income countries." Therefore, the first and foremost task that India should undertake is to expand higher education system further in a planned way so as to cover as large a portion of the eligible age group as possible. But, it will not be possible through the conventional campus based university and college system. This makes it necessary for us to ensure that higher education is accessible to all, at least to all those who desire and deserve it. If we fail to do so, the existing gap between the rich and the poor will further widen. Even if we satisfy ourselves with a target of 20% enrollment ratio to be achieved as early as possible, the existing institutional facilities are severely inadequate. For achieving this target within shortest possible time, we must look for alternative modes of imparting education so as to cover larger number of learners with the limited available resources.

OPEN LEARNING: THE CONCEPT

These circumstances made the government and the policy planners think of alternatives based on part-time and own-time approaches to education, because the limitations of the campus based higher education system had become obvious. The non-conventional modes of education providing for non-residential studies like correspondence courses, which had been fruitfully adopted in developed countries, attracted the attention of the policy makers in India also. The Distance Education (DE) mode, in which it was not necessary to bring all the students together to listen to the face-to-face lectures delivered by the teachers, rather, students while remaining away from their teachers would learn according to their own time, was considered worthwhile. However, in DE system, the provision of occasional meetings between the teachers and the students is made. These meetings are popularly known as Personal Contact Programmes (PCPs). The learners receive their study material through correspondence modes (postal services) and study at home or at their workplace. The efforts of the students are supplemented by assignments, which are checked and evaluated by experts in respective fields of knowledge. More comprehensively, DE is considered as learning taking place in the absence of the teacher through uses of print materials, mechanical and electronic media and occasional face-to-face interaction between the teacher and the taught. This mode of learning is also loosely called "Open Learning". Conceptually, DE is a part and parcel of open learning. In fact, DE system is known by a variety of names such as "Correspondence Education", "Home Study", "Independent Study", "External Study", "Off-campus Study", "Open Learning", "Open Education" etc. In India, three terms are commonly used: "External Appearance" (private appearance), "Correspondence Education" and Distance Education. Sometimes, "Distance Education" and "Open Learning" are used interchangeably. It is argued by some that while distance education is accommodated by open learning system, the opposite premise may not be true (Reddy, 1988), because some of the distance education programs are very rigid and, as such, do not meet the criteria of open learning system. However, there are several similarities between these two concepts. According to Keegan, as quoted by Reddy (1988), distance education has the following characteristics:

The quasi-permanent separation of the teacher and learner throughout the length of the learning process; this distinguishes it from conventional face-to-face education.

The influence of an educational organization both in planning and preparation of learning materials and in the provision of student support services; this distinguishes it from private study and teach-yourself programmes.

The use of technical media; print, audio, video or computer, to unite teachers and learners and carry the content of the course.

The provision of two-way communication so that the students may benefit from or even initiate a dialogue; this distinguishes it from other uses of technology in education.

The quasi-permanent absence of a learning group throughout the length of the learning process so that people are usually taught as individuals and not in groups, with the possibility of occasional meetings for both didactic and socialization processes.

The conventional system, because of is restricted scope and rigid approaches, could serve only a microscopically small section of the Indian society. On the other hand, the open learning system has the potential of reaching out to those who (Chauhan, 2001):

(i) Were left out and could not continue their education beyond secondary stage due to familial and economic constraints;

(ii) Dropped out without completing even the first degree course and joined job-market or the family occupations;

(iii) Looked upon education as a lifelong process, and wanted to continue their education for improvement of knowledge and skills while remaining in employment;

(iv) Lived in geographically isolated areas having peculiar climatic conditions such as forests, hilly tracks and remote villages;

(v) Belonged to socially and economically backward, and weaker sections of the society such as scheduled castes, scheduled tribes and women;

(vi) Could not find a seat in the conventional system for non-fulfilment of the required academic qualifications or because of lack of required aptitude and motivation, but were later on motivated to continue their studies to acquire superior qualifications; and

(vii) Were employed and hence could not pursue regular education but wanted to improve their knowledge and skills in the areas specific to their job.

DISTANCE EDUCATION ABROAD

Open learning, in the form of DE, started at the middle of the 19th century in the form of correspondence education under different nomenclatures such as Home Study Programmes, Radio and Television Universities, Every Man's University, Universities of the

Air, Free University and Open University. The idea of DE took a concrete shape in 1840 when Issac Pitman conducted a postal/ correspondence course in shorthand in England. However, it became more systematic in the last decade of 19th century some other good colleges in UK introduced examination-oriented correspondence courses (Sahu, 1993) on commercial basis. Later on, the Robin's Report (1963) to the government of UK, emphasized the need of expanding universities so as to meet the demands of the qualified school leavers and pleaded for extension of opportunities to all classes of the population as an emergent need in order to replace the 'elite' system of education that had been prevalent in UK for many years (Anand, 1979). The first open university was established in UK, through the Royal Charter 1969, on the basis of the Report of the Open University submitted to the Secretary of the State for Education and Science, which emphasized higher education as a basic right and condemned the denial of the greatest educational opportunity to the greatest number of citizens as unjust to the individual and unwise for the society. This university became the first full-fledged university in the field of distance education and is hailed as a landmark in the history of distance education.

In USA also a humble beginning in the direction of setting up distance education centers was made in 1873 with the formation of the Society for Home Studies (Sahu, 1993). Establishment of institutes of correspondence education in some universities such as Illinois Western University (1874) and Correspondence University at Ithaca, New York (1883) followed this. Subsequently, other institutions like the Institute of Correspondence Schools (1890), American Society for Extension of University Teaching (1890) and National University Extension Association (NUEA) made considerable headway in the field of distance education in that country. In the early part of the 20th century, a non-profit educational association named National Home Study Council (NHSC) was established for setting standards for correspondence schools. By 1967, there were around 70 correspondence institutions, which had joined the NUEA and some hundred institutions had become members of the NHSC.

In the same way, the USSR also established (1926) a correspondence study department in one of the institutions of higher learning, and subsequently, encouraged correspondence education in order to cope with the demand for specialists with higher academic and professional qualifications. By 1967, the institutions of correspondence education had become an organic part of the entire educational system covering all stages of education, elementary, high school undergraduate and postgraduate courses. The geographical conditions of Australia were particularly conducive for the development of correspondence education. Australia started teacher education programmes in the University of Queensland through correspondence education, to begin with, before extending the system to other universities. Today most of the Australian Universities are providing instruction through distance education mode.

During the last three decade of 20th century, there has been tremendous growth in the area of distance education throughout the world in terms of number of institutions and enrollment. After the establishment of British Open University in 1969, there has been a spurt in this process and many countries in the world have set up open universities. Notables among them are: Allama Iqbal Open University (Pakistan), Athabasca University (Canada), Everyman's University (Israel), Fern University (West Germany), Free University (Iran), Sri Lanka Open University (Sri Lanka), Sukhothai Thammathirat Open University (Thailand), Central Radio and Television University (China), University of the Air (Japan), Kyogni Open University (Korea), Korea Air and Correspondence University (South Korea), Open University (Netherlands), Universities Terbuka (Indonesia), Universidad Nacional Abierta (Venezuela), National open University (Nigeria), and Al-Quds Open University (Jordan).

DISTANCE EDUCATION IN INDIA

The Open Learning system in India originated in the form of "Private Appearance" of the candidates in public examinations under which a candidate who could not study as a regular student was also allowed to appear in the examination after undertaking necessary study at home. This system was probably introduced to help the poor and needy, but motivated students to continue their studies further after studying as a regular student for some time. The approach was beneficial to the candidates belonging to socially disadvantaged sections of the society, particularly Scheduled Castes, Scheduled Tribes and women.

Later on, in order to overcome the deficiencies of the private appearance and improve the quality of education, some universities started correspondence courses to cater to the requirements of such students. The correspondence courses constituted, in fact, the second stage of the evolution of the concept of open learning in India. The wide social acceptance of the concept of correspondence education led to the development of the concept of distance education, which in turn, led to the direction of establishment of open universities, the third stage of development of the concept of open learning. The term DE received a formal recognition in 1982 when the four-decade old International Council for Correspondence Education changed its name to the International Council for Distance Education (Satyanarayana, 1988). This happened primarily because the old concept of correspondence education was exclusively associated with print material while the new concept of distance education includes supplementary material being used through non-print media such as radio television computer and satellites. At present, India has two types of distance education institutions. These are:

(i) Correspondence Course Institutions (CCIs) working under the conventional universities, which initially used print media as a main vehicle for delivery of study material with some use radio and television programmes. These institutions may be called the dual mode institutions.

(ii) Newly established Open Universities, which design their programmes by using modern technologies and approach the learners through multimedia technology using computers, satellites and Internet. These may be termed as single mode institutions.

Correspondence Education

The development of correspondence education and subsequently, the concept of distance education throughout the world also had its impact on Indian education. In this regard, the Planning Commission of India pointed out (1960) that in the Third Plan (1961-66) in addition to provision for expansion of facilities for higher education, proposals for evening colleges, correspondence courses, and the award of external degrees were also under consideration.

The proposal of the Planning Commission was accepted by the Central Advisory Board of Education (1961) and the Ministry of Education appointed an Expert Committee headed by Professor D. S. Kothari, then Chairman of the UGC. The committee consisted of 10 members from different organizations like the UGC, Ministry of Education, and eminent scholars drawn from the Universities. In view of the lack of experience in the field of correspondence education, the committee recommended the introduction of correspondence courses at the undergraduate stage in selected subjects to begin with. The committee suggested that (i) such courses should be administered by the universities only, and (ii) that to begin with, correspondence courses should be confined to the first-degree level. These suggestions were aimed at ensuring adequate quality of education imparted through the new approach.

In 1962, the University of Delhi established the School of Correspondence Courses and Continuing Education. This event was an important landmark in the history of distance education in India as it was the first experiment of this kind. The syllabus, examination and the university degree were the same for correspondence course students as for their counterparts in the regular courses. Even at the end of the first year of its operation, it was observed that the performance of the students in the university examination was fairly comparable to that of regular college students. This convinced the public and the government that the experiment was fairly successful.

The views of the Education Commission (1964-66) were also favourable to the system of correspondence education. The Commission stated:

> At present, a student at the undergraduate stage must either be admitted on a full-time basis or go without education altogether. This creates a great demand for full-time seats in colleges and leads to a deterioration of standards as the resources to provide all the seats needed are not available. One solution to this is to keep full-time seats strictly limited on the basis of resources available and to institute correspondence courses, part-time courses, evening courses etc., for those who aspire to a university degree but are not able to get admission to the regular courses. This device is being increasingly used in many countries such as the USA,

> the UK, the USSR, and Japan. The correspondence courses recently started by the University of Delhi as a "pilot project" have proved to be promising experiment and are producing satisfactory examination results...We recommend that the opportunities for part-time education through programmes like evening colleges, and for own-time education through programmes like correspondence courses, should be extended as widely as possible and should also include courses in science and technology (either at the degree or diploma level). They are the only means to provide higher education to those who desire to study further but are compelled, on economic grounds, to take up employment at the end of the school stage. There need to be no fear that they will lead to a deterioration of standards, especially if due care is taken to maintain personal contacts with the students receiving correspondence education by organizing academic programmes during vacations and holidays. We suggest that by 1986, at least a third of the total enrollment in higher education could with advantage be provided through a system of correspondence and evening colleges.

The National Policy on Education, 1968 made it clear that correspondence education would be given the same status as the full-time courses. Subsequently, the Planning Commission, while drafting the Fourth Plan document, emphasized the need of diverting certain portion of enrollment in higher education to correspondence stream in future. In the meantime the government of India sent delegations (1968-71) of experts to the USSR to study the scheme of correspondence education and recommend suitable measures to streamline the existing programmes and start new ones.

The government of India responded positively to the success of the experiment in Delhi University and Professor Noorul Hasan, then Minister of Education, in his convocation addresses at Agra and Mysore, called for a massive programme of general education through correspondence mode. These events encouraged some other universities also to toy with the idea and initiate processes to implement it. Punjabi University Patiala was the second to come forward to implement the scheme (1968). During the same year, Rajasthan University, Jaipur also set up the Institute of Correspondence Studies and Continuing Education. The following year, the Institute of Correspondence Courses and Continuing Education was set up at Meerut University and Mysore University (1969). The decade of 1960s was, therefore, the period during which the concept of correspondence education took strong roots in the Indian soil (Datt, 1986). Only four conventional universities offered correspondence programmes at postgraduate level during the decade 1962-72. During the next decade, 19 universities established the institutes/directorates of correspondence education or CCIs, which provided major thrust to distance education. Some of these universities started correspondence education for postgraduate and diploma/certificate courses also.

A careful examination of enrollment in these institutions indicates that there has been a continuous increase in their share in the total enrollment in higher education from the very beginning. In 1971, when the system of correspondence education was in its infancy, only 48,000 students, constituting 2.32% of the total enrollment in higher education, were enrolled in the correspondence stream. But, these figures increased to 66,000 (2.79%) in 1977-78, 1,60,000 (5.12%) in 1982-83, and 3,32,000 (9.02%) in 1986-87. At present (1999-2000), there are 62 conventional universities, which are offering academic as well as professional courses through DE mode, making it the largest dual mode system in the world. The CCIs are offering more than 400 programmes, about 50% of which are professional in nature. The enrollment in these institutions is of the order of 9,00,000, which forms 11.64% of the total enrollment in higher education in the country. An important point to be noted here is that the growth rate of enrollment in the correspondence mode has been higher than that of higher education in general. As can be observed in the Table 11.1, while the total enrollment in higher education during the period 1971-2000 has grown less than four-fold, the student population in the correspondence mode has increased twenty-fold.

This is a measure of the growing popularity of the distance education mode in India. These institutions differ from the Open universities only in the mode of delivery of instructional material. The correspondence mode institutions use print media for the delivery of the instructional material, which is generally not in the self-learning format, while the modern Open Universities are also using a combination of both multimedia technologies and the print material.

There have been two distinctive features of the DE system in India. First, until recently, the DE mode had confined its scope to Liberal Education imparting education in the areas related to social sciences and arts only. This was, perhaps due to lack of adequate infrastructure because in science subjects, practical work is involved, which require laboratories. Second, this system has mostly benefited the weaker sections of the society, especially, women, scheduled caste and scheduled tribes. It can be said that this system has proved to be a very powerful tool of democratization of education in India.

Table 11.1
Enrolment in the Correspondence Education (1970-2000)

Year	*Total Enrollment in Higher Education (Lakhs)*	*Enrollment in The CCIs*	*Enrollment in CCIs as % of Total Enrollment*
1971-72	20.65	48,000	2.32
1974-75	23.67	66,000	2.79
1977-78	25.65	88.000	3.43
1982-83	31.33	1,60,000	5.12
1985-86	35.71	2,29,000	6.41
1986-87	36.82	3,32,000	9.02
1989-90	47.64	4,33,500	9.10
1991-92	52.76	5,47,600	10.40
1993-94	58.17	5,24.435	9.00
1997-98	70.78	—	—
1999-2000	77.34	9,00,000	11.64

Sources:
(i) Anand, S. P., 1979.
(ii) Venugopal, V. and Manjulika, S., 1996.
(iii) UGC Reports, 1985-86, 1986-87, 1999-2000.

The institutions of correspondence education suffered from certain problems, due to which the quality of education imparted by them was put to criticism. These weaknesses are:

1. The correspondence institutions were somehow considered as second grade institutions as compared to the regular course institutions and functioned as subsidiaries to them.
2. Most of these institutions offered courses in arts and social sciences only, and were not properly equipped for running courses in sciences and commerce.
3. The curricula and examination systems followed by the correspondence institutions were the same as prevalent in the full-time regular courses run by the parent universities. Therefore, the rigidities of the conventional system in the matters related to admissions and examinations were also carried over to the new system.
4. Most of these institutions used only one, *i.e.* print, and largely depended on the Post and Telegraph Department of the Government for delivery of the reading material to the learners. This caused a lot of hardships to the learners. The lack of institutional mechanism for delivery of the material reduced the efficiency of the system.
5. The parent universities did not allocate adequate funds to these institutions expecting them to generate their own funds. But, the funds collected from students in the form of fees and the price for the printed material was inadequate to run the institutions. The UGC also provided meagre amount funds to them.
6. The correspondence institutions lacked coordination among themselves, which led to considerable duplication of efforts and wastage of the limited resources available.

Open Universities

As mentioned earlier, the establishment of the first Open University in UK served as source of inspiration as well as a model for other developed and developing countries of the world. The government of India also considered the matter seriously. The Ministry of Education and Social Welfare organized a seminar on distance education (1970) in collaboration with the Ministry of Information and Broadcasting, the Indian National Commission for cooperation with UNESCO, and the UGC. This seminar recommended the establishment of an Open University in India on an experimental basis and proposed that a committee should be constituted to workout details for this purpose. It was in 1971 that Professor Noorul Hasan, then Union Minister for Education, advocated this novel idea and proposed the setting up a National Open University in India that would take the entire nation in its ambit. Consequently, a committee headed by G. Parthasarthy, then Vice Chancellor of Jawaharlal Nehru University, was appointed by the government to study the feasibility of the British scheme in Indian context and workout the detailed scheme along with financial implications. This committee made favourable recommendation, but the scheme could not be implemented for a period of more than a decade.

In the meantime, the state government of Andhra Pradesh took the lead and appointed a committee (1982) under the chairmanship of Dr. G. Ram Reddy, then Vice chancellor of Osmania University Hyderabad, to examine the end report on academic, organizational, and financial aspects of a proposed Open University in the state. On the recommendation of this committee, the Lagislature of Andhra Pradesh enacted the "Andhra Pradesh Open University Act" in 1982. Consequently, in August 1982, Andhra Pradesh Open University (APOU), the first Open University in India, was inaugurated by Giani Zail Singh, the then President of India. Prof. G. Ram Reddy was appointed its first Vice Chancellor, and the university started functioning in 1983.

This experiment of Andhra Pradesh inspired the government of Maharashtra to examine the feasibility of establishment of an Open University in the state. The state government appointed a committee in 1984 for this purpose, which was headed by Dr. K.G. Deshmukh, then Vice Chancellor of Amaravati University. The committee submitted its report in January 1985 in which it recommended that an Open University should be established in the state at the earliest with its headquarters at Bombay or Pune or Nagpur. The state government accepted the report.

At the national level, the idea of an Open University was revived in 1984, and then Prime Minister Rajeev Gandhi, in his first broadcast to the nation in January 1985, gave an indication to establish an Open University at Delhi. In pursuance of this, the Ministry of Human Resource Development (MHRD) constituted a committee to prepare a Draft Bill and a detailed Project Report on various aspects relating to the establishment of the proposed Open University (Chauhan, 1990). The Union Government introduced a

Bill in the Parliament, and the Indira Gandhi National Open University (IGNOU) Bill was passed by both the Houses of the Parliament in August 1985.

The chief aim of IGNOU is to promote development of distance education system in the country, and to determine and coordinate academic standards in all institutions in the country following DE mode. The major objectives of the university include widening of access to higher education by providing opportunities to larger segments of the population, particularly the disadvantaged groups, organizing programmes of continuing education and initiating special programmes for higher education for special target groups like women, people living in backward regions and hilly areas etc. The university offers more than 50 programmes at present. During the year 1999, the total number of students registered was 1,72,548 and the total number of students on the rolls was 5,16,580. The network of student support services currently consists of 21 regional centers and 440 study centers (GOI, 2000). The university is likely to open two more regional centers at Jalandhar and Ranchi. The programmes of IGNOU are telecast daily on the National Channel of Doordarshan. Interactive radio phone-in-counselling is also a popular programme, which is aired from 21 All India Radio stations. The university has started working for D.D. Gyandarshan, an educational TV channel. Socially relevant programmes on environment, forest management, human rights, HIV-AIDS awareness and food and nutrition are also being introduced.

After the establishment of APOU and IGNOU, some other state governments also decided to implement the scheme. The government of Rajasthan opened the Kota Open University in 1987. The same year, the government of Bihar established the Nalanda Open University at Patna. In 1989, the state government of Maharashtra established the Yashwantrao Chavan Maharashtra Open University at Nasik. Establishment of the Raja Bhoj Open University (1992) at Bhopal, the capital of Madhya Pradesh followed this. The Gujarat government established Dr. Babasaheb Ambedkar Open University at Ahmedabad in 1995, and Karnataka State Open University, Mysore was set up in 1996. The state of West Bengal also established Netaji Subhash Open University in 1997. The government of Uttar Pradesh has also proposed to establish the U.P. Rajrishi Open University at Allahabad (1998). All these universities are state universities while

IGNOU is a Central University. This process continued, and in fact, still continues. By the end of the year 2000, there were 10 open universities in India, which is the largest number in the world. The long-term plan is to have an Open University in each state. It is being proposed that the correspondence education institutions attached to the conventional universities should be upgraded to level of open learning institutions or some of them may be merged into the State open universities. The 8th Five-Year Plan (1992-97) had proposed that in view of the increasing demand for higher education, 50% of the admission seekers should be encouraged to join the DE mode.

These open universities have had a tremendous impact on Indian education in respect of access, quality and equity. All the open universities together are offering about 300 programmes and over 1900 courses of conventional and non-conventional type at different levels. Earlier it was believed that through distance education only education in social sciences and arts could be imparted, but now this belief is over, and the DE mode has proved equally effective in imparting education of science subjects including medicine engineering and technology also. Also the quality of education imparted through DE mode is comparable to the one imparted through the conventional face-to-face mode. The student enrollment in these institutions has increased very fast. When Andhra Pradesh Open University stared functioning in 1983, it enrolled about 6,200 students. In 1986-87, the APOU and IGNOU together enrolled about 17,000 students. By 1990, the number of Open Universities had gone up to 4, which together enrolled 83,600 students in 1989-90. During the later part of 1990s the open learning system attracted a large number of students. In a short period of just three years 1995-98, the annual enrolment of Open Universities in India increased from 2.01 lakhs to 3.50 lakhs, the corresponding cumulative figures being 5.72 lakhs and 10.5 lakhs (Khan, 2000). At present, the annual enrollment of students in all the open universities taken together is a little more than 6,18,300, and the cumulative figure of enrollment has approached 17,85,000 (Rausaria and Bhushan, 2001).

Table 11.2
Enrollment in the Open Universities in India (1984-2000)

Year	*Enrollment in Open Universities*	*Share of OUs in Total Enrollment (%)*	*Enrollment in DE Institutions*	*Share of DE in Total Enrollment (%)*
1983-84	6,231	0.19	2,01,000 *	6.08
1985-86	17,004	0.47	3,35,090	9.00
1987-88	50,569	1.25	4,02,720	9.40
1989-90	83,603	1.83	5,17,148	10.90
1991-92	1,16,417	2.20	6,64,572	12.60
1993-94	2,28,338	3.92	7,52,773	12.94
1995-96	5,72,000	8.90	—	—
1997-98	10,50,000	14.83	—	—
1999-2000	17,85,000 *	23.08	26,85,000 *	34.72

*Estimated
Sources: Same as in Table 11.1.

These universities have established a large network of Regional Offices and Study Centers all over the country in order to ensure effective delivery of instructional material and increase efficiency of student support services. About 38,000 academic counsellors, drawn from the conventional institutions, provide tutorial services through Regional Offices and Study Centers. The Open Universities have employed their own staff also for carrying out academic, ministerial and administrative business. The development of study material and designing of delivery mechanism is the responsibility of the academic and technical staff respectively.

As a part of its mandate for training of distance education personnel, Staff Training and Research Institute in Distance Education (STRIDE) has been set up at the IGNOU headquarters at New Delhi. This institute organizes national and international seminars and workshops to achieve its objectives. A proper mechanism has been evolved to coordinate the activities of the institutions of distance education. A coordinating council, known as Distance Education Council (DEC) has also been constituted for development of correspondence programmes offered by the traditional universities and for taking policy decisions so as to avoid duplication of efforts and ensure exchange of ideas and resources. This council has created network of open universities for joint programme development, sharing of material and delivery of programmes/courses. For example, the APOU is using the "Food and Nutrition" course evolved by the IGNOU, while the Nalanda University (Bihar) has decided to use the "Public Accountancy" programme developed by Kota Open University (Rajasthan). In order to promote cooperation among the Open Universities of Asian countries, the Asian Association of Open Universities has been formed. It is expected that by exchanging course materials among the member countries of the Association, both time and money can be saved.

One essential feature of distance education system is that the teacher and the student are at a distance apart. There is hardly any possibility of face-to-face interaction between the two. Obviously, the communication between teacher and the taught is essential for learning to take place. This communication is made possible through media. As discussed earlier, correspondence education system largely depended on the print media through which learning material was sent to the learners. The usual procedure of transportation of the material involved the mailing of the material in packets through postal services. But, these days, conditions have completely changed. The system is now well-organized having a large network of Study Centers and Regional Centers along with other components of Student Support Services. These are the three major components of the methodology of Distance Education.

NATIONAL INSTITUTE OF OPEN SCHOOLING

Although, the Constitution of India, vide Article 45, puts an obligation on the government to provide for free and compulsory elementary education for all children of the relevant age group, yet many children could not take advantage of this provision due to various reasons. A large group of children is not enrolled in school because of illiteracy among parents, poverty and/or their affiliation to socially and culturally disadvantaged sections of the society. Many children have to dropout of the school due to social, economic, psychological or personal reasons including lack of scholastic aptitude. Such children find it very difficult to enter the formal school system at a later stage when they feel fresh motivation or need to do so. In the geographically isolated and remote areas, the population is highly scattered and the schools are located at distant places, and therefore, are not accessible to many children.

The overall condition of schooling facilities is also not very satisfactory in our country. The existing schools have limited infrastructure in terms of building, playgrounds and equipment. This process forces the existing schools to make admissions on the basis of academic merit for fixed number of seats, thus depriving a large number of aspirant's entry in the formal school system. There are some people for whom education is a life long process. They want to enrich and update their knowledge in certain areas of interest or wish to acquire knowledge in new areas as a hobby. Sometimes, the requirements of the workplace encourage working people to learn new skills in order to be able to discharge their duties more effectively and efficiently. But, such people, for certain compelling reasons, cannot join the full-time formal schools/ colleges. They demand educational facilities suitable to their situations.

These circumstances have forced the educationists to device some alternative system of school education, which would provide for needed flexibility in terms of instructional calendar, entry qualifications, and time limit for completion of courses, admission rules and examination. In addition to this, the alternative system should be cost-effective in the sense that it should reduce the financial burden, not only on the government, but also on the public.

Historical Perspective

As a result, our educational planners thought of new alternative approaches for providing access to education for those who wanted to continue their education. At school level, correspondence education was first introduced in 1965 (IGNOU, 2000), when the Conference of Board of Secondary Education at Pune, recommended correspondence education courses for the private students. Even earlier, the mode of appearance in the examinations as private candidates was in practice. But, the candidates had to prepare for the examination through home study method. The first correspondence school was established at Bhopal in 1965, just three years after the establishment of the first institute of correspondence education for higher studies at Delhi University. Setting up of the Patrachar Vidyalaya at Delhi in 1968 followed this. The same year, the Board of Secondary Education, Rajasthan (Ajmer), also started correspondence courses at school level. After this, the Central Board of Secondary Education, the Institute of Correspondence Education

(Allahabad), the Board of Secondary Education, Orissa, and SCERT, Tamil Nadu also established similar institutions.

However, the correspondence education system suffered from the same weaknesses as the conventional face-to-face system because it followed the syllabus of the conventional schools and the students had to appear in the examination along with the students of the conventional system. Therefore, the traditional rigidities of the conventional system plagued the correspondence system also. The only difference was that the students of the correspondence system did not attend the classes regularly. Consequently, the problem of access could not be fully tackled through the correspondence system. It was felt that Open Learning system could meet the special needs of the out of school children and bring the un-schooled population within the fold of education. The matter was discussed at length in the world conference of the International Council of Correspondence Education (ICCE) held in New Delhi in 1974. In 1979, the Open School was established at Delhi as a Project of the Central Board of Secondary Education. But, it was not an examining body, and the examination of candidates registered with it was conducted by the CBSE. When the National Policy on Education was launched in 1986, the Open Learning system received an overriding priority as a part of its proposals. The Open School was upgraded and became the National Open School (NOS), an autonomous institution. Under its new incarnation, it was empowered to conduct its own examinations and became an independent Board of School Education. Recently, it has been renamed as National Institute of Open Schooling (NIOS).

The main objective of the NIOS is to provide useful and practical education to those who need. Like Open Universities, the target groups of the NIOS are those children or adults who remained partially deprived of formal school education for some social, psychological, or personal reasons, and decide to continue their learning at a later stage when they get motivated or feel its need. By serving the needs of dropouts and left-outs, the NIOS makes a very significant contribution to the UEE. As the doors of NIOS are open to all, it serves as an effective instrument of democratization of school education so as to make it accessible to poor, disadvantaged and disabled citizens. It also provides education at affordable price, and hence, offers cost-effective means of learning. The in-built flexibility and cost-effectiveness ensure equity, and hence, serve the democratic purpose of equalization of educational opportunities at school stage. The NIOS is also offering need based vocational courses for the benefit of those who wish to enrich their knowledge and skills. Such continuing education programmes run by the NIOS are very useful in the evolution of a learning society in India.

The NIOS is not only providing education in the academic areas, but also serving the learners through courses of professional nature like Computer Applications, Word Processing and Secretarial Practices, both at secondary and senior secondary stages. In addition, the NIOS is playing a leading role in the development of a network of open schools in the country, resulting in the establishment of State Open Schools and State Centers for Open Schooling. While State Open Schools in Andhra Pradesh and Tamil Nadu were set up during 1980s, those in Haryana, Rajasthan, Madhya Pradesh, Karnataka, West Bengal, and Punjab came into being during 1990s. Some other states are also planning to establish open schools in near future.

Organization and Functioning

The National Institute of Open Schooling is an autonomous organization set up by the Government of India, Ministry of Human Resource Development under the Societies Registration Act of 1860. It is partly funded by the Government of India. As a society, it has a General Body headed by the Union Minister of Human Resource Development as its President, which is its apex governing body vested with the responsibility of assisting the NIOS society by providing sound professional advice in connection with its functioning. It gives broad policy directions and helps the NIOS to ensure that it remains publicly accountable. In addition, the NOS also has an Executive Board vested with powers to manage the affairs of the society and ensure its smooth-functioning. Its Chairman who is also the Chairman of the NIOS Society heads the Executive Board. The specific responsibilities of the executive Board are to plan all policies and programmes of action, to take appropriate decisions for their implementation and to review the functions of the society.

The Vice Chairman who is appointed from amongst the three Heads of the Departments by rotation assists the Chairman of the NIOS. These are Director Academic, Secretary and Controller of Examinations who look after Academic, Administrative and Examination Departments respectively (NOS Profile, 1999).

Enrollment Trends

Like open universities, the NIOS functions through a network of Regional Centers and Study Centers spread throughout the country. Its Regional Centers are located at Allahabad, Kolkata, Cochin, Chandigarh, Delhi, Guwahati, Hyderabad, Jaipur, Patna, and Pune. The annual enrollment of students at NIOS has increased from only about 40,900 in 1990-91 to over 1,90,000 in 2000-2001. At present, it is estimated that there are over 5 lakhs of students receiving education through NIOS (GOI, 2000-2001). The annual enrollment trends may be understood from Table 11.3. It may be observed in the table that there has been a continuous growth in the number of students seeking registration in the NIOS study programmes during the period of more than one decade since its inception. Secondly, the NIOS has a diverse profile of students with a healthy mix of old and the young learners from all the States and Union Territories of India. The age of learners varies from 14 years to 89 years, though most of them are in the age group 18-24 years, and they are coming from different parts of the country. In 1999-2000, the NIOS had 1,075 accredited institutions all over the country with about 4.5 lakh students on its rolls. The number of study centers and accredited institutions has risen to 1,459 by 2000-2001. The number of accredited vocational institutions, which was only 39 in 1993-94, has gone up to 365 in 2000-2001.

Table: 11.3
Enrollment Trends in National Open School (1991-2001)

Year	*Annual Enrollment*	*Students Certified*
1990-91	40,900	35,510
1991-92	34,800	54,000
1992-93	53,570	79,200
1993-94	62,300	1,13,230
1994-95	64,500	1,33,900
1995-96	75,430	1,70,260
1996-97	93,700	2,12,100
1997-98	1,12,210	2,41,860
1998-99	1,30,000	2,80,000 *
1999-2000	1,60,000 *	3,30,000 *
2000-01	1,90,000	4,00,000 *

*Estimated.

Sources: 1. The NOS Profile 1999.
2. The Annual reports of the MHRD, Government of India, 1999-2000 and 2000-2001.

The NIOS has set up eight regional centers out of ten such centers approved for the Ninth Plan. The NIOS has its study centers outside India also at such places as Dubai, Abu Dhabi, and Muscat in the Middle East. The Commonwealth of Learning has conferred an Award of Excellence on the NOS for its remarkable contribution in the area of distance education at school stage. By the end of the year 2000-2001, about 4 lakh students had completed their studies through the NIOS and had been awarded the Secondary and Senior Secondary School Certificates.

Recently, it has been informed by the NIOS (TOI, April 22, 2002) that currently over 7 lakh students are enrolled in the NIOS for its secondary and senior secondary programmes with over 1 lakh enrolling every year. There are about 1,370 accredited institutions spread over the length and the breadth of the country. In addition, there are 426 institutions offering vocational courses through open learning system. This is a great achievement.

On the whole it may be stated that Open Learning at school stage has been a successful experiment in India and has proved to be a suitable system for our socio-economic conditions. In a country as diverse as India the role of open/distance learning becomes increasingly important for providing educational opportunities to the deprived sections of the society. In this system, the regular formal institutions serve as centers of learning and their teachers assume the role of facilitators of learning as academic councillors.

12

Educational Finance

Educational finance is an important component of national economy. There exists a strong relationship between educational and economic development. However, in India, the educational components of economic development, somehow, could not receive desired degree of attention of politicians and policy planners. This is also not recognized that slow progress of economy during the last several decades is because of slow progress of education, which, in the ultimate analysis may be attributed to less than desirable investment in education. Educational investment is the only investment that yields assured dividend, though, the gestation period is generally larger than that in the case of other industries. Nobel Laureate Amartya Sen has rightly suggested the whole world to invest more money on education and health sectors of economy. According to his theory, all socio-economic disparities are caused by disparities in human capabilities, physical and mental. Both physical and mental energies are necessary for any kind of productive work. While good health ensures needed physical energy, good education is essential for development and proper use of mental capacity. Both social and individual returns of good education are high. Education makes a person capable of getting a job thereby helping him to take advantage of available opportunities, which in turn, enhance his personal freedom in many other activities of life. Therefore, it is essential for developing nations like India that they should invest more money on these two sectors of economy.

Higher literacy rate and basic education facilitate public debates on social needs and encourage informed collective demands for essential services like health and security (Dreze and Sen, 1995). Greater literacy and educational achievements of disadvantaged groups can increase their ability to resist oppression, to organize politically, and to get a fairer deal. The present upsurge in the political awareness among the weaker sections of the Indian society and their aggressive assertion of their political and social rights is a live example. Their increased level of education has enhanced their participation in productive economic activities thus adding their share in the national development. This process, in the long run, leads to reduction in the socio-economic disparities. Increased level of education among girls may result in drastic changes in gender-based inequalities. If, on the other hand, a society is a victim of illiteracy, ignorance and ill health, its progress is likely to be hampered by these factors, and ultimately, it is overpowered by underdevelopment and poverty. This is exactly what has happened in our country. From the very beginning, education has not been an important sector for our successive governments. Let us examine the issues related to educational finance in India, especially, during the post-independence period.

HISTORICAL PERSPECTIVE

During the ancient period, there was no state-funding system of education. Mostly, schools were associated with religious places like temples and were financed by kings and well-to-do members of the society through donation of land, buildings, and other types of endowments. Sometimes, kings and big landlords also donated money in the form of cash and scholarships. There was no system of payment of salaries to the teachers. The teachers, known as pundits, maintained themselves on presents and guru dakshina, which their students offered to them out of devotion in exchange of education imparted. The payment of fees by the students was completely prohibited. During the medieval period also the same pattern continued. Schools were generally attached to mosques under direct control of the Maulvis, who were teachers. The pattern of finance was almost the same as the one prevalent during the ancient period.

The state-funding system of education started during the British period. As mentioned in the first chapter, the East India Company was not much interested in the education of the native population in the beginning, but at a later stage, the Company felt that there was a need to have some system of schooling for the children of the officers of the Company and those of the Anglo-Indians holding high positions in the administrative machinery. The process started with the establishment of schools by the missionaries whose main objective was to spread Christianity among the native people. But, the East India Company did also not fund these attempts; rather, the missionaries managed their funds from the religious organizations located in Britain.

For the first 165 years since its arrival in India, the Company functioned as a commercial concern and, as such, did not consider its duty to educate the people it traded with. However, the Company encouraged the educational endeavor of the missionaries. In 1659, the Court of Directors of the Company expressed its strong desire to spread Christianity among the people of India, and allowed the missionaries to embark on their ships. In 1677, the Company sent to Madras a paid schoolmaster to teach the elements of English and the Protestant religion (Misra, 1962). When the Charter of the Company was renewed in 1698, a missionary clause was introduced desiring the company to maintain ministers of religion at their factories in India and to maintain schools in all the garrisons and bigger factories. Again in 1793, when the British government considered the Charter Act, an attempt was made to clear a resolution in favour of the missionaries being sent out to India, but it failed. However, the efforts continued in this direction and succeeded in 1813 when clause 43 was inserted in the Charter Act of the Company. This clause reads as follows:

> It shall be lawful for the Governor General in the Council to direct that of any surplus which may remain of the rents, revenues, and profits arising from the said territorial acquisition, after defraying the expenses of the military, civil and commercial establishment and paying the interest of the debt, a sum of not less than one lakh of rupees in each year

> shall be set apart and applied to the revival and improvement of literature and the encouragement of the learned natives of India and for the introduction and promotion of a knowledge of the sciences among the inhabitants of the British territories of India; and that any school, public lecture or other institutions for the purpose aforesaid.... Provided always that all appointment to offices in such schools shall be made by or under the authority of the government.

The introduction of this clause was an important milestone in the history of British education in India. It was from this point onwards that the system of financing of education by the government took a definite shape and Company's educational policy was clearly defined. However, the provision also gave the governor a freedom of choice between spending and not spending the earmarked amount for the specified purpose. Secondly, the said amount was to be made available for education only when there was a surplus of funds after clearing all other liabilities including interest on debt. Such a situation was, however, very hard to achieve. Consequently, nothing could be done in this direction at least for a decade to follow. It is said that it took the then government a long period of twenty years to withdraw the first instalment under this provision (Singh, 2001).

The Charter Act of the Company came up for renewal again in 1853, and the British Parliament appointed a Select Committee to enquire into the affairs of the company. This Committee, among other important matters, discussed the issues about education and its development, on the basis of which the Education Dispatch of 1854 was drafted. During discussions, the government realized that the educational efforts of the government alone were not sufficient to meet the growing demand for education among the public. It was, therefore, decided to introduce the system of "grants-in-aid", which would supplement the efforts of the government to ensure accelerated progress of education. The main purpose of the proposal was to draw support of the local public in terms of financial and material resources. In the Dispatch of 1854, the Court of Directors declared, among other things, that;

> ..... in consideration of the impossibility of the Government alone doing all that must be done to provide adequately for

> the education of the people of India they resolve to adopt, in India, the system of grant-in-aid which had been adopted in England with very great success, the system being based on an entire abstinence from interference with the religious instruction conveyed in the school assisted; that no government colleges or schools should, therefore, be founded in future in any district which had a sufficient number of institutions capable, with Government grants, of supplying the local demands for education; and that they looked forward to the time when any general system of education entirely provided by the Government might be discontinued with the gradual advance of the system of grant-in-aid and when many of the existing Government institutions, especially those of the higher order, might be safely closed or transferred to the management of local bodies under the control of, or aided by, the State;....

One important point to be noted here is that it was in the Dispatch of 1854 that the government first approved the official payment of salaries and pension to teachers in India. Another significant development, after the issuance of the Dispatch was the introduction of the levy of a local cess of one anna on every rupee of land revenue of which, 1/3 was to be assigned to education.

SOURCES OF EDUCATIONAL FINANCE

There are two major sources of educational finance in India. The government and the private sectors in indifferent proportions share the entire expenditure incurred on educational activities. The government expenditure, also known as public expenditure, includes funds provided by the central government, state governments, the UGC (in the case of higher education) and local bodies such a municipal corporations, district boards and Zila parishads. The private sector funds, on the other hand, include the financial contribution of parents in the form of fees for the education of their children, and contribution of public in the form of donations and endowments.

There is another way of classification educational expenditure, *viz.*, direct educational expenditure and indirect educational expenditure. Direct educational expenditure is incurred on the maintenance of the institution. This includes expenditure incurred on the payment of the salaries of the teaching and non-teaching staff, recurring expenditure on equipment and maintenance of buildings, contingency expenses etc. Indirect expenditure is that part of the total expenditure which is incurred on construction of new buildings, purchase of new equipment, direction and inspection, scholarships, hostel facilities and other miscellaneous items. The most part of the direct expenditure is recurring in nature. The indirect expenditure, on the other hand, is partly recurring and partly non-recurring. It is worthwhile to study and analyze the financial resources available to education in terms of public and private sector contributions. The discussion regarding pre-independence and post-independence periods is given below.

Pre-Independence period

The details of financial resources made available for education have been presented in the following table (Table 12.1). It can be observed from the table that government funds for education increased from Rs. 17.26 lakh in 1855-56 to Rs. 177.04 lakh by 1901-02, a ten-fold growth during a period of 45 years. The process of increase went on, and by 1946-47, the figure reached Rs. 3436.1 lakh. As a percentage of total expenditure, the government share was 92.2% in 1865-66. Thereafter, it decreased to 88.7% in 1870-71, 56.4% in 1881-82, 51.1% in 1991-92, 44.1% in 1901-02, and then suddenly increased to 51.6% in 1911-12. After this again it started declining and came down to 59.6% in 1946-47. This shows that even during the pre-independence period government financed education sector to a considerable extent. In fact, the government contributed a major portion of the total educational expenditure.

The roll of private sector, including the parents of pupils, was also significant. In the beginning, the proportion of private contribution to educational finance was low but it continued to increase over the years. In 1865-66, the private expenditure on education was Rs. 4.1 lakh, which increased to Rs. 10.5 lakh in 1870-71, Rs. 81.2 lakh in 1881-82, Rs. 149 lakh in 1891-92, Rs. 224.2 lakh in 1901-02, Rs. 380.7 lakh in 1911-12, and reached Rs. 2330 lakh in 1946-47. In terms of percentage of the total expenditure, the share of private sector first increased from 7.8% in 1865-66 to 55.9% in 1901-02, and then came down to 48.4% in 1911-12, and finally to 40.4% in 1946-47. This shows that during the pre-independence period, the private sector and public sector shared the educational expenditure in the ratio of 40:60 and the government encouraged private agencies to come forward and share educational efforts.

Table 12.1
Educational Finance During The British Period (1855-1947)

Year	*Public Expenditure (Rs. in Lakhs)*	*Private Expenditure (Rs. in Lakhs)*	*Total (Rs. in Lakhs)*
1855-56	17.26	—	17.26
1865-66	48.50 (29.20)	4.12 (7.80)	52.62 (100)
1870-71	82.55 (88.70)	10.52 (11.30)	93.07 (100)
1881-82	104.89 (56.40)	81.18 (43.60)	186.07 (100)
1891-92	156.18 (51.10)	149.01 (48.90)	305.19 (100)
1901-02	177.04 (44.10)	224.17 (55.90)	401.21 (100)
1911-12	405.23 (51.60)	380.69 (48.40)	785.92 (100)
1921-22	1,149.61 (62.60)	687.92 (37.40)	1,837.53 (100)
1931-32	1,684.19 (61.9)	1,034.38 (38.10)	2,718.57 (100)
1941-42	1,804.86 (58.50)	1,280.95 (41.50)	3,084.81 (100)
1946-47	3,436.10 (59.60)	2,330.03 (40.40)	5,766.13 (100)

* The figures within brackets indicate percentage of the total.
** Figures compiled from Misra (1962), Educational Finance in India, Asia Publishing House, New Delhi.

Post-Independence Period

The distribution of educational expenditure by sources (in terms of percentages) during the period from 1950-51 to 1990-91 is presented in Table 12.2. It can be observed that the share of government expenditure has been increasing continuously since independence. In 1950-51, the government share was 68.00%, but it went up to 74.50% in 1960-61, 81.30% in 1970-71, 85.00% in 1980-81 and 90.66% in 1990-91. At present, in 2001-02, it might have increased to over 95%. On the other hand, the share of private sector, including fees and donations, has been decreasing in the same proportion. The share of fees and endowments has successively come down from 32.20% in 1950-51 to 25.50% in 1960-61, 18.70% in 1970-71, 15.00% in 1980-81, and 9.34% in 1990-91. It might have further decreased to less than 5% during the last one decade. The available records show that government funds have been increasing in absolute terms, but private funds have not shown significant rise. The share of student fees has successively decreased from 20.4% in 1950-51 to only 3.2% in 1990-91. This has happened because fees have not been revise upwards for a long time and the prices have gone up sharply. With the downfall in the share of private sector, the government expenditure has increased. And education sector receives very high subsidy from the Government.

Within government expenditure, the share of Central Government is very small as compared to the share of the state governments. This is despite the fact that education is in the concurrent list. Though, nominal rise in the allocation takes place, yet as a proportion of the total revenue expenditure of the Union Government it has been declining. The only positive point is increased allocation for elementary education, which has been done at the cost of higher education. This may undermine the quality of higher education in the long run. So much so that the Plan expenditure by the Center is now of the order of 38% of the total plan expenditure on education. In the case of elementary education the share of the Central Government in the plan expenditure has gone up from 11.7% in the Sixth Plan to 38% in the Eighth Plan. This shows that the state governments play a major role in educational finance. The share of the state governments in the overall educational expenditure at present is of the order of 60%. In the state budgets, the share of education sector varies from 25% to 30%, which is a major portion of their total expenditure.

Table 12.2
Educational Finance by Source (%)

Source	*1950-51*	*1960-61*	*1970-71*	*1980-81*	*1990-91*
Government (Centre and State)	57.10	68.00	75.62	80.00	87.63
Local Bodies	10.90	6.50	5.70	5.00	3.03
Total Govt.	68.00	74.50	81.30	85.00	90.66
Fees	20.40	17.20	12.80	12.00	6.14
Endowments etc.	11.80	8.30	5.90	3.00	3.20
Total Private Sector	32.20	25.50	18.70	15.00	9.34
Total	100.00	100.00	100.00	100.00	100.00

Sources: Vaidyanatha Ayyar, R.V. Journal of Educational Planning and Administration, NIEPA, New Delhi, Vol. VII, No. 2, April 1993.
Department of Education, Ministry of Human Resource Development, Government of India, New Delhi (1999-2000).

FINANCIAL PATTERN

Recurring Expenditure

If we analyze the annual educational expenditure in absolute terms, we observe certain interesting trends. Though, overall annual expenditure on education has increased from Rs. 1140 million in 1950-51 to Rs. 3450 million in 1960-61, 11,180 million in 1970-71, Rs. 37,460 million in 1980-81 and 203,520 Million in 1990-91, yet, as a proportion of the Gross National Product (GNP) the increase has been marginal (Table 12.3). The expenditure on education as percentage of the GNP was 1.2 in 1950-51. It increased to 2.5 in 1960-61, 3.1 in 1970-71, 3.9 in 1980-81, 4.0 in 1985-85, and then decreased to 3.9 in 1989-90. Even today it has not touched the figure of 4%. It is clear that expenditure on education as proportion of the GNP has been continuously increasing since the beginning of the First Five Year Plan, but increase has been slow. However, it falls short of the requirements of the large system of education that we have created. The amount invested in education has not been adequate. The Education Commission (1964-66) argued for increased investment in education. It suggested that the proportion of GNP allocated to education should rise from 2.9% in 1965-66 to 6% by 1985-86. The National Policy on Education 1968 also endorsed this target. Again in 1992, the Modified educational Policy on Education 1986 stated that, "the outlay on education will be stepped up to ensure that during the Eighth Five Year Plan and onwards it will uniformly exceed 6% of the national income." The Education Commission had suggested that during the years 1965-85, the stress should be given on school education. The educational planners did not accept this suggestion. The Commission had suggested that after 1985, there should be increased stress on higher education and research.

Non-Recurring Expenditure

After the inception of the strategy of planned development, expenditure on education as a proportion of the GNP has increased marginally, as discussed earlier. In terms of plan expenditure, the share of education as a percentage of total plan outlay has also decreased (Table 12.4). It can be seen from the table that in absolute

Table 12.3
Share of Education in the GNP (%)

Years	*Total (Rs. Millions)*	*As Per cent of GNP*	*Per Capita (Rs.)*	*Per Pupil (Rs.)*
1950-51	1,140	1.20	3.20	35.60
1960-61	3,450	2.50	7.90	53.70
1970-71	11,180	3.10	10.70	141.70
1980-81	37,460	3.90	54.60	337.50
1984-85	71,740	4.00	99.00	283.00
1985-86	1,23,860	4.00	163.50	900.00*
1990-91	2,03,520	3.90	240.00*	1295.00*
1992-93	2,07,500	3.70	238.00	1208.00
1993-94	2,39,090	3.80	265.00*	1360.00*
1994-95	2,71,770	3.90	295.00*	1510.00*

* Estimated

Sources:
1. Azad J.L. Financing of Education in India, Venugopal, V. and Manjulika, S., 1996.
2. Selected Educational Statistics, Ministry of Human Resource Development, Govt. of India, New Delhi 1995-96.

Table 12.4
Plan Expenditure (Rs. in Millions)

Sector	*1st Plan 1951-1956*	*2nd Plan 1956-1961*	*3rd Plan 1961-1966*	*Plan Holiday 1966-1969*	*4th Plan 1969-1974*	*5th Plan 1974-1979*	*6th Plan 1980-1985*	*7th Plan 1985-1990*	*Annual Plan 1990-1992*	*8th Plan 1992-1997*	*9th Plan 1997-2002*
Elementary Education	850 (56)	950 (35)	2010 (34)	750 (24)	2390 (30)	3170 (35)	8360 (33)	28490 (37)	17290 (37)	92010 (47)	118428 (58)
Secondary Education	200 (13)	510 (19)	1030 (18)	530 (16)	1400 (18)	1560 (17)	5300 (21)	18320 (24)	10530 (22)	34980 (18)	26035 (13)
Adult Education							2240 (9)	4700 (6)	4160 (9)	18480 (9)	6304 (3)
Higher Education	140 (9)	480 (18)	870 (15)	770 (24)	1950 (25)	2050 (22)	5590 (22)	12010 (16)	5880 (12)	15160 (8)	25000 (12)
Technical Education	200 (13)	490 (18)	1250 (21)	810 (25)	1060 (13)	1070 (12)	2730 (11)	10830 (14)	8230 (17)	27860 (14)	23735 (12)
Others	9 (140)	10 (300)	12 (730)	11 (370)	14 (1060)	14 (1060)	4 (1080)	3 (1980)	2 (1180)	4 (7510)	4314 (2)
Total	1530 (100)	2730 (100)	5890 (100)	3230 (100)	7860 (100)	9120 (100)	25300 (100)	100 (76330)	47270 (100)	196000 (100)	203816 (100)

Sources: Same as in Table 12.2.

Note: Figures in the brackets indicate percentages.

terms, the plan allocation for education sector has increased from Rs. 1,530 million in the First Five Year Plan (1951-1956) to Rs. 2,03,816 million in the Ninth Five Year Plan (1997-2002). If the distribution of plan-allocation is studied, certain interesting trends are observed (see Table 12.5).

SECTOR-WISE PRIORITIES

If we look at the share of education in the total plan outlay, we find that education has not been the favourite sector for the successive governments. The share of education sector as been dwindling over the years since independence (Table 12.5). It was 7.86% of the Total Plan Outlay in the First Plan, 5.83% in the Second Plan, 6.87% in the Third Plan, and then came down further over the plans and reached 2.70% in the Sixth Plan. After this, there was a reverse trend and the share of education increased to 3.55% in the Seventh Plan and to 4.9% in the Eighth Plan. In the Ninth Plan, it is estimated to be around 5.00%. The share of elementary education, which was 56% during the First Plan, came down successively to 24% during the period of Plan Holiday (1966-1969), and than increased to 47% during the Eighth Plan (1992-1997). During the Ninth Plan (1997-2002), it was 58%. The share of secondary education increased from 13 per cent in the First Plan to 24% in the Seventh Plan (1985-1990), and then decreased successively to 13% in the Ninth Plan. In the same way, the share of higher education also first increased from 9% in the First Plan to 25% in the Fourth Plan (1969-1974), and then declined to 8% in the Eighth Plan. However, in the Ninth Plan the share of higher education was raised to 12%.

This shows that the government funds for higher education are being reduced gradually. At the same time the allocation for elementary education has been continuously increasing after the Sixth Plan. In the case of technical education, the share of funds has been kept frozen at 11-14% level during the period from Fourth to Ninth plans. But, earlier, there was an increase from 13% in the First Plan to 25% in the Fourth Plan.

Table 12.5
Share of Different Sectors of Education in Five Year Plans (%)

Plans	*Share of Education (All Sectors)*	*Share in Total Plan Outlay (%)*				
		Elementary Education	*Secondary Education*	*Higher (General)*	*Higher (Technical)*	*Other Sectors*
I	7.86	56	13	9	13	9
II	5.83	35	19	18	18	10
III	6.87	34	18	15	21	12
Plan Holiday	4.86	24	16	24	25	11
IV	5.04	30	18	25	13	14
V	3.27	35	17	22	12	14
VI	2.70	33	21	22	11	13*
VII	3.55	37	24	16	14	9*
Annual Plan	3.80	37	22	12	17	11*
VIII	4.90	47	18	8	14	13*
IX	5.00**	58	13	12	12	5*

* Includes share of Adult Education also.
** Estimated
Sources: Same as in Table 12.2.

ISSUES AND PROBLEMS

Today, India has a very large educational system with 8.40 lakh elementary schools, about 1.17 lakh secondary and senior secondary schools, more than 11,000 colleges and about 270 universities. These institutions have enrolled about 192 million students. The number of teachers working in these institutions is about 5.3 million. As far as size is concerned, we have one of the largest educational systems of the world. As the system of education in India has been growing in size during the post-independence period, the private sector contribution to educational finance has been dwindling. Due to this development, the dependence on government funds has considerably increased It has been very unfortunate that education has always enjoyed the status of a residual sector despite official acceptance of the fact that this sector of economy needs to be strengthened, and, hence requires more funds. The unfortunate part of the whole episode is that in the years to come the social services in general, and education sector in particular, may continue to be low priority areas as indicated by one of the terms of reference of the Tenth Finance Commission that fiscal deficit as a proportion of GDP be reduced not only at the central level but also at the state level without expecting any transfer from the Center (Shah, 1993). At present, we are spending about 4% of the GNP on education against the recommendation of Education Commission (1964-66) for 6%, thus recording a shortfall of about 33%. Moreover, the target of spending 6% of the GNP on education should have been achieved by 1985-86. We are already late by 17 years. In order to feed the present system properly we should spend around 8% of the GNP. In this connection, there are two major issues that need our attention:

1. We are spending less on education sector than what it actually needs. Many of our ambitious developmental plans for education are not properly implemented for want of required funds. Whenever a financial cut is exercised, it is always from education.
2. Whenever we feel that certain sector of education, say primary education sector, needs more funds, this requirement is met at the cost of some other important sectors, say higher and/or technical education sectors.

The Question of Subsidy

There are three main sources of educational finance in India—Central and State governments, local bodies, and private sector including the students who are its potential beneficiaries. As the system of education grew in size, it required increased funds even for its maintenance. Consequently, the government contribution to educational finance increased from about 57% in 1950-51 to about 90-95% during 1990s. During the same period the contribution of students in terms of fees decreased from about 20% to less than 5%. Moreover, the allocation of funds for education over the nine five-year plans has not shown noticeable improvement, rather, in relative terms, it has been declining continuously. Therefore, in order to augment additional funds for education, we need to adopt a two-pronged strategy. On the one hand the allocation for education needs to be increased substantially so as to achieve the target of spending 6% of the GNP in the shortest possible time with an objective to raise it to 8% in the long run, and on the other hand, the students' fees should be revised upwards at all levels so as to recover at least 25% of the expenditure incurred on their education at school stage and 50% at college stage.

In the developing societies, higher education is considered as a speedy vehicle for upward social mobility, especially by the socially and economically deprived and underprivileged sections. Mostly the upper and middle-income groups demand it. As higher education is considered as a social service, it is highly subsidized by the government. A survey conducted by the NCERT during 1960s showed that 80% of university and high school completers came from the top 20% of the income groups. A similar study conducted by the UGC during 1970s revealed that 70% of the university students came from top 20% of the income groups. On the other hand, 70% of the government revenue came from indirect taxes paid by all citizens of which 60% were living in poverty. This shows that the poor people who are deprived of education of any kind are forced to pay for the education of the well to do through subsidy. This justifies the reduction of subsidy and enhancement of fees. In a democratic society, poor people cannot be taxed for the benefit of the rich.

Those who are benefited by the subsidy in higher education do not demand better quality because they are not paying for it. When a beneficiary of a service has to pay (as in the case of public schools), he expresses concern about its quality. But, in the case of higher education, the amount of fees is nominal and has not been subjected to significant upward revision for several decades. As higher education has been monopolized by the well to do, the major part of the subsidy is going to those who do not need it. Another paradox is that the more expensive the course (such as medicine, engineering and management), the larger the subsidy. A graduate in general education pays about 14% of the cost of his education while a graduate in more expensive professional courses pays only 9 per cent. Here is a case for increasing fees so as to cover at least 50% of the cost in general education. In professional education, the fee may be even higher because these courses lead to higher personal returns. Even at elementary stage, some fees should be charged because anything available free of cost is not valued by the society.

The Expenditure Reforms Commission (ERC) set up by the Union Government has recommended (AIU, September 2002) that tuition fees in the universities and colleges, which have been static at Rs. 15 per month for decades, should now be raised to a range of Rs. 300-500 per month for "general academic courses". This step has been taken after considering that a fair number of students attending private and public schools pay monthly fees of Rs. 500 or more and also considering the general level of economic well being among the families availing the higher education. The ERC also feels that this level of fees cannot be said to be beyond the reach of an average family.

While observing that the "tuition fee in colleges and universities have no relation to the cost of education in such institutions", the ERC has noted that the universities have looked to the UGC to take responsibility and issue a directive for increase of fees, while the UGC has passed the same to the government resulting in freezing of fees at the same unrealistic level. Although, Section 12-A (2) of the UGC Act places responsibility on the UGC to lay down limits for revising fees, it has refrained from specifying any such levels. The individual universities also have powers to under the relevant university acts to increase fees but the general trend has been against increasing fees obviously because it will meet with some opposition from the student community.

Accepting that there would be some students from the poorer families for whom the fee suggested would be a burden, the ERC has suggested that universities could be allowed to retain a portion of about 25% of the additional realizations from increase of fees for being used for extending free-ships to students from poor families. As per the ERC, additional funds raised could cover both merit-based and means-based scholarships. The ERC has also suggested that the present grants-in-aid system should be changed, as the educational institutions are not showing any initiative to increase fees due to this.

Privatization as a Global Trend

According to our cultural traditions, teaching or providing education in any way is considered as a sacred task and a service to mankind. Therefore, it was provided free of cost in the past. It was during the British period that the official government funding of education started. So far, we have been following the same model. But, because of certain socio-economic changes having taken place globally, it has become difficult for governments of almost all the countries to provide liberal financial support to higher education sector. The main reason of this shift is that the size of the system has outgrown the capacity of the governments to finance it. The other reason is that recognition of larger social benefits of primary and elementary education, compared to higher education, has shifted the focus of the government to invest more in these sectors of education than on higher education. Moreover, the demand of the market economy all over the world is increasingly compelling the universities and other academic institutions to introduce skill-oriented courses, which require higher investment but fetch smaller social benefits. This situation has led to increased privatization of higher education. What do these circumstances imply for India? The answer is very simple. We must privatize and globalize higher education, willingly or unwillingly, by forging partnerships with the big business houses, producing sellable skilled graduates, and/or by increasing student fees. The process has already started with the emergence of a large number of capitation-fee charging colleges of technical and professional education in the southern states of Tamil Nadu and Karnataka. Interestingly, these institutions have larger enrollment of students than the government funded or aided colleges. Similar institutions established in Manipal, which are rated by the NAAC as 5-star institutions, have developed into institutions deemed to be universities.

Recently, the state government of Delhi has decided that state-run schools of Delhi with poor results in examination may be handed over to private trusts with permission to raise fees and some grant by the state (TOI, Feb. 2, 2002). About 50-100 schools having 15% result are being considered for the scheme. Most of these schools are located in the colonies inhabiting the poor people. The idea is to improve their quality with increased funds and physical facilities created by the trusts. The land and the building would remain under the control of the government. The trusts would be free to recruit their own teachers as the existing ones neither are acceptable to them nor are ready to remain with them. The government will pay grant of Rs. 400/- per student against the current expenditure of Rs. 800/- per student, thus saving government expenditure and improving quality of education. This decision of the government of Delhi clearly indicates that Government also agrees that under their control schools cannot give good results. This puts a question mark on the capability of the government to manage its own educational institution and justifies the involvement of private sector. The government says that some areas have remained neglected in this regard and need schools, which would provide decent education to the children of these localities, who have remained at a disadvantage. This means that the government accepts that the schools set up and managed by it are unable to provide quality education for which dependence on private bodies is inevitable.

We seem to have some confused thinking on financing of higher education. From 1st to 7th Plan, the average allocation for higher education was 17.3% of the total allocation for education, but in the Eighth Plan, it came down to 8%, almost half of the average of the first seven plans. In the 9th Plan there is a slight improvement to 12 %. It is said that larger allocation has to be made for primary education, and therefore, funds for higher education are being reduced. This argument does not sound reasonable because the two sectors of education are not in competition with each other. The highest of education for a few is as important as the basic education for all in a large country like India, the former provides necessary leadership in all areas of activity while the latter creates an enlightened and literate society, capable of taking advantage of development in the field of science and technology. The department of economic affairs (GOI) has classified higher education as a non-merit service and has recommended that the subsidy on it must be reduced. This viewpoint is completely misguided and has in it, a potential for disastrous consequences. The allocation for S&T research stood at 1% of the GNP in 1987-88, the maximum ever reached; but since then, it has been continuously decreasing and reached 0.81% in 1994-95. These developments do not augur well for the future of science and technology.

The Future of Indian Universities

A few months ago, the report prepared on a "Policy Framework for reforms in Education" by a couple of eminent industrialists as a part of Prime Minister's Council on Trade and Industry recommended that the government's role should be 'maximum' in the sphere of primary education, but should be 'minimum' at the stage of higher education. This report of evoked a strong objection from the university teaching community. It has mooted the idea of establishing private universities and suggested the Government to legislate a Private Universities Bill for this purpose. The report said that a redefinition of government's role in higher education would call for a major privatization of university education system in India. The report has also recommended that all educational institutions in India, that is schools, colleges, institutions and universities, must be rated by independent agencies analogous to CRISIL in the financial sector. It has also strongly recommended that the funding should be linked to the rating. In a scathing indictment of the universities, the report observes that, "our universities have become the hotbeds of politics" and that "the teachers turned politicians in the universities are largely responsible for falling standards and commitment. University unions are seen as nurseries for political careers". The report also stated that the content and curriculum are not in tune with the needs of the society, which has resulted is an increasing level of educated unemployment. The report lamented that there are no innovation in teaching and research and criticized the existing scheme for continuous learning of faculty as being not adequate. The outcome of such schemes is ill-equipped faculty members. While pointing out that most of the outlays on social sector are spent on salaries and wages, the report has stressed the need for the government to ensure that primary education is compulsory and free. The report said that there must be a political will and conviction that compulsory and free primary education is an investment in India's future. The report also said that the government should continue to support the disciplines that have no market orientation, besides providing financial guarantees for student loans.

It is learnt that a series of proposals is under consideration of the World Trade Organization (WTO) to ensure that the process of export and import of higher education is covered under its complex rules and legal arrangements. If WTO, and similar organizations at national level, come in the picture, higher education will be subjected to free trade. This kind of commercialization implies devaluation of the social benefits of higher education, and individual returns would acquire greater significance. The logical implication of such a development is that beneficiaries of higher education should pay for it like they pay for electricity, telephone and water services. The universities, which were traditionally viewed, as custodians of knowledge, would function like business concerns looking for 'buyers' of their 'products' all over the world in order to increase their profits.

These trends must caution us and we should evolve a sound policy of educational finance suited to our requirements, and at the same time, commensurate with the globalization of market economy. The needed changes in the financial pattern of education sector should not be effected abruptly, rather, necessary adjustments should be made in a phased manner.

Bibliography

1. Ahmad, R. Issues and Development of Higher Education in India, Are New Policies Succeeding? Keynote Address, Conference of Executive Heads of Commonwealth Universities, New Delhi, Jan. 14-18, 1991.
2. Altekar, A.S. Education in Ancient India (Fourth Edition), Nan Inshore and Bros. Bananas (Variance) 1951.
3. Ahmad, I. Educational Development of Minorities in India, Journal of Educational Planning and Administration, NIEPA, New Delhi, 1987.
4. Ahmad, Faros Bach. Plight of Urdu Schools, The Hindustan Times, July 26, 1993.
5. Aikara Jacob quality of Educational Opportunities: The Case of Scheduled Castes in India, Journal of Educational Planning and Administration, NIEPA, New Delhi, Vol. X, No. 1, 1996.
6. Anand, C.L. The Constitution of India, in the Teacher and Education in Emerging Indian Society, NCERT, New Delhi, 1983.
7. Anand, C.L. The Educational Demands of Independent India, in the Teacher and Education in Emerging Indian Society, NCERT, New Delhi, 1983.
8. Anand, S.P. University Without Walls, Vikas Publishing House Pvt. Ltd. New Delhi, 1979.
9. Azad, J.L. Changing Complexion of Higher Education—A Study of the Impact of Emerging Socio-economic

Configuration, University News, AIU, New Delhi, March 13, 2000.

10. Balachander, K.K. Financing of Higher Education in India: The Role of Fees, in Landmarks in Management, Mathur, B.L. Arihant Publishers Jaipur, 1993.
11. Bhatnagar, R.P. The Junior Research Fellowship Test: An Evaluation, University News, AIU, New Delhi, March 23, 1992.
12. Bordia, A. The NAEP: The Background and Prospects, in Shah, A.B. and Bhan, S. Non-formal Education and the NAEP, Oxford University Press, New Delhi, 1980.
13. Chanana, K. Availability of Higher Education: Problem of Educating Women, Minorities, Scheduled Castes and Scheduled Tribes in contemporary India, Pariprekshya, Vol. 4, No. 3, NIEPA, New Delhi, 1993.
14. Chauhan, C.P.S. Emerging Priorities in Indian Education, Education and Society, Vol. 8, No. 1, James Nicholas, 1990.
15. Chauhan, C.P.S. Education for All: The Indian Scene, International Journal of Lifelong Education, Vol. 9, No. 1, Jan-March 1990.
16. Chauhan, C.P.S. Higher Education in India: Achievements, Failures and Strategies, Ashish Publishing House, New Delhi, 1990.
17. Chauhan, C.P.S. An Innovative Look at Teacher Education, University News, AIU, New Delhi, Oct. 25,1999.
18. Chauhan, C.P.S. University Funding in the 21st Century, University News, AIU, New Delhi, Nov. 29, 1999.
19. Chauhan, C.P.S. Contemporary Issues in Higher Education, University News, AIU, New Delhi, Dec. 4, 2000.
20. Chauhan, P. Towards Improved Student Support Services in Open Learning, University News, AIU, New Delhi, Jan. 8, 2001.
21. Choudhary, K. Dilemma of Secularism: State Policy towards Education of Muslims in India after Independence, Journal of Educational Planning and Administration, Vol. X, No. 4, NIEPA, New Delhi, Oct. 1996.
22. Competition Success Review, Jan. 2002.
23. Desai, A.S. Women in Higher Education and National Development, University News, AIU, Vol. 39 No. 9, March 1, 1999.
24. Deshmukh, K.G. Universities and Higher Education in the 21st Century, University News, AIU, New Delhi, July 13, 1998.

25. Dutt, R. New Education Policy: Role of Distance Education, University News, AIU, New Delhi, April 1, 1986.
26. Gautam, H. Infancy to Excellence—Developmental Stages of Educational Institutions, University News, AIU, New Delhi, Oct. 18, 1999.
27. Gore, M.S. Post-Independence Development in India and Higher Education, University News, AIU, New Delhi, Jan. 28, 1991.
28. Gopalan, K. Education for All—New Initiatives, University News, AIU, New Delhi, Jan. 1, 1996.
29. Govt. of India. Report of the Secondary Education Commission, Ministry of Education, New Delhi, 1952-53.
30. Govt. of India. Report of the National Committee on Women's Education, Ministry of Education, New Delhi, 1959.
31. Govt. of India. National Policy on Education, 1968, Ministry of Education and Culture, New Delhi, 1968.
32. Govt. of India. Draft National Policy of Edcation, 1979, MHRD, New Delhi, 1979.
33. Govt. of India. Challenge of Education: A Policy Perspective, Ministry of Human Resource Development (MHRD), New Delhi, 1985.
34. Govt. of India. National Policy on Education (NPE), 1986 and its Revised Version-1992, MHRD, New Delhi, 1986 & 1992.
35. Govt. of India. NPE-1986: A Program of Action, MHRD, New Delhi, 1986 & 1992.
36. Govt. of India. National Literacy Mission, MHRD, New Delhi, 1988.
37. Govt. of India. Towards an Enlightened and Humane Society, Report of the Review Committee for NPE-1986, MHRD, New Delhi, 1990.
38. Govt. of India. Learning Without Burden, Report of the National Advisory Committee, Ministry of Human Resource Development, New Delhi, 1993.
39. Govt. of India. Education for All: The Indian Scene, MHRD, New Delhi, 1993.
40. Govt. of India. Selected Educational Statistics, MHRD, New Delhi, 1993.
41. Govt. of India. Development of Education in India (1993-94), MHRD, New Delhi, 1994.
42. Govt. of India. Annual Reports of the Department of

Education: 1994-95, 1995-96, 1999-2000 and 2000-01, MHRD, New Delhi.

43. Hartog, P. Some Aspects of Indian Education: Past and Present, Joseph Payne Lectures delivered at the Institute of Education, University of London, Oxford University Press, 1939.
44. Hasan, S. Noorul. New Pattern of School Education, Inaugural Address to a Seminar on National Policy on Education, Journal of Indian Education, NCERT, New Delhi, May 1975.
45. The Hindustan Times. One crore married girls below 11 years, New Delhi, July 11, 1988.
46. The Hindustan Times. Sharp rise in Muslim Population, New Delhi, Nov. 8, 1995.
47. The Hindustan Times. To hell with the Child Marriage Act, New Delhi, Jan. 6, 1999.
48. The Hindustan Times. Children's scheme has failed to deliver, New Delhi, Jan. 20, 2001.
49. Jain, Justice Sobhagmal, Five Departmental Memos of the Department of Personnel, Rashtriya Sawran Dal—Mukh Patra, Feb-March, 2000.
50. Khan, A.W. IGNOU Plans New Programs, University News, AIU, New Delhi, July 6, 1998.
51. Khan, A.W. Distance Education in the Twenty-first century, in The World of Distance and Open Learning, by Venugopal Reddy V. and Manjulika S. (Ed.), Viva Books Pvt. Ltd. New Delhi, 2000.
52. Kurup, M.R. Accreditation to Autonomy, University News, AIU, New Delhi, Oct. 2, 2000.
53. Manorama Yearbook 2000: Malayala Manorama, Kottayam (Kerala), 2000.
54. Menon, R. The Mother Courage, The Hindustan Times, New Delhi, Jan. 5, 2001.
55. Misra, A. Educational Finance in India, Asia Publishing House, New Delhi, 1962.
56. Mitra, C.R. Cost of Higher Education, University News, AIU, New Delhi, Feb. 22, 1993.
57. Mitra, N.L. Reservation in University Teaching Posts, University News, AIU, New Delhi, Sept. 30, 1991.
58. Naik, J.P. Non-formal Education in India: A Retrospect and a Prospect, in Shah A.B. & Bhan, S. Non-formal Education and the NAEP, Oxford University Press, New Delhi, 1980.

59. Naik, J.P. Education Commission and After, Allied Publishers Private Limited, New Delhi, 1982.
60. NCERT. Education and National Development, Report of the Education Commission (1964-66), New Delhi, 1971.
61. NCERT. National Curriculum for Primary and Secondary Education: A Framework, New Delhi, December 1985.
62. NCERT. National Curriculum Framework for School Education, New Delhi, 2000.
63. NIEPA. Education for All By 2000 A.D., New Delhi, 1990.
64. NIEPA. Development of Education in India 1988-90, MHRD, Govt. of India, New Delhi, 1990.
65. Nurullah, S. and Naik, J.P. History of Education in India During the British period, Macmillan & Co. Limited, Bombay, 1943.
66. Powar, K.B. Assuring Equity and Quality in Mass Higher Education: The Indian Context, University News, AIU, New Delhi, May 27, 1996.
67. Powar, K.B. Higher Education in the Twenty-first Century, University News, AIU, New Delhi, December 4, 2000.
68. Prasad, L.M. Educational Policy for the Scheduled Castes and Scheduled Tribes and its Implementation, The Indian Journal of Public Administration, IIPA, New Delhi, Vol. XXXII, No. 4. 1986.
69. Premi, M.K. India's Population: Heading Towards a Billion, B.R. Publishing Corporation, New Delhi, 1991.
70. Rajagopalan, S. Education for All at Snail's Pace, The Hindustan Times, New Delhi, May 19, 1987.
71. Rajput, J.S. A Problem of Dropouts, The Hindustan Times, New Delhi, July 10, 1993.
72. Rajput, J.S. Elementary Education—Alternative Strategies, The Hindustan Times, New Delhi, June 10, 1994.
73. Rao, M.R. Management of Affiliated Colleges, University News, AIU, New Delhi, July 29, 1991.
74. Rausaria, R.R. and Bhushan B. Institutional Models for Distance Learning in India, University News, AIU, New Delhi, July 2-8, 2001.
75. Ray, Ash Narain. Operation Blackboard: A Tardy Progress Due to States' Lack of Interest, The Hindustan Times, New Delhi, May 31, 1993.
76. Ray, Ash Narain. Education for All; An Elusive Dream, The Hindustan Times, New Delhi, Dec. 13, 1993.

77. Reddy, B. Shiva. Financing Education and Health in India, Journal of Educational Planning and Administration, Vol. V, No. 4, NIEPA New Delhi, Oct. 1991.
78. Reddy, G. Ram: Distance Education: What, Why and How? In Studies in Distance Education, Koul B.N., Singh B. & Ansari M.M., AIU and IGNOU, New Delhi, 1988.
79. Reddy, P.A. & Kumaraswamy, P. Towards Cent Percent Literacy, University News, AIU, New Delhi, Aug. 20, 1990.
80. Rogers, A. (Ed). Partners in Literacy: A Pilot Attitudinal Survey of Literacy Animators in Tamil Nadu, India, Education for Development, Norfolk, 1989.
81. Ruhela, S.P. Education and Social Transformation: Religion, Caste and Tribe, in Teacher and Education in Emerging Indian Society, NCERT, New Delhi, 1983.
82. Sahu, P.K. Higher Education at a Distance, Sanchar Publishing House, New Delhi, 1993.
83. Saini, S.K. Development of Education in India, Cosmo Publications, 1980.
84. Saiyadain, K.G. *et al.* Compulsory Education in India, Universal Book House, New Delhi, 1966.
85. Saraf, S.N. Education for All: Dimensions and Dilemmas, University News, AIU, New Delhi, June 1, 1985.
86. Saraf S.N. Professional Development of Teachers: Nature, Concept and Potentialities, in Professional Status of Teachers, NCTE, New Delhi, 1997.
87. Satyanarayan, P. Distance Teaching Universities, University News, AIU, New Delhi, August 15, 1988.
88. Saxena, N.C. Public Employment and Educational Backwardness among Muslims in India, Man and Development, Vol. 4, No. 4. 1983.
89. Shah, K.R. Education: Plea for Higher Plan Allocation, Journal of Educational Planning and Administration, Vol. VII, No. 2, April 1993, NIEPA, New Delhi.
90. Shah, S. Shamim, Educational Survey Report on Muslim Managed Schools and Colleges in India, Hamdard Education Society, New Delhi, 1987.
91. Singh, R.P. Non-formal Education: An Alternative Approach, Sterling Publishers Private Limited, New Delhi, 1987.
92. Singh, R.P. A Critique of Indian Education: Developing Insights, University News, AIU, New Delhi, Vol. 39 No. 40, Oct. 2001.

93. Singh, S.N. Teaching Profession in India: Past, Present and Future, in Professional Status of Teachers, NCTE, New Delhi, 1997.
94. Singhal, R.P. Implementation of Ten Plus Two: The Indian Experience of School Education, Journal of Educational Planning and Administration, Vol. VI, No. 3, 1992, pp. 251-265.
95. Sharma, C.L. Crisis of Character in India: The Need for Moral Education, Education and Society, Vol. 8, No. 1, James Nicholas, 1990.
96. Sharma, I.P. Adult Education in India—A Colossal Challenge, Education and Society, Vol. 8, No. 1, James Nicholas, 1990.
97. Sharma, I.P. Adult Education in India, National Book Organization, Delhi, 1985.
98. Sharma, I.P. Adult Education in India: A Programme of Action, Indian Journal of Public Administration, IIPA, New Delhi, Vol. 32, 3, 1986.
99. Stella, A. In Defence of Autonomy, University News, AIU, New Delhi, July 24, 2000.
100. Takwale, R. IGNOUs Challenges of Quality, Quantity and Equity, University News, AIU New Delhi, May 27, 1996.
101. The Times of India. Accreditation scheme comes a cropper, New Delhi, September 25, 2002.
102. Tope, T.K. Universities and Law Courts, University News, AIU, New Delhi, April 11, 1988.
103. Tope, T.K. Constitutional Provisions Relating to Education, University News, AIU, New Delhi, Jan. 30, 1989.
104. University Grants Commission. Towards New Educational Management, Report of the Gnanam Committee, New Delhi, 1990.
105. University Grants Commission. UGC Funding of Institutions of Higher Education, Report of the Punayya Committee (1992-93), New Delhi, 1993.
106. University Grants Commission. Annual Reports for the Years 1959-60, 1993-94, 1995-96 and 1998-99, UGC, New Delhi.
107. UNESCO. Education for All, Summit of Nine High-Population Countries (Final Report), New Delhi, Dec. 12-16, 1993.
108. University News, 40 (35), Fees Hike, AIU, New Delhi, September 2-8, 2002

109. Vaidyanatha Ayyar, R.V. Educational Planning and Administration in India: Retrospect and Prospect, Journal of Educational Planning and Administration, Vol. VII, No. 2, NIEPA, New Delhi.

110. Venugopal Reddy V. and Manjulika S. Distance Education in India: A Model for Developing Countries, Vikas Publishing House Pvt. Ltd. New Delhi, 1996.

Index